Confrontations

Confrontations

Studies in the intellectual
and literary relations between Germany,
England, and the United States during
the nineteenth century

*

By René Wellek

PRINCETON, NEW JERSEY
PRINCETON UNIVERSITY PRESS
1965

Copyright © 1965 by Princeton University Press

ALL RIGHTS RESERVED

L.C. Card 65-10841

Publication of this book has been aided by
the Whitney Darrow Publication
Reserve Fund of Princeton University Press

Printed in the United States of America
by Princeton University Press

Preface

✱ In this book I have collected a number of my scattered studies on German-English and German-American literary and philosophical relations during the Romantic age. The earliest of these pieces was published in an Anniversary volume in Prague in 1929 and is now almost inaccessible; four others date from the war years, 1943 and 1944, and were published in American periodicals with very small circulation, while the article which introduces the volume is a hitherto unpublished lecture given in 1963. All the papers have been carefully revised, though not changed except in details, and notes have been added drawing attention to new discussions of these issues.

The volume should be supplemented by my other writings. *Immanuel Kant in England 1793-1838* (Princeton University Press, 1931), of which I am preparing a completely revised edition, contains fuller discussions of Carlyle and De Quincey in relation to Kant; Carlyle and De Quincey are treated as literary critics in the third volume of my *History of Modern Criticism*, to be published by the Yale University Press in 1965; and Emerson, as an aesthetician and critic, is examined, also in relation to the Germans, in a contribution to *Worte und Werte. Bruno Marckwardt zum 60. Geburtstag* (eds. Gustav Eichmann and Alfons Eichstaedt, Berlin, 1961), a piece which will also be reprinted in the *History*. There and in the first two volumes much attention is paid to German-English relations. The paper, "The Concept of Romanticism in Literary History," reprinted in *Concepts of Criticism* (Yale University Press, 1963), takes up related topics in a wider context. There is a

Preface

survey of Coleridge scholarship in *The English Romantic Poets: A Review of Research* (ed. T. M. Raysor, *MLA*, New York, 1956), which contains a section on Coleridge's German sources.

The spread of German philosophical and critical ideas to England and the United States has been a constant theme of my work. I believe that it is of crucial importance for an understanding of intellectual history in the nineteenth century. I can only trust that these studies have helped uncover some new links and survey the evidence without the grinding of any national axe. In all my work I wish to keep the totality of Western thought in mind.

RENÉ WELLEK

New Haven, Conn.
October 1963

✻ Contents

Preface — v

Chapter One
German and English Romanticism:
A Confrontation (1963) — 3

Chapter Two
Carlyle and German
Romanticism (1929) — 34

Chapter Three
Carlyle and the Philosophy
of History (1944) — 82

Chapter Four
De Quincey's Status in the History
of Ideas (1944) — 114

Chapter Five
The Minor Transcendentalists and
German Philosophy (1943) — 153

Chapter Six
Emerson and German Philosophy
(1943) — 187

Index — 213

Confrontations

CHAPTER ONE

German and English Romanticism: A Confrontation*

✷ In 1949 I published a long paper, in the first two numbers of the newly founded periodical, *Comparative Literature*, in which I tried to refute A. O. Lovejoy's famous attempt to show that "the 'Romanticism' of one country may have little in common with that of another."[1] I met Lovejoy's challenge to exhibit "some common denominator" by arguing that "we find, throughout Europe, the same conceptions of poetry and of the workings and nature of poetic imagination; the same conception of nature and its relation to man, and basically the same poetic style, with a use of imagery, symbolism and myth which is clearly distinct from that of eighteenth century neoclassicism."[2]

In a new paper, "Romanticism Re-examined," included in a recent volume of my essays (*Concepts of Criticism*), I surveyed the debate of the last fourteen years and could come to the conclusion that, on the whole, students of the issue agree with my general view or have arrived independently at the same or similar results. "In all of these studies," I said, "however

* A lecture given at a Conference on Romanticism at Ohio State University, Columbus, Ohio, on April 6, 1963. Unpublished.
[1] "On the Discrimination of Romanticisms," *PMLA*, 29 (1924), 229-53. Reprinted in *Essays in the History of Ideas* (Baltimore, 1948), pp. 228-53.
[2] "The Concept of Romanticism in Literary History," in *Comparative Literature*, 1 (1949), 1, 147.

German and English Romanticism

diverse in method and emphasis, a convincing agreement has been reached: they all see the implication of imagination, symbol, myth, and organic nature, and see it as part of the great endeavor to overcome the split between subject and object, the self and the world, the conscious and the unconscious. This is the central creed of the great Romantic poets in England, Germany, and France."[3]

In this paper I should like to shift the perspective radically. I shall assume, however rashly, that the basic argument has been won, that there is a common core of Romantic thought and art throughout Europe. I shall also try, as far as possible, to ignore the history of critical ideas in the Romantic age, which I have discussed amply in my *History of Modern Criticism*. I shall rather examine first the English-German and German-English literary relations during the first decades of the nineteenth century, and then attempt to present a comparison between German and English Romanticism which will try to bring out the distinct and original features of the German movement.

In considering the question, we have first to make up our minds whom we consider Romantic in the two countries. There is little difficulty about England. Actually, there seems today hardly any disagreement that only six poets survive: Blake, Wordsworth, Coleridge, Byron, Shelley and Keats. Among the Romantic novelists only Scott commands contemporary attention. Among other prose writers only Lamb, Hazlitt and De Quincey are still read today. All the other figures who were conspicuous in their time—Southey, Rogers, Campbell, Thomas Moore, Leigh Hunt, Jeffrey—have dis-

[3] *Concepts of Criticism* (New Haven, 1963), p. 220.

German and English Romanticism

appeared into the limbo of specialized interests, while one has the impression that marginal figures such as Thomas Love Beddoes, George Darley, John Clare and James Hogg have remained the exclusive property of a few enthusiasts.

The question whom we should consider a Romantic writer in Germany is, however, much more difficult to answer. I myself argued that from a European perspective, the German *Sturm und Drang* is parallel to what in the West we have become accustomed to call Preromanticism, and that even Goethe and Schiller, in spite of their Classicist phases and Classicist tastes, will appear Romantic in this wide general sense. In Germany, for reasons I have discussed in the old paper, the term "Romantic school" has become confined to two groups of writers: the early group comprising the two Schlegels, Wackenroder, Tieck and Novalis, and the younger group of whom Arnim and Brentano are the best known names. In addition, most German literary histories cite E. T. A. Hoffmann as a particularly Romantic writer, though he had only slight personal associations with the two Romantic groups: he met Tieck and Brentano very casually.[4] Also Joseph von Eichendorff, who knew Arnim and Brentano well, has been increasingly recognized as a typically Romantic poet. But this traditional focus on two groups of friends obscures to my mind the all-pervasive Romantic attitude in the Germany of the time and isolates such great writers as Hölderlin, Jean Paul and Heinrich von Kleist needlessly by emphasizing their disagreements with the professedly Romantic groups. I cannot see why one should divorce even

[4] Harvey W. Hewett-Thayer, *Hoffmann: Author of the Tales* (Princeton, 1948), pp. 78, 81.

German and English Romanticism

Uhland, Mörike, Lenau or the early Heine from Romanticism; a play such as Büchner's *Leonce und Lena* (1836) strikes me as arch-Romantic, and so is much of Grillparzer and Grabbe. I mention these names to suggest the plethora of interesting writers in the Germany of that time. I need hardly point to the fact that one can label as "Romantic" several great thinkers, Fichte, Schelling, Schleiermacher and Hegel, and that Romantic feeling penetrated German natural science, political theory and painting. And who can forget German Romantic music, though today it is usually called "Classical," especially Beethoven, since he emancipated himself from his models, Schubert, Schumann, Weber and Mendelssohn.

Still, for the purposes of this paper I shall recognize the narrow limits put on the term Romanticism in German literary history and examine first the historical question of the contact between the English Romantic poets and the two German groups as defined above. As to personal contacts, we must conclude that they were very meager. In 1798 Wordsworth and Coleridge visited Germany, but, of all writers, they called only on old Klopstock in Hamburg for a brief and awkward visit.[5] In 1806 Coleridge, on his return from Malta, met Tieck in Rome, "but was not aware of his eminence as a poet."[6] Sophie Bernhardi, Tieck's sister, wrote to August Wilhelm Schlegel (then at Coppet) about a "wonderful Englishman who had studied Kant, Fichte, Schelling, and the old German poets and admires Schlegel's trans-

---

[5] See Coleridge's account in "Satyrane's Letters" utilizing a letter to Thomas Poole, Nov. 20, 1798. See *Collected Letters*, ed. E. L. Griggs (Oxford, 1956), vol. 1, 441ff.

[6] According to H. C. Robinson, see *Blake, Coleridge, Wordsworth, Lamb . . .* , ed. E. Morley (Manchester, 1922), p. 31 (Nov. 15, 1810).

German and English Romanticism

lation of Shakespeare unbelievably," but she had forgotten his name.[7] Coleridge renewed his fleeting acquaintance with Tieck on the occasion of the latter's visit to London in 1817; there they met only twice. From Henry Crabb Robinson's reports and some letters of Coleridge,[8] we know that they met at the Gillmans' in Highgate, conversing on the authenticity of Shakespeare's plays, German mysticism and animal magnetism. Coleridge wrote several letters of recommendation for Tieck and wrote him one letter, only recently come to light, which speaks of Goethe's *Farbenlehre* and animal magnetism. Two letters by Tieck to Coleridge have been preserved.[9] In 1828 Wordsworth and Coleridge went on a trip along the Rhine and for the first time met August Wilhelm Schlegel in a large company at Bad Godesberg; they had not met when Schlegel was in London in 1814 and 1823. Coleridge and Schlegel exchanged compliments about their respective translations of Shakespeare and Schiller; and supposedly Schlegel had to ask Coleridge to speak in English as he could not understand his German.[10] On a tour in 1837, Wordsworth met Brentano by chance on a street in Munich. He "rattled in French about religion in a way that could but half amuse and half disgust" Wordsworth.[11] Byron had met

[7] Feb. 6, 1806, in *Krisenjahre der Frühromantik. Briefe aus dem Schlegelkreis*, ed. J. Körner (Brünn, 1936), vol. 1, 291-92.

[8] June 13 and 24. See E. Morley, *Henry Crabb Robinson on Books and Their Writers* (London, 1938), vol. 1, 207-208, *Collected Letters*, ed. E. L. Griggs (Oxford, 1959), vol. 4, 738, 739, 742-43, 744.

[9] *Ibid.*, vol. 4, 750-51 (July 4, 1817). For Tieck's letters cf. "Ludwig Tieck and Samuel Taylor Coleridge," *Journal of English and Germanic Philology*, 54 (1955), 262-68.

[10] Charles Young, *Memoir of Charles Mayne Young* (London, 1871), pp. 112, 115.

[11] Morley, *op. cit.*, vol. 2, 530-31 (July 17, 1837).

German and English Romanticism

A. W. Schlegel at Coppet, in 1816, but did not care for him.[12] This is apparently the sum total of all personal and epistolary contacts between the two Romantic groups. No friendships developed, no letters (except three between Tieck and Coleridge) were exchanged. The meagerness of these contacts has induced a recent student of the question, Eudo C. Mason,[13] to make extravagant claims for the one man, Henry Crabb Robinson, who had met the two Schlegels and Clemens Brentano as a youngster in Germany, and later knew both Coleridge and Wordsworth in England. Robinson is an appealing figure, and his letters and diaries are a mine of information; but I cannot see that he accomplished anything important as an intermediary between the two groups. Whatever his understanding of German Romantic literature may have been, it is not documented publicly, and certainly in his own time Henry Crabb Robinson was strictly a "private person." It is legend that Robinson influenced Madame de Staël's *De l'Allemagne*. His own not very numerous articles attracted no attention. The most curious is a piece on Blake which appeared, in German translation, in a short-lived Hamburg review in 1811.[14] Neither Blake nor Shelley nor Keats nor Lamb nor Hazlitt nor De Quincey had any German contacts, and those few that Walter Scott had were not with the German Romantics.

Personal and epistolary contacts matter less than the impression made by the reading of books. But even in

---

[12] *Letters and Journals*, ed. Lord Prothero (London, 1898), vol. 3, 341; vol. 4, 161; vol. 5, 101-102, 333, 334.
[13] *Deutsche und englische Romantik* (Göttingen, 1959).
[14] *Vaterländisches Museum*. See H. C. Wright, "Henry Crabb Robinson's 'Essay on Blake,'" in *Modern Language Review*, 22 (1927), 137-54 which reprints the essay.

German and English Romanticism

strictly literary relations the contact between the two groups was exceedingly slight. Blake, Wordsworth, Byron, Shelley and Keats knew nothing of German Romantic writing in our narrow sense, except that Byron and Shelley read in the lecture courses of the two Schlegels in French or English translation.[15] But of course Coleridge and De Quincey are the exceptions. Coleridge was importantly influenced by German Romantic aesthetics and criticism. I cannot understand how it is still possible to deny this fact proved by all the rules of evidence. Certainly the whole Romantic-Classical, organic-mechanical contrast is derived from Schlegel, as Coleridge himself admitted.[16] The basic ideas of August Wilhelm Schlegel's *Lectures on Dramatic Literature* impressed also Hazlitt and De Quincey, though Hazlitt had his reservations and De Quincey attacked both Schlegels ferociously.[17] But the influence of German Romanticism on actual imaginative writing was negligible. An instance worth mentioning may be Coleridge's free version of Tieck's "Herbstlied" inserted in his play *Zapolya*.[18]

[15] Byron's *Letters and Journals*, ed. Lord Prothero (London, 1899), vol. 3, 343. Mary Shelley's *Journal*, March 16, 19, 21, 1818, quoted in Edward Dowden, *Life of P. B. Shelley* (London, 1886), vol. 2, 187-88, tells that Shelley read Schlegel (probably August Wilhelm Schlegel's *Lectures* in English) aloud to his two female companions on his trip to Italy.

[16] Cf. A. W. Schlegel, *Ueber dramatische Kunst und Literatur* (Heidelberg, 1811), vol. 3, 8, with Coleridge, *Shakespearean Criticism*, ed. T. M. Raysor (Cambridge, Mass.), 1930, vol. 1, 224. Coleridge himself refers to a "continental critic." See G. N. Orsini, "Coleridge and Schlegel Reconsidered," *Comparative Literature*, 16 (1964), 97-118.

[17] On Hazlitt and Schlegel see my *History*, vol. 2, 189, 209. For De Quincey see my "De Quincey's Status in the History of Ideas," below pp. 114ff, esp. p. 128, n. 57.

[18] "Glycine's Song" beginning "A sunny shaft did I behold," see

German and English Romanticism

Coleridge read some of Tieck's fiction expressly in anticipation of their meeting in 1817, but he did not like it.[19] (I may mention that the translation of Tieck's *Love Charm*, with a highly laudatory postscript on Tieck, reprinted in Masson's edition of De Quincey is not by De Quincey, but by Julius Hare.)[20] E. T. A. Hoffmann's reception in England was very lukewarm; Walter Scott wrote an almost wholly damning article "On the Supernatural in Fictitious Composition" (1827); and Carlyle's introduction to his translation of *Der goldene Topf* (The Golden Pot) in the same year is patronizingly condescending to the poor drunken Bohemian.[21]

The influence of the English Romantics is also negligible if we restrict ourselves to the influence of the German Romantic groups. Wordsworth and Coleridge (and of course Blake) remained unknown in Germany, as did Shelley and Keats for a long time. Freiligrath's translations of "The Ancient Mariner" and "The Solitary Reaper" did not appear until 1836.[22] Gutzkow wrote an essay on Shelley in 1838 out of sympathy for a persecuted atheist and revolutionary.[23] But of course Byron proved to be, as everywhere, an enormous influence. Goethe's

---

S. T. Coleridge, *Poems*, ed. E. H. Coleridge (Oxford, 1912), pp. 426-27.

[19] See letters to H. C. Robinson, 20 June 1817, and to J. H. Green, Dec. 13, 1817, in *Collected Letters*, ed. E. L. Griggs (Oxford, 1959), vol. 4, 743, 793. *Sternbald* "is too like an imitation of Heinse's *Ardinghello* . . . it is a lewd day-dream, in which the Dreamer at once *yawns and itches*."

[20] See Hans Galinsky, "Is Thomas De Quincey the Author of the Love-Charm?" in *Modern Language Notes*, 52 (1937), 389-94.

[21] In July, 1827 Number of *The Quarterly Review*. Carlyle's *German Romance*.

[22] See *Sämtliche Werke* (New York, 1858), vol. 3, pp. 122, 129.

[23] *Götter, Helden, Don Quixote* (Hamburg, 1838), pp. 3-17.

German and English Romanticism

admiration helped, though it was hardly indispensable. But Byron's influence—which is rather an influence of a mood and of a hero-type than of actual poetry—comes *after* the Romantic movement. He could not affect the Schlegels, Tieck, Novalis, Arnim, Brentano or Hoffmann. Heine and Lenau were the real German Byronists.[24] The same is true of Walter Scott: he determined the rise of the German historical novel after the Romantic movement. Only Hoffmann has the Serapion brothers discuss Scott's *Guy Mannering* very favorably.[25] But Arnim's historical novel, *Die Kronenwächter* (The Guardians of the Crown, 1816), is apparently still untouched by Scott; only Willibald Alexis' novels from Prussian history and Wilhelm Hauff's *Lichtenstein* bear the mark of the Magician of the North, and the late historical novels of Ludwig Tieck show that he could not resist Scott's all-pervasive influence.[26]

We cannot escape the conclusion that personal, epistolary and literary relations between the two groups were extremely tenuous. Among the English, only Coleridge and De Quincey show the influence of German Romantic ideas; among the Germans, English Romantic influences from Byron and Scott come later. The two movements existed at the same time, but they ran parallel without making deeper contacts, if we except Coleridge, whose very isolation points to the gulf between the two movements. But lack of historical contacts does not, of course, preclude similarities and even deep affinities. I have tried to generalize about them before; as partial explanation one can point to common antecedents in

---

[24] Cf. Lawrence Marsden Price, *English Literature in Germany* (Berkeley, 1953), pp. 316-28, and bibliography.
[25] See *Werke*, ed. G. Ellinger (Leipzig, 1912), vol. 8, 161-62.
[26] See Price, *op. cit.*, pp. 329ff., and bibliography.

German and English Romanticism

history, e.g. the very general similarity between the thought of Wordsworth and Coleridge and that of Schelling and thus generally of the German Romantics is marked even before Coleridge had read Schelling.[27] It is due to the common background in the tradition of Neo-Platonism, in mysticism such as Böhme's, and in varieties of pietism. Rousseau and hence Goethe's *Werther* supply the common ancestry for the two groups in eighteenth-century sensibility and sentimentality. The Gothic tradition can be found in Coleridge, Shelley and Scott as well as in Tieck, Arnim, Brentano and E. T. A. Hoffmann. Ideas and folk themes migrate most easily and form a common European heritage.

But there are obvious and startling differences between the two literatures which should be described in other terms than a different emphasis on specific ideas or a different use of universal themes. The differences will appear most sharply if we focus on the important poetic productions of the time and look at the differences in the hierarchy of genres. This is a difficult and elusive problem. It can be solved only by bold critical judgment which will necessarily profit from the hindsight acquired by our time. There can be hardly any dispute that in Germany the Romantic lyric had assumed a central status in the hierarchy of genres. It differs profoundly from the English lyric—the odes, the lyrical ballads, and the meditative blank verse of the English poets. The Germans established the "artificial folk song" as the norm of the lyric, a kind of poem which can be described as the expression of a subjective mood

---

[27] See Donald E. Hirsch, *Wordsworth and Schelling* (New Haven, 1960). On Coleridge and Schelling see my *Immanuel Kant in England* and *History of Modern Criticism*, vol. 2.

German and English Romanticism

rendered by loosely, or even abruptly, joined images; the poems are usually in the four-line stanza of the folk song, in a rhythm and sound pattern which tries to achieve musical effects. We must distinguish this German Romantic lyric from the folk song of a Burns or Thomas Moore, which is social, implies often a definite addressee, and conveys some, however rudimentary, logical statement. The German lyric suggests immediacy of personal experience, even inspiration, unconscious solitary speaking, without logical or even imagistic coherence. It is a poetry of the famous *Gemuet*, of the cultivation of the soul. It lacks what T. S. Eliot calls an "objective correlative." It comes near to the Romantic ideal of an identification of subject and object, man and nature, the self and the world. I am thinking of such poems as Eichendorff's "Dämmerung will die Flügel spreiten" (1811), "Ich wandre durch die stille Nacht" (1826) or Brentano's "Abendständchen": "Hör, es klagt die Flöte wieder." Max Kommerell, Emil Staiger and Käte Hamburger[28]—three of the best German scholar-critics who have discussed the issue—agree remarkably in taking this type of lyric as the ideal of pure poetry, which serves, often strangely, to devaluate anything which deviates from this pattern. In English poetry of the time there is, I believe, hardly anything which corresponds to it closely. Possibly Shelley's song "A Dirge: Rough wind, that moanest loud" or "O World, O Life, O Time" come nearest, but even "Music, when soft voices die," which sounds similar, turns out on closer inspection to be a

[28] Max Kommerell, "Vom Wesen des lyrischen Gedichts," in *Gedanken über Gedichte*, 2nd ed. (Frankfurt, 1956), pp. 9-56. E. Staiger, *Grundbegriffe der Poetik* (Zürich, 1946). Käte Hamburger, *Die Logik der Dichtung* (Stuttgart, 1957).

German and English Romanticism

series of conceits and even an allegory.[29] In France we would, I believe, have to go to Verlaine before we find anything parallel.

When we look at prose, the divergence between the two countries is equally striking. The English essay preserved its high standing derived from the eighteenth century. There were two distinct types of English fiction, the Gothic novel and the novel of manners, until Scott established the vogue of the historical novel, which draws on these two traditions. In Germany, Goethe's *Wilhelm Meister*—ridiculed in England by Francis Jeffrey and De Quincey as immoral, vulgar and absurd[30]—established the genre of the educational novel. With the German Romantics, a hybrid type (drawing on the educational novel, but more closely related to Sterne's *Tristram Shandy*), became the central form—a mixture of irony and fantasy for which Friedrich Schlegel prescribed a program in his "Letter on the Novel."[31] His own *Lucinde* (1799)—a medley using such forms as the letter, the dialogue, the idyll, the fantasy and allegory—is not successful as fiction, though it does contain, intermittently, much wit, charm, erotic atmosphere and even good sense about love and marriage. Rather, Jean Paul is the main German Romantic novelist, the *magnus parens* of German fiction, and E. T. A. Hoffmann, Heine, Stifter and Keller begin with him. Matthew Arnold was quite off the mark when, in 1854, he ridiculed the idea

---

[29] See F. R. Leavis' analysis in *Scrutiny*, 13 (1945), 66-67.

[30] *Contributions to the Edinburgh Review* (London, 1844), e.g. vol. 1, 263. De Quincey, *Collected Writings*, ed. D. Masson (London, 1890), vol. 11, 222-58.

[31] Friedrich Schlegel, "Brief über den Roman," part of *Gespräch über die Poesie* (1800), in *Kritische Schriften*, ed. Wolfdietrich Rasch (Munich, 1956), pp. 318-28.

German and English Romanticism

that the whole literary movement in Germany in the last fifty years could be ascribed to Jean Paul and Novalis.[32] Jean Paul is known (if he is known at all) in the English-speaking world largely through Carlyle's translations, which are confined to the grotesque idylls, to *Schmelzle's Journey to Flaetz* and to the *Life of Quintus Fixlein*. Carlyle himself, in his three essays on Jean Paul, aptly characterized Jean Paul's style as a combination of imagination and religious vision.[33] One must know the "Speech of the Dead Christ from the Vault of Heavens that there is no God"[34] to appreciate Jean Paul's reach into the sublime or know the scenes of doubles and mirrors, the dream world strangely mixed with the world of the German small burghers and the little courts to recognize a type of fiction which is outside the main stream of the novel of manners. Brentano's novel *Godwi*, a "novel gone wild,"[35] is an obvious imitation and almost parodistic exaggeration of Jean Paul's manner, and Hoffmann's *Opinions of Kater Murr* exploits some of Jean Paul's technical devices to the limit. The supposed reminiscences of the tomcat Murr alternate with fragments of the biography of Kapellmeister Kreisler which were written on the reverse pages of the wastepaper the tomcat had used for his writing. Everything was then printed continuously just as it came into the printer's

[32] Letter to Sainte-Beuve, Sept. 28, 1854, in Louis Bonnerot, *Matthew Arnold: Poète* (Paris, 1947), pp. 521-22. Cf. "Heinrich Heine" in *Essays in Criticism*, First Series, beginning, for similar statement.

[33] See my "Carlyle and German Romanticism," reprinted below, pp. 34-81.

[34] "Rede des todten Christus vom Weltgebäude herab, dass kein Gott sei," forms "Erstes Blumenstück" in *Blumen Frucht und Dornenstücke (Siebenkäs)*, 1796.

[35] *Godwi, ein verwilderter Roman* (Bremen, 1801).

German and English Romanticism

hand. Carlyle, in *Sartor Resartus*, learned something from Jean Paul, for he aims at the same combination of educational novel, humorous rhapsody and imaginative fantasy. But there was nothing similar in English before Carlyle's novel, and it was difficult to get *Sartor Resartus* published.[36]

In addition to this peculiar kind of novel, or rather hybrid form of romance and satire, the German Romantics cultivated two genres which were hardly known in England at that time: the artificial fairy tale and the *Novelle*. Novalis had proclaimed the "fairy-tale the canon of poetry,"[37] and his own novel, *Heinrich von Ofterdingen*, though something of an educational novel set in a fanciful Middle Ages, assumes quickly the mood and uses the devices of the fairy tale: "Die Welt wird Traum, der Traum wird Welt."[38] Tieck had set the pattern for the Romantic fairy tale with "Der blonde Eckbert" (1797), and the other Romantics vary it: Brentano's fairy tales draw often on the seventeenth-century Neapolitan, Basile, and his grotesque baroque gambols and verbal arabesques, while Hoffmann, in his fairy tales, seems rather to have learned from Gozzi and the tradition of the *commedia dell' arte*. There is nothing so fanciful, verbally inventive, and absurdly grotesque as some of Brentano's fairy tales, e.g. in *Gockel, Hinkel und Gackeleia* the castle is made out of sucked egg shells and its roof of hen's feathers. Nothing is so eerily fantastic as Hoffmann's *Golden Pot*, which shifts from the prosaic to the weird and uncanny with graceful ease.

[36] It was written in 1830-31, published in *Fraser's Magazine*, 1833-34. In book form, Boston, 1836, at Emerson's urging, London, 1838.
[37] *Gesammelte Werke*, ed. C. Seelig (Zurich, 1945), vol. 4, 165.
[38] *Ibid.*, vol. 1, 304.

German and English Romanticism

The old applewoman turns into a grinning door knocker; the student Anselmus finds himself imprisoned in a glass bottle on a shelf in the library. Brentano and Hoffmann seem to me to have created a type of fairy tale which is far removed from ostensible folklore. The better-known Romantic German fairy tales—such as Tieck's *Runenberg*, which is a version of the Rip van Winkle legend, or Chamisso's *Peter Schlemihl*, who sold his shadow to the devil, or Fouqué's *Undine*, the water sprite who wants to acquire a human soul—are nearer to actual folklore, to straight narrative, to the short story, the *Novelle*, and thus to the main stream of fiction.

The German *Novelle* has, because of its great artistic successes, attracted much critical attention and much effort has been expended and, I am afraid, wasted to give a definition of the genre. I cannot see how the *Novelle* can be distinguished from the short story and how it differs, basically, from the formal pattern established by Boccaccio and Cervantes, the models very much in the mind of its German practitioners. It seems to me impossible to confine the *Novelle* to stories told within a framework, a technical device established by the *Decamerone* and in Germany made popular by Goethe's *Unterhaltungen deutscher Ausgewanderte* (Entertainments of German Emigrants, 1795).[89] Nor can one confine the *Novelle* to stories which have the much discussed "falcon" of Paul Heyse's theory of the *Novelle*. Kleist's *Novellen* have no framework and need none, and that of Hoffmann's *Serapionsbrüder* is an external device which brought together stories published independently and does not distinguish the stories collected in *Serapions-*

[89] See Fritz Lockemann, *Gestalt und Wandlungen der deutschen Novelle* (Munich, 1957).

German and English Romanticism

brüder from stories collected without any framework. There is no discernible "falcon" in many a German *Novelle* to which it would be difficult to refuse the title. I fail to see what is achieved for the definition of the genre or its criticism when Bernhard von Arx tries to establish a concept, "Novellistisches Dasein," which seems to mean something inferior, unfree, hurried, pressed, implying the overrating of a single case. The writer of *Novellen*, we are told, "works out of poverty" and is unable to build a world, the world of a large-scale novelist.[40] In bombastic Heideggerian terms we merely learn that *Novellen* are short stories and not long novels and are thus apt to tell of a single event which is taken to be representative and universal. But this of course is the procedure of all art: stories claim to be "exemplary" as Cervantes knew. We don't need existentialism, the frame or the "falcon" to appreciate *Michael Kohlhaas*, or *Die Marquise von O. . . .* who advertises for the man who violated her, or any number of striking *Novellen* by E. T. A. Hoffmann. Hoffmann's stories seem to me best when they do not approximate realistic genre pictures or fairy tales but are stories of eccentric artists or simply horror stories. Though he draws on the Gothic novel tradition and specifically on "Monk" Lewis for his long novel, *Die Elixiere des Teufels*, his art can be matched in English only later by Edgar Allan Poe, or elsewhere by Mérimée or by Pushkin's *Queen of Spades*.

If we glance finally at the German Romantic drama, the difference from the English situation is equally striking. In England there was a deep gulf between the stage and the closet drama which was very rarely bridged. The

---

[40] Bernhard von Arx, *Novellistisches Dasein* (Zurich, 1953), p. 175: "So arbeitet der Novellist aus einer gewissen Armut heraus."

German and English Romanticism

best poetic drama of the time was probably Shelley's *Cenci*, a pastiche of Shakespeare and Webster which is effective on the stage but could not be performed then because of its theme: the incest of father and daughter. There were also the mythological poems cast in dramatic form, such as Shelley's *Prometheus Unbound* or Byron's *Cain*, which were written only for an imaginary theater. In Germany, however, there were dramatists who produced effective stage plays which constitute something like a genre: the tragedy of fate. I know that Schiller's *Bride of Messina* was the first example and that, in its lower reaches, the *Schicksalstragödie* degenerated into sensational horror plays such as Werner's *24th of February* or Müllner's *Guilt*. But much of Kleist, beginning with *Die Familie Schroffenstein*, the wonderful fragment *Robert Guiscard* and *Kätchen von Heilbronn*, or even Grillparzer's *Ahnfrau* cannot be dismissed as mere popular entertainment.

In the tragedy of fate the German Romantics found a peculiar form for what is, it seems, the basic outlook on life, the attitude, the "vision" of the German Romantics—their feeling for the uncanny, the menace, the sense of evil lurking behind the façade of the world. German Romanticism, in contrast with English and French Romanticism, is not Rousseauistic: it lacks the trust in goodness, the trust in God and Providence, or the belief in progress which inspires Wordsworth and Coleridge, and, in a secular form, Shelley or, in a messianic prophetic version, Blake (who must not be misinterpreted as a Satanist or a forerunner of Nietzsche). In the best things of Tieck, Brentano, Arnim and Hoffmann a sense of the double bottom of the world is conveyed—a fear that man is exposed helplessly to sinister forces, to fate, to chance, to the darkness of an incomprehensible mystery.

This in itself is, of course, an age-old feeling, but the Germans convey it by methods not paralleled in England at that time: by the grotesque and by Romantic irony. The grotesque is a term which is used so widely that it often means little more than the bizarre or odd, but if we follow its historical association with the grotesque decorative work of Raphael and see it particularly as abolishing the difference between the human and the animal realms, we can arrive, as Wolfgang Kayser does in his book,[41] at a more precise meaning. The grotesque assumes the horror and the menace of the world and a fateful determinism which reduces man to a helpless puppet in the hands of superior powers. This is why puppets and automatons or homonculi, such as Arnim's mandrake and Golem, are favorite figures in German Romantic fiction, particularly in Hoffmann; it also explains why Kleist, in his profound essay on the Puppet Theater, chose the puppet as metaphor for his philosophy of history. The world of Brentano, Arnim, Hoffmann and even Büchner in *Leonce und Lena* is filled with bored puppets, twitching, jerky, human dolls which have little in common with the apparent models: the heroes and heroines of Shakespeare's comedies or the sweetly melancholy figures of Musset's *Phantasio*.[42] I

---

[41] *Das Groteske, seine Gestaltung in Malerei und Dichtung* (Oldenburg, 1957). English translation, 1963, Bloomington, Indiana.

[42] Arnim Renker in *Georg Büchner und das Lustspiel der Romantik*, 16 (Berlin, 1924), showed that *Leonce und Lena* draws on Musset's *Phantasio*, but the ethos is quite different. On the play cf. Rudolf Majut, *Studien um Büchner* (Berlin, 1932); and Gustav Beckers, *Georg Büchners "Leonce und Lena": Ein Lustspiel der Langweile* (Heidelberg, 1961), an existentialist reading.

German and English Romanticism

cannot think of English parallels at that time: possibly the *dance macabre* of Beddoes' *Death's Jest Book* is somewhat similar in mood.

The grotesque can be repulsive or simply in bad taste, but it is often lifted into the realm of art by the detachment of the author, the psychic distance, the irony, the playing with the material which is cultivated with particular insistence by the German Romantics. Today it is frequently forgotten that devices considered strikingly modern were common among the German Romantics: the deliberate breaking of illusion, the interference of the author, the manipulation of the conventions of the novel or the play. Brentano's Godwi refers to the page of the first volume on which he has fallen into a pond.[43] In Tieck's *Puss in Boots* a character discusses the play *Puss in Boots* which is just being performed.[44] Zerbino in another of Tieck's satirical plays pushes the play backwards, as if it were a machine in reverse motion, so that the preceding scenes come back into view.[45] But this breaking of the illusion, which as a device dates back to the whole "Rehearsal" tradition and in the novel had its immediate model in Sterne, is only a superficial symptom of Romantic irony as expounded theoretically by Friedrich Schlegel and Solger. To them, irony means complete objectivity, and ultimately an insight into the contradiction of all existence and the nothingness of aes-

---

[43] *Godwi*, ed. Heinz Amelung, in *Sämtliche Werke*, ed. C. Schüddekopf (Munich, 1909), vol. 5, 310. "Dies ist der Teich, in den ich Seite 143 im ersten Bande falle."

[44] *Der gestiefelte Kater* (1797). The original, shorter version reprinted in *Satiren und Parodien*, ed. Andreas Müller, vol. 9 of *Reihe Romantik* in *Deutsche Literatur*, ed. H. Kindermann (Leipzig, 1935), p. 50.

[45] *Prinz Zerbino* (1798), in *Schriften* (Berlin, 1828), vol. 10, 330ff.

German and English Romanticism

thetic illusion. Hegel and Kierkegaard found Romantic irony ethically irresponsible, mere play-acting, mere aestheticism; but in the best Romantics it is more than a realization that art is only art, that imagination is free and capricious: it is an insight into the chance existence of man, his insignificance, and his sovereignty over his insignificance which must have repelled a cosmic optimist like Hegel or a deeply troubled, agonized believer like Kierkegaard. This Romantic irony is completely absent from the English Romantic writers, even when they laugh or joke or parody. Wordsworth, Coleridge, Shelley, Keats are earnest, even solemn people, though Shelley may ridicule Wordsworth and Coleridge or savagely satirize Swellfoot the Tyrant and Keats may write funny doggerel on his trip to Scotland. Lamb may be whimsical, Scott broadly humorous, but no Englishman —with the possible exception of Byron—at that time has the sense of art as play, of life as Nothingness, of the artist as an outsider.

This ironical detachment is obviously related to the whole problem of what today is called the "alienation" of the artist, which was so much greater in Germany than in England. Wordsworth was a lonely man, Blake lived in a world of vision, Byron and Shelley flouted and attacked their society. The Germans hate and ridicule the Philistines, they wage savage war against the burghers, and Hoffmann, at least in his fiction, shrinks at the mere contact with the world of merchants and artisans who disturb the dream world of his artists. The books of the German Romantics are peopled with eccentrics, odd fellows, riders of hobbyhorses—sometimes as harmless as Uncle Toby or Walter Shandy, but more often sinister

German and English Romanticism

and dangerous.[46] Some are merely grotesque fools: Jean Paul's Dr. Katzenberger eats spiders and sucks junebugs alive in the presence of his bride. Others are criminals obsessed with a fixed idea like René Cardillac, the jeweler in Hoffmann's *Das Fräulein von Scuderi*, who has to murder the buyers of his works of art; others are sinister figures, charlatans or hypnotists like the *Magnetiseur*. Often they are divided, torn apart, "zerrissen" (split personalities, we would say today), sometimes represented as actual physical doubles.[47] The theme of the double, so characteristic of German Romanticism, may be merely humorous, as it was in Plautus' *Menaechmi*, in Shakespeare's *Comedy of Errors* and in Molière's *Amphitryon*. In Jean Paul, who apparently coined the German term, *Doppelgänger*, it assumes a sinister doubt of the identity of the ego. Schoppe would suddenly look at his hands in company and say: "Here sits a man and I am in him, but who is it?" He hates his image in the mirror gallery, the orang-outangs multiplying endlessly.[48] In Hoffmann the double is often simply the other self, the criminal self within man: the Mr. Hyde against the Dr. Jekyll of Stevenson's much later romance. Contemporary interest in "animal magnetism," in Mesmerism, gave scientific support to this idea of an irrational self in every man. Or the double, as in the remarkable poem of Chamisso's, "Erscheinung," may be the other self who usurps the place of the original self, yet it is impossible to decide who is the

---

[46] See Herman Meyer, *Der Typus des Sonderlings in der deutschen Literatur* (Amsterdam, 1943).

[47] On doubles see Otokar Fischer, "Dějiny dvojníka," in *Duše a slovo* (Prague, 1929), pp. 161-208. Ralph Tymms, *Doubles in Literary Psychology* (Cambridge, 1949).

[48] *Titan*, from *Sämtliche Werke*, ed. E. Berend, vol. 9, 322. "Da sitzt ein Herr leibhaftig und ich in ihm, wer ist aber solcher?"

German and English Romanticism

right one—the idealist or the cowardly, lying scoundrel.[49] The theme which received its most profound treatment in Dostoevsky, the concreteness of human existence, the problem of the stability and fixity of the human self, is clearly stated by the German Romantics.[50] It is not merely alienation from society, or the conflict between the artist and society; it is a much profounder *malaise* about the utter elusiveness of reality, the discontinuity of our self, the impossibility of human freedom.

In the most complex, most clearly elaborated figure of the divided, half-mad romantic artist, Hoffmann's Kapellmeister Kreisler, art becomes the salvation from division and madness. Kreisler is a musician not only because Hoffmann was one, but because music is to Hoffmann and to the German Romantics the highest art, the art which leads us into the dark abysses of our soul and the mystery of the world.

Here again the contrast with the English Romantic poets is painfully obvious. They have no, or hardly any, deeper relation to music, which in England had ceased to be a creative art. I am not aware of a single significant reference to Mozart, Beethoven or even Handel among the English Romantic poets. Wordsworth reportedly fell asleep at a musical-evening party.[51] Shelley speaks himself of his "gross idea of music": he went to the opera at the persuasion of Thomas Love Peacock in London and again in Milan, and he listened with delight to Jane

[49] (1828) in *Gesammelte Werke*, ed. Max Koch (Stuttgart, s. d.), vol. 2, 18.
[50] See Dmitri Chizhevsky, "The Theme of the Double in Dostoevsky" in *Dostoevsky: A Collection of Critical Essays*, ed. R. Wellek (Englewood Cliffs, N.J.), 1962, pp. 112-29.
[51] *Henry Crabb Robinson on Books and Their Writers*, ed. E. Morley (London, 1938), vol. 1, 293 (April 5, 1823).

German and English Romanticism

Williams playing the guitar.[52] Keats admits that "through Hunt he is indifferent to Mozart." Still, he indulged with his brothers and friends in an after-dinner parlor game of imitating vocally some musical instrument, Keats himself apparently imitating the bassoon.[53] Among the essayists a definite deprecation of music seems to be the pattern. Lamb wrote a semi-serious "Chapter on Ears" where "he must avow that he has received a great deal more pain than pleasure from this so cried-up faculty."[54] De Quincey comments on the "obstinate obtuseness" of the English in regard to music.[55] Hazlitt, who on occasion reviewed performances of operas and oratorios, consistently disparaged the genre and describes approvingly the indifference of the English public.[56] Music bores him as it presents "no distinct object to the imagination": it makes an "uninterrupted appeal to the sense of pleasure alone"; it is like "color without form: a soul without a body."[57] In commenting on a performance of Mozart's *Don Giovanni*, Hazlitt voices his disapproval of attempts to exalt the opera above the common run. It is a "kind of scented music." Zerlina's aria "La ci darem" gives him

[52] Letter to John Gisborne, June 18, 1822, in *Letters*, ed. Roger Ingpen (London, 1909), vol. 2, 976-77. On opera see vol. 2, 592 and 599.
[53] Letter to George and Georgiana Keats (Dec. 16, 1818–Jan. 4, 1819), *Letters*, ed. Maurice B. Forman, 4th edition (London, 1952), p. 251. On parlor game, *ibid.*, pp. 73, 129.
[54] *The Works*, ed. T. Hutchison (Oxford, 1924), vol. 1, 520.
[55] "Style" (1840), in *Collected Writings*, ed. D. Masson (London, 1897), vol. 10, 135.
[56] "The Italian Opera" (1816), in *Complete Works*, Centenary, ed. P. P. Howe (London, 1930), vol. 5, 325. Cf. vol. 5, 196.
[57] "The Oratorios" (1816), *ibid.*, 296-97. Hazlitt echoes British eighteenth-century views. See M. H. Abrams, *The Mirror and the Lamp* (New York, 1953), pp. 91-94. Cf. Herschel Baker, *William Hazlitt* (Cambridge, Mass., 1962), p. 297.

German and English Romanticism

"more pleasure than all the rest of the opera put together."[58] Only Coleridge is an exception among the English writers, though his interest in music seems almost entirely theoretical. Still, we know that very early the idea of writing an opera libretto crossed his mind.[59] Only recently, an entry in a late notebook was published in which Coleridge speaks of music as "this mighty magic," regretting his own ignorance, but romantically asserting that "music seems to have an immediate communion with my life." "It converses with the life of my mind, as if it were itself the Mind of my Life."[60] But this reflection is quite isolated and points again to Coleridge's singular position and special relationship to the Germans.

In general, it may be not unfair to contrast the metaphor of the Aeolian harp as "the corresponding breeze" (rightly pointed up by Meyer H. Abrams as the characteristic image of the English poets' sense of the unity of the universe)[61] with Hoffmann's use of the Devil's voice, which he professed to have heard as a boy on the seashore in East Prussia: a weird sound which filled him with profound terror and piercing compassion.[62] This natural

---

[58] "Don Juan" (1817), in *Complete Works*, Centenary Ed., vol. 5, 364.

[59] Letter to George Coleridge, April 7, 1794, in *Collected Letters*, vol. 1, 79. Coleridge then knew a musician, Charles Clagget, who set four of his poems to music. (On Clagget see *DNB*.)

[60] In *Inquiring Spirit*, ed. K. Coburn (London, 1951), pp. 214-15.

[61] "The Correspondent Breeze: A Romantic Metaphor" in *The Kenyon Review*, vol. 19 (1957), 113-30. Also in *English Romantic Poets: Modern Essays in Criticism*, ed. M. H. Abrams (New York, 1960), pp. 37-54.

[62] "Die Automate," in *Werke*, ed. G. Ellinger (Berlin, 1912), vol. 6, 95. Hoffmann himself refers to his source, G. H. Schubert, *Ansichten von der Nachtseite der Naturwissenschaft* (Dresden, 1808), p. 65.

German and English Romanticism

music is an image of the singing which kills the daughter of Rat Krespel, or it may be the demonic violin playing of Kreisler—a voice from the upper world which brings salvation or lures to destruction. Hoffmann is no exception among the Germans. He is preceded by Wackenroder, whose musician Berglinger, like Kreisler, feels music as a divine inspiration and perishes in the conflict with the world. In Wackenroder's last sketch, the strange "Oriental Legend of a Naked Saint,"[63] written shortly before his early death, art is conceived as the way to salvation from the incessant deafening roar of the wheel of Time, which the saint has to imitate with ecstatic mad gestures until he is freed by the saving sounds of a song. This saint's legend seems almost to anticipate Schopenhauer, who celebrated the effect of art in "stopping the wheel of Ixion"[64] and temporarily and illusorily alleviating the pain of existence. For the German Romantic artists and for Schopenhauer, who, we must remember, was their contemporary in spite of his belated fame, music is the central, the highest art. Thus also the hierarchy of the arts differs in Germany and England, as does the hierarchy of genres in literature.

We might ask whether we can account for these differences in causal terms. Do the economic and social differences between the two countries determine the literature? It would be easy to describe them, e.g. the contrast between the German particularism, with its many small states and lack of a single center, and England with its great metropolis, London.[65] Industrially, England was un-

[63] *Werke und Briefe* (Berlin, 1948), pp. 197ff.
[64] *Sämtliche Werke*, ed. A. Hübscher (Leipzig, 1937), vol. 2, 231. "Das Rad des Ixion steht still."
[65] Two books by W. H. Bruford, *Germany in the Eighteenth*

German and English Romanticism

doubtedly far more advanced than Germany. But the concrete bearing on literature of such knowledge seems, in this age of Marxism, greatly overrated. As to social provenience, the two groups in both countries represent a similar mixture of upper and lower *bourgeoisie* and aristocracy: Byron and Shelley were noblemen, as were Novalis, Arnim and Eichendorff. Coleridge was the son of a clergyman, as were the two Schlegels. Tieck was the son of a rope-maker in Berlin. Keats's father managed a livery stable in London. If we examine the economic resources of the two groups, we are led to the conclusion that only Byron and Scott made a fortune by writing, that Wordsworth had the luck of receiving an inheritance, that Shelley lived by borrowing on his expectations as the grandson of a Baronet, that Keats drew a small annuity, and that Coleridge had a patron in the china manufacturer Thomas Wedgwood, but also fended for himself eking out a living from journalism, lecturing and some royalties. Lamb was an official of the East India Company. The situation in Germany was not so very different. August Wilhelm Schlegel was for years a member of the household of Madame de Staël and later a Professor of the University of Bonn. Friedrich Schlegel became a high official in Metternich's Austria. Novalis was a salt-mine supervisor. Arnim and Eichendorff were Prussian landowners. E. T. A. Hoffmann was a law official, though for several years he tried to earn his living as an orchestra conductor and theater manager. It seems to me difficult to generalize with such data and

---

Century: The Social Background of the Literary Revival (Cambridge, 1935), and *Culture and Society in Classical Weimar 1775–1806* (Cambridge, 1962), contain much material.

easy to exaggerate the economic hardships which were suffered by a few of these writers at some time.

Politically, the outlook of both groups was necessarily deeply influenced by the French Revolution and the Napoleonic wars. In England the distinction of two generations is obvious: Wordsworth and Coleridge were young men at the outbreak of the Revolution and were carried away by enthusiasm for it; they were disappointed by its excesses and repelled in their patriotism and therefore moved into a conservative position which later showed also as hostility to the industrial revolution fostered by the liberals. In Wordsworth particularly, the enmity toward the city and an admiration for the "perfect republic of shepherds"[66] in the Lakes were important factors of his politics. The younger generation—Byron, Shelley and Keats—grew to manhood in the stifling atmosphere of the Restoration and were liberals of diverse shades. Shelley was the most radical, though his radicalism remains quite Utopian in spite of his exhortation to "The Men of England" to "forge arms—in your defence to bear."[67] The Germans were politically conservative, but in different degrees. The upsurge of patriotic fervor against the French, and hence against the ideas of the Enlightenment, was shared by all. Novalis, in his essay "Christianity or Europe" (1799) was, to quote Lukács, the first to recommend "the simple exchange economy of the Middle Ages, the totality of labor in arts and crafts against the rising fragmentation

---

[66] Wordworth's own term, see *Guide to the Lakes*, ed. E. de Selincourt (London, 1926), p. 67.

[67] "Song to the Men of England" (1819. Published 1839), in *Complete Poetical Works*, ed. T. Hutchison (Oxford, 1933), p. 568.

of capitalist economics."[68] Others put the conservative creed in purely political and religious terms. Friedrich Schlegel, Adam Müller and Zacharias Werner were converted to Roman Catholicism, E. T. A. Hoffmann administered somewhat reluctantly the laws persecuting the German *Burschenschaften*,[69] and Eichendorff served as an official of the Prussian Ministry of Education in charge of Catholic Ecclesiastic Affairs. Thus the German Romantics believed in an alliance of conservativism and nationalism accepted only by the older English group. This is a great distinctive feature of German nineteenth-century history, for elsewhere, in Italy and the East European countries, nationalism and liberalism were firmly allied. The fervor of German medievalism, the passionate interest in the German past and in peasant folklore can be associated with this general revolt against the leveling and centralizing tendencies of the Enlightenment, the Revolution and Napoleon. In England we have to go to Carlyle, Ruskin and the Oxford Movement to find similar conceptions of the Middle Ages as social norm: as a realm of order, tradition and joyful handicrafts.

For the concrete literature, economic and political conditions and ideologies are less important than the relation to philosophical and religious traditions. Some of this is implied in the economic and political attitudes: obviously the Catholic conversions were also politically motivated. In England both the Enlightenment and

[68] "Hölderlins Hyperion," in *Goethe und seine Zeit* (Bern, 1947), p. 120.

[69] Gottfried Fittbogen, "E. T. A. Hoffmanns Stellung zu den 'demagogischen Umtrieben' und ihrer Bekämpfung," in *Preussische Jahrbücher*, 189 (1922), pp. 79-92. Cf. H. Hewett-Thayer, *op. cit.*, pp. 91-93.

German and English Romanticism

established religious tradition were in a paradoxical combination stronger than in Germany. Blake, a nonconformist by background, was the one obvious exception. Coleridge for a time was a Unitarian, and Hazlitt was the son of a Unitarian preacher. In England, there was no parallel to the German idealistic philosophy; academically, Common Sense philosophy was in the saddle, and unofficially, the influence of Utilitarianism was spreading at that time. Thus the relation to religious and philosophical tradition was very different in the two countries. The German Romantics were confronted with the enormous prestige of the philosophy of Kant and Fichte and had a systematic philosopher and ally in Schelling. Friedrich Schlegel and Novalis were themselves engaged in technical philosophical speculation,[70] while Kant and Fichte affected the layman by a misunderstood interpretation—as propounding either a crushing skepticism or an irresponsible solipsism. Kleist felt that Kant had taken away all certainty of knowledge, and Tieck drew from Fichte the view that "Things are because we thought them."[71] In England, only Coleridge tried to speculate as a philosopher, and he drew heavily on the Germans; Shelley and Wordsworth were either confined to the British empiricist tradition or went back to Plato. In Germany, Lutheran orthodoxy had disintegrated, but there was always the alternative of Roman

---

[70] Friedrich Schlegel's independence and importance as a philosopher has been argued by Josef Körner in the introduction to *Neue Philosophische Schriften* (Frankfurt, 1935). On Novalis see Theodor Haering, *Novalis als Philosoph* (Frankfurt, 1955).

[71] "Die Wesen *sind,* weil wir sie *dachten,*" in *William Lovell* (1795), in *Schriften* (Berlin, 1828), vol. 6, 178. Cf. Fritz Brüggemann, *Die Ironie als entwicklungsgeschichtliches Moment* (Jena, 1909), a misnamed book on Romantic subjectivism.

German and English Romanticism

Catholicism which offered a refuge in uncertainty, and Friedrich Schlegel went the way to Rome. Brentano, a Catholic by birth, became fervently religious and spent years taking down the visions of a stigmatized nun, Katharina Emmerich. Only August Wilhelm Schlegel preserved an eighteenth-century skepticism,[72] though he had sympathized and played with all kinds of philosophies.

The distinction between the two countries is equally obvious when we look at the writers' relations to literary tradition. The Germans were confronted with the overwhelming presence of their classics; Goethe lived until 1832, producing incessantly during the heyday of Romanticism. He in particular was the great model and the great challenge. Shakespeare then came as a revelation and an intense connection was established with the older Romance literatures; Cervantes and Calderón especially were widely known and influential. With the Spanish poetry came its meters, and the German use of the four-beat trochee of the Spanish drama and romances has no parallel in England. The first popular example in English is *Hiawatha* (1855). In England there were no immediate models of great authority. The later eighteenth century, at least in poetry, seems barren, and the classicism of the age of Queen Anne was no longer a formidable foe. Spenser, Shakespeare and even Milton were remote in time, and thus they could be drawn upon very freely: the poetic antiquarianism rarely produced self-conscious *pastiche* if we except Coleridge's *Ancient*

---

[72] *Berichtigung einiger Missdeutungen* (Berlin, 1828), and the letter, "Sur la religion chrétienne," dated August 13, 1838, in *Œuvres écrites en français*, ed. E. Böcking (Leipzig, 1846), vol. 1, 189ff.

German and English Romanticism

Mariner, especially in its earlier archaic version, and Keats's "Eve of St. Mark." Rather, the great English Romantic poets used a younger tradition which they lifted into a higher region, the Augustan Miltonic poem, or the ode of the type of Collins and Gray, or the eighteenth-century octosyllabic verse tale. The German Romantics felt much more strongly that they had to break with the Hellenic classicism of Goethe. They drew more consistently on folk forms or on forms of Romance art poetry which they often misinterpreted as popular. In prose, the Germans represent most clearly a case of "rebarbarization": an attempt to raise such popular genres as the Gothic novel, the fairy tale and the anecdote into the realm of higher art.

Something thus can be done to account for the differences between the two literatures at that time, but I would be the first to admit that causal explanation and even historical antecedents do not accomplish much. We must leave something to chance, to genius, to a constellation of circumstances, possibly to that obscure force, national character. Why not agree that we are faced here with some ultimate *data*? It is variety that is the spice of life and of literature. The literary historian and the comparatist has done what he can do if he has accurately described, analyzed, characterized and compared what he has seen and read.

CHAPTER TWO

Carlyle and German Romanticism*

Carlyle is usually considered a Victorian. His great influence began with the success of *The French Revolution* in the very year of the accession of Queen Victoria (1837), and he lived until 1881, revered as a sage and consulted as an oracle. But we must realize that Carlyle was born in 1795, in the same year as John Keats, and that he was twenty-four years older than Ruskin, who is usually coupled with him. In 1837 he was forty-two. *Sartor Resartus*, the final version of which was written in the winter of 1830-31, anticipates in all essentials the whole of Carlyle's later development. His philosophy is clearly formulated in this early work, and it is no exaggeration to say that every fundamental idea found its expression in this final effort to sum up the convictions of his youth. Thus there seem to be good reasons to associate Carlyle with the Romantic rather than with the Victorian age. Obviously Carlyle has many things in common with Romanticism. First of all, and most glaringly, he has a common enemy in the rationalism of the eighteenth century. He fought against it from his first articles in the *Edinburgh Review* to the last lines of his old age. In the realm of philosophy he attacks rationalism and sensualism. He disagrees with the

* Originally in *Xenia Pragensia Ernesto Kraus septuagenario et Josepho Janko sexagenario ab amicis collegis discipulis oblata* (Pragae, 1929), pp. 375-403. Slightly revised.

Carlyle and German Romanticism

whole development of English philosophy since the times of John Locke; he charges it with giving solely a genetic theory of the mind without even answering the real philosophic questions on the relation of mind and matter, necessity and freedom, man's relation to God, to the universe, to time and space. With even greater vigor and prophetic conviction, he assails the moral creed of the "Enlightenment," the Loss-and-Profit Philosophy of Utilitarianism and Eudaemonism. He opposes the economic ideas of the rationalists, the whole political and social liberalism of Adam Smith, Bentham and Mill. And in all aesthetic matters he stands on the side of Romanticism versus the rules, the rationalistic explanations of the creative processes of the artist, against a narrow formalism, against the suppression of imagination, sublimity and wonder. He recognizes that the bargaining for a reconciliation between science and religion extirpated real religiosity, and he suspects Deism and its different versions of an ill-concealed atheism. His conception of history is certainly violently opposed to the most cherished beliefs of the eighteenth century: he suspects the idea of progress; *Past and Present* glorifies the social order of the Middle Ages.

It is unnecessary to continue, as his position is so obvious that it never could be mistaken by anyone. The real question arises if we inquire how far he stood positively on the side of Romanticism, for we can very well imagine an antagonism to the eighteenth century on different grounds from those of Romanticism. It seems at the first glance that Carlyle shares the Romantic creed. He certainly is an idealist, he preaches the freedom of the will, he dreams of a collectivistic organization of society, and he clings steadfastly to the belief in poetical

Carlyle and German Romanticism

inspiration and the metaphysical meaning of art as a revelation of the absolute. He sees in history a divine plan which is nothing but a self-revelation of the will of God.

This first impression, however, is superficial. Carlyle showed in every field of human thought a deep distrust of Romanticism, which he took sometimes as a welcome ally, but which he never understood properly and which was radically opposed to his own temperament. It would be interesting to prove how completely Carlyle misunderstood and misinterpreted German idealism, how he did not, and could not, see the implications of its aesthetics, ethics and political philosophy. It can be shown in detail that Carlyle's relationship to the English Romanticists was indifferent and even hostile. But probably even more illuminating than a study of his relation to Coleridge, to Wordsworth, to Scott, to Byron and others would be a detailed examination of his relation to the German Romanticists. The reasons for this preference are obvious: with respect to the German Romanticists, we can use a fairly systematic body of opinions which Carlyle formulated very frequently for print and did not divulge, as he did most of his opinions about his English contemporaries, in private letters which sometimes poorly conceal, or rather exhibit, the violence and rashness of his judgment and the hearsay evidence which is used against them. On the other hand, Carlyle's judgment about the Germans is little distorted by oral reports and is very frequently—because of the lack of any material about the private personality of the man in question—free from his chief critical vice: his inordinate submission of the aesthetic judgment to the judgment of the private man. And, last but not least, there

Carlyle and German Romanticism

is a growing body of scholarship which defines and describes so well the characteristics of the different German writers that we are provided with a modern standard which enables us to judge Carlyle's pronouncements with a fairly unbiased scale of values as it was developed quite independently of Carlyle's opinions.

Carlyle's relation to German literature has been scrutinized more or less minutely several times. The sources of many phrases of the most characteristic "Carlylese" have been revealed. Such stock formulas as the "Worship of Sorrow" or the "Open Secret" come from Goethe, the concept of "self-annihilation" is a translation of Novalis' "Selbsttötung," the distinction between a philosophical head and a bread-artist is drawn from Schiller, the passages about the Bungler and Mongrel and of the Divine idea of the world come from Fichte, such phrases as the "ästhetische Springwurzeln" from Jean Paul. But, of course, these borrowings are not of much importance. The verbal loans were very frequently suggested by a passage which came to Carlyle's attention in the course of translating German works. He was confronted with the problem of rendering a strange German term, which clung to his memory because of its very strangeness, or frequently a little trick of speech impressed him because of its quaintness. It would be absurd to speak of anything like influence in such cases, e.g. of Carlyle's taking the titles of the central chapters of *Sartor Resartus* (the "Everlasting No" and the "Everlasting Yea") from a book of the exceedingly unimportant literary historian and ill-famed commentator of Shakespeare, Franz Horn, or his piecing together the title of Teufelsdrökh's book—*Die Kleider, ihr Werden und Wirken*—from Wachler's *Über Werden und Wirken der Literatur*, which Goethe had sent him on June 14, 1830.

It would not be very difficult to trace the sources of Carlyle's knowledge of German literature. But we have to agree with Jean-Marie Carré[1] that the value of Carlyle's German studies has been very much exaggerated by the Germans. From the point of view of modern scholarship or criticism, the value of Carlyle's essays is insignificant. It might be worthwhile to point, at least, to the interesting passages on the dramatic structure of the *Nibelungen*,[2] or to the remark about the similarity between Novalis' *Hymnen an die Nacht* and Herder's poetry[3] (which was proved in detail only fairly recently by Rudolf Unger),[4] or to some of his observations on Jean Paul, which will be discussed later in their proper connection. Obviously the purely factual, i.e. biographical and historical, information which Carlyle used is drawn from German books, and it would be of not much intrinsic value to distinguish in detail among these sources. In order to do this, we would have to track down all the manuals, dictionaries and literary histories Carlyle used as so much raw material, whose analysis would tell us as little as would the analysis of his daily food. History should not only know the limits of its knowledge, but it should also inquire whether it is sometimes worthwhile to know what we can obviously discover with a bit of searching.

For example, we could show that Carlyle used for his introduction to Musaeus in *German Romance* Kotzebue's

---

[1] *Goethe en Angleterre* (Paris, 1920), p. 102.
[2] Carlyle, *Essays*, II, 238. I quote the Centenary Ed. (London, 1899).
[3] *Ibid.*, p. 44.
[4] *Herder, Novalis und Kleist* (Frankfurt am Main, 1922).

Carlyle and German Romanticism

introduction to Musaeus' *Nachgelassene Schriften*; in this introduction Carlyle sometimes translates literally, sometimes paraphrases very freely and sometimes simply uses the information for his own purposes.[5] We could show in detail whence his facts about Hoffmann are drawn,[6] or his information about Jean Paul, Novalis, or Werner. We could even show the sources of some of his judgments. His estimate of Maler Müller is derived from Tieck.[7] His criticism of Musaeus' technique of fairy tale is similarly derived from Tieck; the condemnation of Gessner comes probably from A. W. Schlegel, while several details of his sketch of Lessing apparently are taken from Franz Horn.[8] This has been sometimes a necessary preparatory work, for it is important to distinguish Carlyle's own contribution, his own mental characteristics, from mere paraphrases and digests. But the problem is not solved by such an analysis whose results could be indicated only in passing. We should merely get an exact knowledge of the extent and depth of Carlyle's study of German literature. But the result is more or less clear from the very outset: Carlyle studied what could be studied in the Edinburgh of the early nineteenth century, and neither his intentions nor the means at his command permitted him to exhaust the materials which even then were accessible in Germany.[9]

---

[5] Cf., e.g. *Nachgelassene Schriften* (Mannheim, 1813), p. 7, with Carlyle, *German Romance*, I, 15; also cf. *Nachgelassene*, p. 10 with *German*, p. 16; and *Nachgelassene*, p. 17 with *German*, p. 13.

[6] Chiefly E. Hitzig, *Aus Hoffmanns Leben und Nachlass* (Berlin, 1823).

[7] Possibly through the medium of Horn, who quotes the passage in his *Poesie und Beredsamkeit der Deutschen* (Berlin, 1822-29); cf. *Phantasus*, I, 446-70 and Horn, III, 309.

[8] Cf. *Essays*, I, 46-48 with Horn, III, 119.

[9] Werner Leopold, in *Die religiöse Wurzel von Carlyles literarischer*

Carlyle and German Romanticism

Carlyle's task was the writing of articles, introducing translations—in short—the duties of a propagandist. Only for a brief time (1829-30) did he have in mind a systematic history of German literature,[10] and the articles, "The Nibelungenlied" and "German Literature of the 14th and 15th Centuries," were the only ones planned for such a whole. And it is not mere chance that just these papers are the most colorless and unoriginal Carlyle ever wrote. He used this material in a lecture-course he gave in 1838 on German literature, of which only very scanty transcripts have been preserved. Nor do these fragments make us especially regret this loss. For his own purposes, which were not those of a scholar, and for a Scotchman of his age, his knowledge of German literature was both surprisingly wide and accurate. What the general standard was at that time can best be judged from William Taylor's *Historic Survey of German Poetry* (3 vols., 1828-30), which cannot by any means be considered the effort of a chance layman but which nevertheless teems with gross misstatements and elementary blunders. Carlyle did not miss the opportunity to expose them in his sharp though justified review of the lifework of this early pioneer of German literature.

It will be our main concern to appreciate and analyze

Wirksamkeit (Halle, 1922), in an article "Carlyle and Franz Horn" in *Journal of English and Germanic Philology*, XXVIII (1929), 215-19 and later in an appendix, "Carlyle's Handbooks on the History of German Literature," in C. F. Harrold's *Carlyle and German Thought* (New Haven, 1934), pp. 238-47 has investigated these sources thoroughly. Also Hill Shine's edition of *Carlyle's Unfinished History of German Literature* (Lexington, Ky., 1951), contains further details in the introduction and notes.

[10] Since then Hill Shine edited *Carlyle's Unfinished History of German Literature*. The manuscript is in the Yale University Library.

Carlyle and German Romanticism

Carlyle's deeper relation to German literature. This has been done before from different angles of approach. Jean-Marie Carré's *Goethe en Angleterre* (Paris, 1920) gives an excellent account of this chief relation in a fair and well-balanced spirit, and though I am not able to agree with some of his minor conclusions, the whole is so satisfactory that another examination of this well-tilled field seems superfluous. The thin and not very fully informed essay by C. E. Vaughan[11] sees equally well the central point of this relation. And F. Küchler's detailed paper, "Carlyle und Schiller,"[12] is in all respects satisfactory. Carlyle's debt to Schiller is in any case rather slight, though he wrote his first book on him and as late as the fifties translated long supplementary passages on Schiller's family for the second edition of his *Life*. Herder (though there are a number of extracts from Herder in Carlyle's *Note Books*),[13] and especially Wieland, did not play any significant part in Carlyle's picture of German literature, nor is his relation to Lessing more than cold respect for the skeptic who deserved to be a believer.[14] All the information about Schubart and Musaeus is more or less literally translated,[15] nor is there any necessity to dwell on his incidental remarks about Gessner, Heinse, Maler Müller, or Bürger. Nor

---

[11] "Carlyle and His German Masters" in *Essays and Studies*, I (1910), pp. 168-96.

[12] *Anglia*, XXII (1903), 1-93, 393-446. Note the same author's *Carlyle und Schiller* (Halle, 1902), a discussion of Carlyle's *Life of Schiller* which is not identical with the *Anglia* articles.

[13] See, however, Hill Shine, "Carlyle's Early Writings and Herder's *Ideen*: The Concept of History," *Booker Memorial Studies* (Chapel Hill, N.C., 1950), pp. 1-33.

[14] *Essays*, I, 47-48.

[15] The *Life* of Schubart in the appendix to Schiller's *Life* from Jördens' *Gelehrtenlexikon*, the Musaeus from Kotzebue's introduction.

Carlyle and German Romanticism

had Carlyle any particularly close relations with the new literature of Young Germany. Obviously the scanty references to Heine,[16] whom he calls a "blackguard worth very little," or the references to Börne,[17] to Menzel,[18] and to Count Pückler[19] show little sympathy and apparently only a slight acquaintance with the newest developments of German literature. Thus Romanticism remains as an unexplored field which will lead, I trust, to interesting results for the general problem of Carlyle's historical position.

For practical reasons, the advantages of which will become apparent, I shall survey first Carlyle's relation to the younger generation of the German Romanticists. It is characteristic that the chief poets of the period, Brentano and Arnim, remained unknown to Carlyle and that he apparently had no firsthand knowledge of Kleist, whom he mentions briefly in his introduction to Fouqué,[20] though we may note this passage as the first allusion to the great dramatist in English (1826). Only three of the major writers of the younger generation became the object of Carlyle's passing interest: Fouqué, E. T. A. Hoffmann and Zacharias Werner. All three were received by Carlyle with equal sympathy. Even very late in his life he refers with respect to Fouqué's

---

[16] See letter to Varnhagen of Nov. 7, 1840, in *Last Words of Thomas Carlyle* (London, 1892), p. 203, and letter to Emerson, Nov. 5, 1836 in *The Correspondence of Thomas Carlyle and Ralph Waldo Emerson*, ed. C. E. Norton (Boston, 1883), I, 109.

[17] Reference to his speech on Jean Paul, *Essays*, I, 4 and to his *Briefe aus Paris*, *Essays*, III, 209.

[18] Letter to Emerson, Nov. 5, 1836, *loc. cit.*

[19] To Mill, Aug. 28, 1832, in *Letters of Thomas Carlyle to John Stuart Mill, John Sterling and Robert Browning*, ed. Alexander Carlyle (London, 1923), p. 16.

[20] *German Romance*, I, 208.

Carlyle and German Romanticism

Undine, which he originally planned to translate for his collection *German Romance*, until he discovered that an English translation was already in existence.[21] The translation of the tale "Aslauga's Ritter"[22] was apparently only a makeshift, for in the second edition Carlyle suppressed this piece. The introduction to this little fairy tale is not without some interest, and the sketch in it of Fouqué is very sharp-eyed and just. Carlyle rightly stresses the inner weakness and delicacy of the heroes, which is in such striking contrast to their enormous physical strength. The formula, "meek heroism," "soft-hearted and strong-armed," is very neat and is substantially in accordance with Heine's much more venomous and much less polite description of Fouqué's Siegfried: "Er ist stark wie die Felsen von Norweg und ungestüm wie das Meer, das sie umrauscht. Er hat soviel Mut wie hundert Löwen und so viel Verstand wie zwei Esel."[23] Carlyle touches lightly on the bloodlessness of this aristocratic art and hints at the inner relationship between Fouqué and Spanish art (which could be explained by Fouqué's ancestry).

Carlyle's relation to E. T. A. Hoffmann is more illuminating, though it speaks very little for his aesthetic appreciation. Carlyle translated the *Golden Pot*, this miracle of fancy and severe structure, with apparently not much enthusiasm, and in the second edition he deleted it. The inherent trouble—a trouble which constantly mars his attitude to his English contemporaries—

---

[21] Cf. the letter to John Carlyle of Dec. 24, 1835, in *Letters*, ed. C. E. Norton (London, 1888), II, 439. *German Romance*, I, 210.

[22] From the third number of the review *Die Jahreszeiten* (Berlin, 1814).

[23] *Die Romantische Schule*, III.

Carlyle and German Romanticism

with Carlyle's relation to Hoffmann was that he unluckily knew too much about Hoffmann's private life and character, or at least was under the illusion that he knew all about it, when he had read Hitzig's *Aus Hoffmanns Leben und Nachlass*.[24] Carlyle admitted that this introduction was the worst.[25] Carlyle displays here an unpleasant side of his character, that of the inhuman preacher who looks down, with a condescending pity, upon his poor sheep strayed from the path of righteousness, the moralist who freely distributes posthumous censures and advice as to how to avoid the terrible fate of artistic Bohemia which met poor Hoffmann. E. T. A. Hoffmann was, according to Carlyle, a man without principles, without a creed, without an aim in life. He had neither belief nor the courage for disbelief: he was politically indifferent. His art (which Carlyle apparently knew only from the *Phantasiestücke in Callots Manier*, comparatively immature writing) has no aim and is merely the effusion of his changing moods. He did not love art with pure love as a well of beauty; it was to him rather the source of refined pleasure. He did not long for heavenly peace, but for earthly excitement, an argument which Carlyle used only a few months later in his attack on Byron.[26] Hoffmann, he tells us, never recognized the truth—that our life cannot be a mere string of passive pleasures or agreeable sensations. In his character there is something insincere, something of the manner of an actor (which is apparently Carlyle's reaction to Hoffmann's Romantic irony). And finally, he had in him-

[24] Berlin, 1823.
[25] Letter of May, 1826, in *Letters*, ed. Norton, II, 350-51.
[26] *Wotton Reinfred*. Printed in *Last Words of Thomas Carlyle* (London, 1892).

Carlyle and German Romanticism

self only the raw material for a poet, but he could not rule himself: "In fact, he elaborated nothing; above all, not himself."[27] He belongs to these pitiful beings such as Callot, Teniers, Rabelais, Beckford, who now and then find still a few admirers. Hoffmann can be proud of this society in hell, which is for Carlyle the hell of beings who have nothing else to do than tell stories. As a matter of fact, Hoffmann had little luck in England in contrast to his splendid fortunes in France and Russia. Here he had been translated even before Carlyle.[28] The essay by Walter Scott, "On the Supernatural in Fictitious Compositions and Particularly on the Works of E. T. A. Hoffmann,"[29] which for years to come determined the English idea of Hoffmann as a teller of gruesome stories, is superficial and shallow.

Zacharias Werner, who is, as a personality and a writer, certainly the most problematic of all the Romantic tribe and who is in everything the antipode of Carlyle, curiously enough attracted a great deal of attention which was not always hostile. Carlyle devoted to Werner a very long paper in the *Foreign Review* of 1828, in which he retells his life fairly completely according to Hitzig's biography and gives, obviously from firsthand acquaintance with the texts, a full account of *Die Söhne des Thals, Das Kreuz an der Ostsee, Martin Luther* and *Die Mutter der Makkabäer*, interspersed with quotations in his own, rather clumsy, verse-translation. This is not in itself a sign of great personal sympathy, as Carlyle had

[27] *German Romance*, II, 19.
[28] The tales "Das Majorat," "Das Fräulein von Scudery," and "Meister Floh" and the full-length novel, *Die Elixiere des Teufels* (Edinburgh, 1824).
[29] In *Foreign Review*, 1827, reprinted even in the French edition of Hoffmann's works, translated by Loève-Veimars.

Carlyle and German Romanticism

to write a long and detailed paper for financial reasons. But his personal interest flashes up at intervals. Although he is not always enthusiastic about Werner, Carlyle admits that in his whole conduct there was never a vestige of insincerity—a large concession, if we know what sincerity means in Carlyle's scale of values, and the more remarkable as Werner has been frequently suspected of acting. Werner had, according to Carlyle, real religion throughout his whole life; he thirsted after truth as the highest possession of mankind and therefore stands *eo ipso* above the unbeliever. Carlyle grants him great artistic abilities, too, when he praises *Das Kreuz an der Ostsee* for its severe structure. He is not blind, however, to Werner's shortcomings: his imagination is uncouth and untamed, his reason weak and his will broken. Carlyle recognizes the disparity between Werner's ambitious plans and the meager results; he shrewdly notices his Asiatic (or rather Catholic) passivity and languid mysticism. But Carlyle hesitates in his condemnation and even admits that he does not understand him completely, a humility altogether too rare in Carlyle's rash pronouncements about people. We can explain Carlyle's interest in Zacharias Werner by purely human motives: Werner attracted his interest mostly as a convert to Catholicism. Curiously the puritan Carlyle had no marked aversion to such converts as Friedrich Schlegel and Zacharias Werner. It could be that he was much too sure of his own Protestantism to feel a serious danger in Catholicism. He stood so much outside the act of conversion that he could give it the disinterested curiosity of a man who is fascinated by religious conversions in general, who had himself gone through a crisis of inner illumination, but who could not possibly feel the

Carlyle and German Romanticism

temptation of a conversion from Calvinism to Catholicism. Carlyle tries to explain the conversion, though he admits that his explanation is far from complete. He offers the psychological interpretation—Catholicism as a quiet haven, as a refuge of a shipwrecked man—and he gives a historical interpretation, which is more enlightening for Carlyle's convictions than for the actual fever of conversion raging in Germany. Carlyle thinks that the Germans consider denomination as a purely exterior form (he cites Johannes Müller, Schelling and Herder as witnesses), or in the language of Teufelsdrökh, as a "mere cloth of belief." But this is no explanation of the reasons why the stately dress of Catholicism was preferred to the humbler clothes of Luther. This psychological problem is obviously the one point of interest which dominates Carlyle's mind. But in other respects, also, Werner's doctrine is not altogether distasteful to Carlyle: he speaks with approval of his philosophy of self-forgetting, of the necessity to submerge the I in the Idea, which corresponds to Carlyle's usual phrase of "Self-annihilation." He quotes with apparent approval his hatred of Eudaemonism and of the doctrine of heavenly rewards, and he did not translate without wholehearted support a very recondite passage in a note to *Das Kreuz an der Ostsee*, where Werner speaks of Protestantism: "There is another Protestantism, however, which constitutes in Conduct what Art is in Speculation, and which I reverence so highly, that I even place it above Art, as Conduct is above Speculation at all times."[30] With the exception of this essay, there is little of Werner in the other writings of Carlyle. In a

[30] *Essays*, I, 132.

Carlyle and German Romanticism

decisive passage of *Sartor Resartus*, at the end of the famous scene in the Rue St. Thomas de l'Enfer, Carlyle speaks of his spiritual New-Birth, or "Baphometic Fire-Baptism," a curious term derived from the second scene of the fifth act of Werner's *Templer von Cypern*, which Carlyle had translated in his long paper.[31] And a quotation in the chapter on Old Clothes comes from the same monstrous drama.[32]

In this connection it may be not amiss to refer to Carlyle's criticism of Franz Grillparzer. In a review "German Playwrights" published in the *Foreign Quarterly Review* (1829), he speaks rather condescendingly of the great dramatist, who was known to him from *Die Ahnfrau*, *Sappho* and *Ottokar*. He considers him a very innocent, meek, graceful and pure soul, a misjudgment which is inexplicable to us who know something of his bitter fight with Austrian narrowness and bureaucracy. Curiously enough, Carlyle thinks that Grillparzer was induced to play-writing only by the prevailing fashion and that he would have been more proficient either in prose or in a minor province of poetry, in the sonnet or in the elegy; this is again a judgment refuted by Grillparzer's rather bulky but decidedly uninspired and sluggish poetry. But Carlyle rightly recognizes the essential egocentricity of his character and his whole art, which is little more than an expansion of his own personality, and he sees well the relation between *Ottokar* and Schiller's *Piccolomini*. (Today we could not overlook the connecting link, the dramas of Mathias Collin.) Yet the essay is worth mentioning as one of the first

---

[31] Cf. *Sartor*, p. 136 with *Essays*, I, 100-101.
[32] "The Prison men call Life," cf. "he cast him forth and shut him in a prison called Life." Cf. *Sartor*, p. 192 with *Essays*, I, 109.

Carlyle and German Romanticism

accounts of Grillparzer outside Germany[33] and as a striking illustration of Carlyle's critical weaknesses when confronted with a work about whose author he apparently knew nothing whatsoever, for he says that he "seems to be an Austrian."[34]

Naturally Carlyle's relation to the older generation was much closer, not only because it was much more interesting philosophically, but also for chronological reasons: it was much more established and less the center of controversy than the second generation, which was coeval with Carlyle. The brothers Schlegel are usually considered the leaders and founders of German Romanticism. Their philosophical originality is sometimes doubted today—though the newest research shows that Friedrich Schlegel was not altogether the passive recipient of Fichte's and Novalis' ideas—and it would be absurd to ascribe the whole change of literary taste mainly to their activities. But outside Germany they were the most important representatives of the Romantic movement, chiefly because Madame de Staël had presented August Wilhelm as its spokesman in *De l'Allemagne*. For Carlyle they were the natural starting-point for a discussion of his own conception of Romanticism, because only through them had the word "romantic," in the sense of a literary program, became known in England. Carlyle rightly disbelieves Madame de Staël's contention that three young men (the Schlegels and Tieck) in a little town like Jena could have effected such a sweeping change. He thinks that there is not much of a gulf be-

---

[33] See, however, Byron's high praise of *Sappho*, Jan. 12, 1821, *Letters and Journals*, ed. R. E. Prothero (London, 1901), v, 171-72 and reviews in *Blackwood's*. Cf. Artur Burkhard, *Franz Grillparzer in England and America* (Vienna, 1961).

[34] *Essays*, I, 361.

tween them and the so-called Classics. They apply in literary criticism the principles of Goethe and Schiller,[35] and they propagate successfully the ideas of Kant, Herder, Schiller, Goethe and Richter, which they try to harmonize;[36] they are only the defenders and justifiers of Goethe and Schiller.[37] Certainly this is a great simplification of the complicated and intricate relationship between the two brothers and the Weimar Classics. Carlyle rejects the idea that the struggle of the Schlegels is a struggle against Schiller and Goethe and considers it rather as the old fight against the general rule of shallowness and mediocrity, simply as a fight against the Enlightenment.[38] There is, according to Carlyle, a single critical movement from the *Xenien* to Tieck, Wackenroder and the Schlegels.[39] This is at least a consistent conception, consistent especially from an English point of view, since in England we can really speak of a continuous stream from the first reaction against the eighteenth century up to the summits of Romanticism. Hence Carlyle had to look upon the German development through Storm and Stress, Classicism and Romanticism as a parallel to the English situation. German literary history of recent times (especially H. Korff in his excellent *Geist der Goethezeit* and in *Humanismus und Romantik*) begins again to minimize the differences between the single stages of the great development and to stress more and more the unifying idea—irrationalism attacking the rationalism of the eighteenth century. Carlyle's position, though it is much too simplified and much too clear-cut to grasp the manifold variety of historical reality, is as a whole perfectly defensible and

[35] *German Romance*, I, 261.   [36] *Essays*, I, 53.
[37] *Ibid.*, p. 71.   [38] *Essays*, II, 18.   [39] *Ibid.*, p. 353.

Carlyle and German Romanticism

consistent. He, of course, does not miss the opportunity to launch the second and strongest reason for his contention: German Romanticism is not exclusively a German phenomenon, but is generally European in its scope. He cites the new enthusiasm for Shakespeare and Elizabethan literature and the reaction against Pope and the French taste in England as a parallel. Even in France they began to doubt the value of the three unities and to undermine the authority of Corneille.[40] Again Carlyle saw the general situation clearly enough; but his view was colored by his characteristic disregard for the finer shades of difference among the several Romantic movements, for he personally was interested in the one common trait, the enmity toward the Enlightenment.

Carlyle respects the Schlegels, though he protests against an exaggeration of their importance. He draws a great deal of information from them, while occasionally disputing their opinions. In the *Life of Schiller* he disagrees in favor of Schiller with some of A. W. Schlegel's judgments on *Kabale und Liebe* and *Die Jungfrau von Orleans*.[41] At other times he quotes with approval Friedrich Schlegel's opinion of *Wilhelm Meister*,[42] or of English philosophy since Hume;[43] he reproduces Friedrich's parallel between the Reformation and Kant's critical philosophy,[44] or quotes August Wilhelm Schlegel's opinion of Tieck.[45] In his essay about the great philolo-

---

[40] *German Romance*, I, 261.

[41] Cf. *Life of Schiller*, p. 36, with A. W. Schlegel's *Vorlesungen über dramatische Kunst und Litteratur*, 2nd ed. (Heidelberg, 1817). III, 407; also cf. Carlyle, *Schiller*, p. 169, with Schlegel, *op. cit.*, III, 412, where he speaks of "das rosenfarb erheiterte Märtyrtum der Jungfrau von Orleans."

[42] *Wilhelm Meister*, I, 7.   [43] *Essays*, I, 80.
[44] *Ibid.*, p. 77.   [45] *German Romance*, I, 258.

Carlyle and German Romanticism

gist Heyne,[46] Carlyle refers to the brothers Schlegel as the founders of a new and more humane view of Greek and Roman antiquity, and in the lectures on *Heroes and Hero-Worship*, he praises A. W. Schlegel's remark which called the histories of Shakespeare a kind of "National Epic."[47] But Carlyle hardly appreciated their historical importance, especially in criticism, philology and philosophy. He even confused them in his memory, as he wrongly ascribes a passage from Friedrich to August Wilhelm.[48]

Later the much more literary and scholarly August Wilhelm Schlegel almost disappeared from Carlyle's horizon, and the more speculative Friedrich remained as an object of his vivid interest. He comments in a very tolerant mood about Friedrich's conversion,[49] and he devotes one of his greatest essays, "Characteristics" (1831), to Friedrich Schlegel's last philosophical work: *Philosophische Vorlesungen, insbesondere über Philosophie der Sprache und des Wortes* (Vienna, 1830). What Carlyle says about Schlegel's book is in the main not an actual comment about Schlegel, but simply Carlyle's confession about his relations to metaphysics. He stresses Schlegel's spiritualism, in which—according to Carlyle— all Matter is evaporating into a Phenomenon, and terrestrial Life itself, with its whole doings and showings, is a Disturbance (*Zerrüttung*) produced by the *Zeitgeist*

---

[46] *Essays*, I, 351.   [47] *Heroes*, p. 109.

[48] Cf. *Essays*, I, 80: "This is August Wilhelm's verdict: given in words equivalent to these." The original publication in the *Edinburgh Review* (1827) has: "This is Schlegel's view, his words are not before us." The passage occurs in Friedrich's *Geschichte der alten und neuen Literatur* (Vienna, 1816), 2nd part, p. 224. This was first pointed out by Werner Leopold in *Die religiöse Wurzel*, *loc. cit.*

[49] Speaking of Werner's conversion *Essays*, I, 144.

Carlyle and German Romanticism

(Spirit of Time).[50] The underlying spiritualism of Schlegel is nothing very peculiar to him, and what Carlyle reproduces here of Schlegel's original speculation is so indistinct, and even incorrect, that we can confidently ascribe it to Carlyle's general inability to comprehend any more abstract speculation. The Force which dislocated Time from Eternity is in Schlegel identical with the original sin of "individuation" or even with the principle of Evil, with the very Devil, and this force is called the "Spirit of Time,"[51] which has therefore nothing to do with the Voltairean conception of an "Esprit des Temps." Then, continues Carlyle, Schlegel considers Time and Space as mere forms of man's mind and does not ascribe to them any external reality and existence,[52] again an idea which is common in epistemological idealism and not at all characteristic of Friedrich Schlegel, who, on the contrary, protests against the phenomenalism implied and would not exclude the concept of Time from the essence of things.[53] Carlyle, it seems, did not understand Schlegel's ideas but simply ascribed to him the idealism which he liked and which he understood in his own way. Schlegel's whole book serves as only a pretext for a long and brilliant polemic against the spirit of Carlyle's time, against the English Enlightenment, whose influence he felt as oppressive throughout his whole life.

Several years later, the older brother, A. W. Schlegel, reappeared on Carlyle's horizon. A. W. Schlegel visited London in 1832, but Carlyle apparently avoided a meet-

---

[50] *Essays*, III, 54.
[51] Cf. *Sämtliche Werke*, 2nd edition (Vienna, 1846), XV, 90-91.
[52] *Essays*, III, 54.
[53] *Sämtliche Werke*, loc. cit., p. 84.

Carlyle and German Romanticism

ing, leaving a calling card and entering in his notebooks some (probably true) reports that he painted his face.[54] A. W. Schlegel did not take offense, for he recommended Carlyle to Hayward shortly afterwards as the only Englishman who could write a general appreciation of Goethe, "who had just died."[55]

The third young man who—according to Carlyle—did not effect a literary revolution, Ludwig Tieck, meant necessarily much less to Carlyle than either of the brothers Schlegel. It is true that he translated some of his short stories for *German Romance* ("Der blonde Eckbert," "Der getreue Eckhard," "Der Runenberg," "Die Elfen" and "Der Pokal"), but the introduction to these translations is especially empty and insignificant. It is obvious that he knew very little about Tieck, as he otherwise could not have considered the drama *Kaiser Oktavianus* a novel. And his attempt to characterize Tieck is singularly awkward. Carlyle himself admits that the first paragraph of this sketch could be equally well applied to any real poet.[56] Then he proceeds to define Tieck's imagination as an imagination of the character and not of the intellect, a definition which I confess sounds very obscure at first. But if one supposes that "character" is intended to mean the German "Gemüt," then this hazy definition assumes at least some meaning. Carlyle acknowledges Tieck's merits in the history of the fairy tale and even calls his style "chaste and simple." This is about all he can say about Tieck the writer. The man was more

---

[54] *Two Note-books*, ed. C. E. Norton (New York, 1898), p. 258.

[55] Cf. Hayward's letter to Carlyle, April 6, 1832, first printed in D. A. Wilson's *Carlyle till the French Revolution* (London, 1924), p. 284.

[56] *German Romance*, I, 264. A detailed account in E. H. Zeydel's *Tieck and England* (Princeton, 1931), pp. 114-24.

Carlyle and German Romanticism

interesting to him, but apparently he did not know much about him, as the scanty biographical facts show. Tieck is to him a man of negation who arrived at faith. At this stage—there, where his scale of values became stabilized—he had to solve the problem of how to translate "honorable feelings into a suitable language, the language of deeds." Here Carlyle's activistic creed intrudes so glaringly that we are tempted to doubt the value of most of his judgments. Later on, Carlyle frequently used Tieck's judgment and information. He translated a good deal from his introduction to Novalis' writings, and he quotes his introduction to the *Minnelieder aus dem schwäbischen Zeitalter*,[57] or a remark about Dante's *Divine Comedy*.[58] Even from such a comparatively late date as 1843, we have a detailed criticism of Tieck's *Vittoria Accorombona* (1840), which Carlyle read on his journey to Paris.[59] But it is safe to say that the relation was always a cool and correct one, simply because there were no matters of friction and no local proximity between them.

On his first belated trip to Germany, Carlyle called on Tieck in Berlin on October 7, 1852. He made a very unfavorable impression on Tieck, while yet remaining friendly. Carlyle wrote to Jane: "Yesterday I saw old Tieck, beautiful old man; so serene, so calm, so sad." And in an interview he spoke of Tieck as "a genial, nobly gifted man, with almost the finest head I ever saw."[60]

[57] Cf. *Essays*, II, 275, 276 with Tieck's *Kritische Schriften* (Leipzig, 1848), I, 196.
[58] In *Heroes and Hero-worship*, p. 90, from Tieck's introduction to Novalis, also translated by Carlyle, in *Essays*, II, 53.
[59] Cf. letter from July 12, 1843, quoted by J. A. Froude, *Thomas Carlyle: A History of His Life in London* (London, 1884), I, 258.
[60] Zeydel, pp. 122-28.

Carlyle and German Romanticism

Novalis exerted a much greater charm on Carlyle. He pays him deep respect and expresses his gratitude: "Novalis is an Anti-Mechanist—a deep man—the most perfect of modern spirit seers. I thank him for somewhat."[61] Though Carlyle could not and would not understand the fragmentary mind of a Coleridge, he felt drawn to the German mystic for the power of his personal charm. Carlyle's essay in the *Foreign Review* (1828) is an honest attempt to understand a foreign point of view, one of the few examples of a sympathetic approach in Carlyle's dogmatic writings. He even admits that not all is clear to him, that much study is still needed to unravel the marvelous texture of his subtle speculations. Carlyle's essay is in a way an introduction to a hostile reader: it gives a prolix defense of mysticism, it tells the story of his life according to Tieck's account and it translates a rather manifold selection of passages from "Lehrlinge von Sais," a number of the Fragments, two scenes from *Heinrich von Ofterdingen*, and the third "Hymne an die Nacht." Again Carlyle explains the general characteristics of German idealism in rather elementary terms: idealism (pointing to Indian philosophy as a parallel), phenomenalism, which is rightly understood as a purely epistemological idea, the irreality of Space and Time and the marvelous abilities of Reason in contrast to Understanding. Here he quotes Jacobi ("it is the instinct of Understanding to contradict Reason")[62] as if he were supporting Kant, though Kant of course could not have approved of this opposition. In Novalis, Carlyle sees a radical champion of these ideas: a spiritualist, for whom reality has lost its meaning, and

[61] *Two Note Books*, ed. Norton, p. 140.
[62] *Essays*, II, 27.

Carlyle and German Romanticism

a herald of the new god "reason." In his ethics he sees an identification of the Good and the Beautiful and a union between the Christian God with the Platonic Eros, and he recognizes the stress on organism and the hidden meaning of the universe in Novalis' outlook on Nature. This is practically all he can say about the thinker, if we disregard the general praise that he bestows freely on his wonderful subtlety of intellect and power of intense abstraction.

The poetical tale, *Heinrich von Ofterdingen*, is more closely and more critically examined by Carlyle. It does not seem to him especially great: "In his professedly poetical compositions there is an indubitable prolixity, a degree of languor, not weakness, but sluggishness, the meaning is too much diluted . . . he speaks in a low-voiced, not unmelodious monotony." Carlyle quite rightly protests against the usual judgment which prefers *Ofterdingen* to all the other works of Novalis. His criticism culminates in a dissection of Novalis' human character, which he finds wanting: it is too weak and sensitive, it lacks violent energy, it is passive, tender and chaste. He formulates his impression in a well-balanced metaphor: "He sits, we might say, among the rich, fine, thousandfold combinations, which his mind almost of itself presents him."[63] Carlyle calls him—as he did Werner—an "Asiatic character." But what in the case of Coleridge is a charge which condemned the victim is told about Novalis in a quiet and objective manner. Where he could not possibly sympathize, as in the question of the influence of the death of Novalis' young love, Sophie von Kühn, Carlyle simply opposed the authority

[63] *Ibid.*, p. 52.

Carlyle and German Romanticism

of Tieck. His healthy realism seized upon the fact of Novalis' engagement to Julie von Charpentier, which took place soon after the death of Sophie; his instinct saw here the sober truth.

We still have to define the reasons for Carlyle's interest and tolerance. It seems that he was more attracted by some of the perfect, deeply paradoxical aphorisms, by some of the great verbal charm of this supreme "goldsmith of words," than by his human personality and his convictions. It is true that Carlyle agreed in a way with his position, for he manifestly welcomed in him an ally against rationalism; but, on the other hand, there is little evidence that he could have followed him into his subtle associations, philosophical puns and paradoxes. He appreciates Novalis' desire to unite philosophy and religion. He quotes with satisfaction his great attack on the Enlightenment from "Christenheit oder Europa,"[64] placing it at the end of his great paper on, or rather against, Voltaire. There are other passages which charmed Carlyle. Foremost among them is the Fragment "Der echte philosophische Akt ist Selbsttötung; dies ist der reale Anfang aller Philosophie."[65] The term "annihilation of self" or "Self-annihilation" recurs quite often in the pages of Carlyle, though, we suspect, in a meaning little to the taste of Novalis, who did not think of the Christian sacrifice of the self for ethical reasons, but rather of the submergence of the individuality in the ecstasy of mysticism. In a central passage of *Sartor Resartus* in the chapter "The Everlasting Yea," it is used in this sense, as the first preliminary moral act, "Annihilation of Self" (*Selbsttötung*). Another Fragment was curiously

---
[64] *Schriften*, ed. J. Minor (Jena, 1923), II, 32. Cf. *Essays*, I, 465-66.
[65] *Schriften*, ed. Minor, II, 178. Cf. *Essays*, II, 39.

Carlyle and German Romanticism

enough liked by Carlyle, though there is no contrast more striking than that between his puritanism and the hedonistic and sensualistic mysticism implied in Novalis: "Es gibt nur einen Tempel in der Welt, und das ist der menschliche Körper. Nichts ist heiliger als diese hohe Gestalt. Das Bücken vor Menschen ist eine Huldigung dieser Offenbarung im Fleisch. Man berührt den Himmel, wenn man einen Menschenleib betastet."[66] Carlyle felt the similarity between this idea and his own clothes-philosophy: the body is the garment of God. And this is probably the reason why he quotes this Fragment frequently.[67] Another phrase became part of the stock of Carlyle's phraseology. Novalis describes the effect of the rationalistic philosophy in these striking words: "Er (i.e. the philosopher of the eighteenth century) macht die unendliche schöpferische Musik des Weltalls zum einförmigen Klappern einer ungeheuren Mühle, die vom Strom des Zufalls getrieben und auf ihm schwimmend, eine Mühle an sich, ohne Baumeister und Müller und eigentlich ein echtes Perpetuum mobile, eine sich selbst mahlende Mühle sei."[68] Carlyle translated this passage,[69] and from that point on, apparently, we meet in his writings a number of logical, self-grinding mills, or mills of death.[70] Some smaller phrases come from Novalis, as his calling man the Messiah of Nature, which occurs in *Sartor*, in the Novalis essay and in the "Dr. Johnson."[71] But this simply leads to little tricks of speech which are not illuminating for our purpose of describing the spiritual relationship between the two men.

[66] *Schriften*, ed. Minor, II, 226.
[67] *Essays*, II, 39. *Sartor*, pp. 190-91. *Heroes*, 10.
[68] *Schriften*, ed. Minor, II, 33.   [69] *Essays*, I, 466.
[70] E.g. *Sartor*, pp. 53, 130, 133.
[71] *Sartor*, p. 175. *Essays*, I, 40; III, 90.

Carlyle and German Romanticism

The man who meant more to Carlyle than anyone else except Goethe remains to be considered. Carlyle's great love for Jean Paul (Johann Paul Friedrich Richter) is, especially in English books, treated with a pitying condescension as the weakness of a great man for a temporary celebrity. Of course, this point of view must be charged at least partly to German literary scholarship, which until comparatively recent times held Jean Paul in the background, partly for artistic reasons, as it objected to an art conforming so little to the ideals of German Classicism, and partly for personal reasons, as it was apt to neglect anyone who disputed the infallible authority of the established classics. But his time has come: with Hölderlin, Herder and Hamann, Jean Paul now receives the attention which he amply deserves. An artist of such severe and subtle artistic discipline as Stefan George ranks him as "die grösste dichterische Kraft der Deutschen (nicht der grösste Dichter, denn der ist Goethe)."[72] A host of literary historians and critics have begun to till this vast and comparatively neglected field. Topping the zeal of German enthusiasts, his new biographer, Walther Harich, prefers him openly to Goethe. As much as this enthusiasm overshoots the mark, we must recognize Jean Paul as one of the great moving forces of nineteenth-century German literature. His historical importance is, indeed, very great. We now see clearly how much he meant for the style and the imagery of the German Romantic movement and Young Germany (Börne and Heine), how much he meant for the beginning of realism, especially Adalbert Stifter, whom

[72] Introduction to George's anthology *Deutsche Dichtung* (Berlin, 1923), I, Jean Paul, p. 5; cf. also George's "Lobrede auf Jean Paul" in *Tage und Taten* (Berlin, 1925), p. 60.

Carlyle and German Romanticism

Ernst Bertram rightly calls "eine Provinz aus dem Reiche Jean Pauls,"[73] or for Gottfried Keller.[74] In contrast to the usual ideas, we can confidently say that Carlyle's estimate of Jean Paul supposes a certain independence of judgment (though, of course, he was introduced to Jean Paul's importance by such a critic as Franz Horn, whom he consulted for reference very frequently), a free and unrestricted intuition which sees—without regard for English tradition—greatness in a strange though kindred soul. Also in regard to the different works of Jean Paul, Carlyle conserved an independence from the then current German rating. He was disappointed by *Titan* and says expressly that he chose for translation "Schmelzles Reise nach Flätz" quite independently, without knowledge of any German opinion.[75] Today, this work is almost universally recognized as one of the most successful minor pieces of Jean Paul's humor.

It is necessary first to remove a misunderstanding which stands in the way of a right comprehension of Carlyle's debt to Jean Paul. It is frequently asserted that Carlyle's style is derived from Jean Paul's. Küchler's formula—Goethe determined the contents, Jean Paul the form of *Sartor Resartus*—seems to be almost generally accepted. Only Bernhard Fehr suspected this conclusion.[76] We cannot, of course, contradict this statement in the simple way Froude does—by asserting that there is not the slightest resemblance between the two styles.

---

[73] *Nietzsche* (Berlin, 1922), p. 238.

[74] Cf. the monograph by Frieda Jäggi, *Gottfried Keller und Jean Paul* (Bern, 1913).

[75] *Essays*, II, 138-39. *German Romance*, II, 129.

[76] B. Fehr, "Der deutsche Idealismus in Carlyles *Sartor Resartus*," *Germanisch-Romanische Monatsschrift*, V (1913), 100: "Die Behauptung, die man in so vielen Büchern findet, Carlyles Stil rühre von Richter her, muss erst bewiesen werden."

Carlyle and German Romanticism

Nor can we accept Edmond Scherer's verdict of the complete dependence of Carlyle's style on Jean Paul's, a sweeping assertion which was repeated by Lowell, Thoreau and some Germans, such as Streuli and Pape.[77] Carlyle himself decided the question: "As to my own poor style, Edward Irving and his admiration [probably derived from Coleridge, we may add] of the old Puritans and Elizabethans, his and everybody's doctrine on that head played a much more important part than Jean Paul upon it. And the most important by far was that of nature, you would perhaps say, if you ever heard my father speak, or my mother, and her inward melodies of heart and voice."[78] It is not nature simply, but the family tradition (which is steeped in the language of the Bible and the great Anglican and Puritan tradition of pulpit eloquence). But certainly one element which contributed to the make-up of Carlyle's style had been forgotten at that moment. We find a new secular influx in the style of Laurence Sterne (who in his turn perpetuates some of the great traditions of the seventeenth

[77] J. A. Froude, *Thomas Carlyle: A History of the First Forty Years of his Life* (New York, 1882), I, 323: "Carlyle's 'style,' which has been a rock of offense to so many people, has been attributed to his study of Jean Paul. No criticism could be worse founded." Edmond Scherer, *Études sur la littérature contemporaine* (Paris, 1882), VII, 67. James Russell Lowell, *My Study Windows* (Boston, 1871), p. 124: "In 'Sartor' the marked influence of Jean Paul is undeniable, both in matter and manner." Henry David Thoreau, *Miscellanies* (Boston, 1894), p. 100: "In his graphic description of Richter's style Carlyle describes his own pretty nearly; and no doubt he first got his tongue loosened at that fountain, and was inspired by it to equal freedom and originality." Wilhelm Streuli, *Thomas Carlyle als Vermittler deutscher Literatur und deutschen Geistes* (Zürich, 1895), pp. 33ff. Henry Pape, *Jean Paul als Quelle von Carlyles Weltanschauung und Stil* (Rostock, 1904), pp. 50ff.

[78] Froude, *History of the First Forty Years*, I, 323 and *History of his Life in London*, I, 35-36.

Carlyle and German Romanticism

century such as Burton's *Anatomy of Melancholy*). Sterne belonged to Carlyle's early favorites, and his influence was soon discernible; as early as 1814 his friend Thomas Murray found evidence for a "Shandean turn of expression."[79] But though there are many passages in the letters[80] which give evidence of his reading and his admiration for Sterne, and which show in all essentials the characteristics of what we are accustomed to call "Carlylese," there is no doubt that on the whole, the *Life of Schiller*, the introductions to *German Romance*, *Wotton Reinfred* and the first essays are written in the style of the eighteenth century. The great stylistic change—which substantially means a return to older forces and a conscious practice of principles long ago recognized—has to be ascribed to the influence of Jean Paul. Carlyle himself confesses this influence in a letter to Jane Welsh, July 19, 1826: "It is singular what a mock-bird I am. I am writing here unconsciously in the very note of J. P. Richter, on whose works I have been labouring for the last four weeks."[81] This influence is undeniable, though the whole development of Carlyle tended in this direction and Jean Paul himself drew partly from the same sources as Carlyle: the Bible and Sterne. (Sterne also affected Jean Paul indirectly through Hippel.) Of course, *Sartor Resartus* and the numerous quotations of the imaginary Professor Sauerteig are not reliable witnesses for the question of Jean Paul's influence, because in *Sartor* Carlyle exaggerates purposely

---

[79] Froude, *History of the First Forty Years*, I, 322, 29.

[80] E.g. the second passage in the *Early Letters*, ed. C. E. Norton (London, 1886), pp. 2-5.

[81] Letter to Jane Welsh, July 19, 1826, in *The Love Letters of Thomas Carlyle and Jane Welsh*, ed. Alexander Carlyle (London, 1909), II, 305.

Carlyle and German Romanticism

some characteristics of this style to heighten the "Germanism" of these supposed translations. Even a very close imitation has here its good artistic justification. Later, however, even writings which do not pretend to look and sound German, *The French Revolution*, the lectures on *Heroes*, and *Latter Day Pamphlets*, are written in this style, though Carlyle could always use the more sober and normal style of his youth, as is evident not only in the *Life of Sterling* and *Reminiscences*, but also largely in *Frederick the Great* and *Past and Present*. These two styles occur in Carlyle rarely entirely separately, but there is this difference between the two, and obviously Carlyle uses the more "baroque" type, which shows the reading of Jean Paul, just in grotesque or rhetorical passages. Carlyle quotes Jean Paul very frequently, and usually in prominent passages of his writings or in intimate letters; he likes to use his imagery, and he takes from him curious and quaint German names. But it is difficult to imagine that this fascination came only from Jean Paul's style. This influence of the style can be only a symptom, a necessary accompaniment of something which is much more powerful and much more important. It is partly the influence of Jean Paul's thought and partly the charm of his personality and character, which in Carlyle's eyes was always more than a purely literary relation. This strong impression was possible only by the striking likeness of the two great men. I do not want to underrate their differences, which are obvious and could be easily elaborated, but the similarities are close enough to explain the fascination which Jean Paul exercised over Carlyle. If we read Carlyle on Jean Paul we feel as if he were speaking of himself.

Carlyle and German Romanticism

The very first sketch of Jean Paul[82] shows his conception quite clearly: it is not a narrow interpretation and is not confined to one side of his work. Carlyle recognizes very well his formal principle, which is different from the Classicist's insistence on clear outlines and just proportions, on structure, finish, economy and unity. In Jean Paul's art "the elements of his structure are vast, and combined together in a living and life-giving, rather than in beautiful or symmetrical order."[83] This contrast approaches Schlegel's distinction between mechanic and organic art. Starting from a passage in Goethe's notes to the *Westöstlicher Divan* (under the heading "Vergleichung"), Carlyle compares Jean Paul's imagery with Oriental poetry and finds also a temperamental similarity between him and Oriental poets.[84] Goethe's comparison sees only one side of the matter, however; the purely formal characteristics of his imagery, and a comparison of the ideas, would find a similarity with the Far East rather than with the poets of Persia and Arabia, who were in Goethe's mind. Jean Paul did not have any special knowledge of any of the Oriental literatures; his friend Emanuel Samuel introduced him to Hebrew literature, and the Indian Emanuel in *Hesperus* became a conventionalized picture of this sage and learned man. Carlyle hints briefly at a comparison with Gothic, and speaks of his "rich stately foliage,"[85] a parallel which was elaborated at great length by Jean Paul's first admirer, Caroline Herder, the wife of the great critic. But the comparison with the

---

[82] In the introduction to the translation in *German Romance*, II, 117-30, written in 1826.
[83] *German Romance*, II, 121.
[84] *Ibid.*, p. 125.   [85] *Ibid.*, p. 124.

Carlyle and German Romanticism

"baroque" style is much more to the point: Carlyle refers rightly to the style of Burton and jokingly, one suspects, of Jeremy Bentham.[86] It may suffice to quote the greatest Jean Paul authority, Eduard Berend, who puts this relationship very succinctly: "Eine ganz ähnliche Mischung und Durchdringung von Rationalismus und Mystik, von Gefühl und Witz, dieselbe Vorliebe für kostbare Gleichnisse und gespitzte Antithesen, für schroffe Stimmungskontraste und nicht selten für Geschmacklosigkeiten und Schwulst."[87] This passage might apply equally well to Carlyle's style. Carlyle recognizes the deep musicality of Richter's structure,[88] which is well in accordance with the comparison used by Harich and others between Jean Paul's works and the polyphonic art of Bach.

In this first and as a whole rather undistinguished and colorless essay, Carlyle also defines Jean Paul's position in the history of thought. He does not confine him to the narrow field of his idyls—on the contrary, his reservations about *Quintus Fixlein* show that he saw the one-sidedness of this example—nor to the airy realm of dreams, but stresses his severe and clear outlook on reality; he recognizes his ardent social feeling, his deep intimacy with nature and, at the suggestion of Richter's *Vorschule der Aesthetik*, he shows the identity of his humor with that of Cervantes and Sterne. But what Carlyle was most interested in was Richter's belief in God and the immortality of the soul. This is a miracle for Carlyle: Jean Paul is to him the only true believer among the modern Germans. He exempts both Herder

---
[86] *Ibid.*, p. 130.
[87] *Deutsche Rundschau*, vol. 52 (Nov. 1925), p. 125.
[88] *German Romance*, II, 128.

Carlyle and German Romanticism

and Jacobi and shows some knowledge of Richter's love for them. By these names, Jacobi and Herder, Jean Paul's position in the history of thought is characterized in the best possible manner. Jacobi was almost his only philosopher, and he paid tribute to Herder's genius almost all his life (e.g. in the conclusion of the *Vorschule der Aesthetik*). Carlyle could find a eulogy of Jacobi in *Die Unsichtbare Loge,* the first of Richter's long series of novels,[89] a passage which he certainly knew from Horn[90] if not from the novel itself. Also in its phrasing of details this first essay is exceedingly successful (especially compared to the introductions to Tieck, Musaeus and Hoffmann which were written about the same time), e.g. when he explains Richter's clumsiness and heaviness by the nice and subtle metaphor that he is not moving with one faculty of the soul, but with his whole being: with intellect, sublimity, wit and humor. He points out very well the complexity of Richter's personality, a quality which differentiates him from the more single-track and straightforward minds of the Enlightenment, which cultivated only one human faculty (especially reason or sensibility or sensuality) at the expense of the others or at the expense of the harmony of its different components. Here we feel already Carlyle's strong human interest in Jean Paul, though he did not then know very much about his life. He calls him "one of the truest, deepest and gentlest hearts that ever lived in this world" and stresses his tenderness and "true sensibility."[91]

The second and more mature article on Jean Paul marks an important period in Carlyle's work. It was his

[89] *Sämtliche Werke* (Berlin, 1826), I, 158.
[90] *Poesie und Beredsamkeit,* II, 404.
[91] *German Romance,* II, 126n, 119, 123.

Carlyle and German Romanticism

first article in the *Edinburgh Review*, to which he began to contribute early in 1827, and it introduces, therefore, the first volume of the *Essays*. The point of view is, on the whole, the same as in the earlier essay, since the difference in time between them was not much more than a year. But the greater length and his deeper reading give enough individual coloring to this essay to distinguish it from the preceding one, which is much more abstract and bloodless. Carlyle starts with a severe criticism of Döring's *Jean Paul Friedrich Richters Leben*[92] and then goes on to analyze Richter's personality vividly and even gracefully (as much as Carlyle was at all capable of the light touch). The description of the style is promisingly more concrete, less impressionistic, much more eager to get at an objective description of its characteristics: his liking for parentheses, dashes and subsidiary clauses, his inexhaustible inventiveness for new terms, which gives new life to old words and chains and pairs and packs even the most distant ones into jarring new combinations, his fertility of images and metaphors and allusions to all the provinces of Earth, Sea and Air, his epigrammatic breaks, vehement outbursts, or sardonic turns, interjections, quips and puns. Carlyle goes on to describe his technique of framework, which always explains how the author got hold of the manuscript and his inclination for a disguised representation of the author. He points to the peculiarity of his digressions, his "Extrablätter,"[93] and compares his method with the methods of a Rhapsodist.[94] Again he compares his style with that of the great prose-writers of the seventeenth

[92] Gotha, 1826. [93] Cf. *Die Unsichtbare Loge* and *Hesperus*.
[94] *Essays*, I, 12-13.

Carlyle and German Romanticism

century, with Milton, Hooker, Taylor and Browne.[95] Even the name of Rubens, as the greatest painter of the "Baroque," occurs in this connection.[96] Again, and now with much more emphasis, he points to the ethical meaning of Jean Paul's work. Amusement is for Richter only a means to the moral end, and essentially he is—however he may disguise it—a philosopher and moral poet whose only study has been human nature.[97] Carlyle mentions with praise that Richter never attempted to create supernatural figures, because he could not write without belief.[98] And much more than in the older essay, Carlyle stresses Richter's humor, which is to him the central light of his soul, the central fire which illumines and enlivens his whole being. Humor, of course, is to Carlyle inseparably bound up with love and sensibility, and his theoretical discussion of humor is strongly reminiscent of German aesthetics and especially of Jean Paul's own *Vorschule der Aesthetik*.[99] The passage which defines humor as a sort of inverted sublimity, exalting as it were into our affections what is below us, while sublimity draws down into our affections what is above us, corresponds with Schiller's conception, which was attacked by Jean Paul[100] and is therefore a new proof that Carlyle's theoretical position was by no means very clear and consistent. The remarks on Shakespeare, Swift, Sterne, Cervantes, Ariosto and Molière are similar to the discussion in the sixth and seventh "Program" of Jean Paul's *Vorschule*.[101] Again great stress is laid upon the

---

[95] *Ibid.*, pp. 18, 25.   [96] *Ibid.*, p. 15.
[97] *Ibid.*, p. 9.   [98] *Ibid.*, pp. 21-22.
[99] *Vorschule* (Stuttgart und Tübingen), especially p. 187 of 2nd edition, 1813.
[100] *Vorschule*, p. 183.
[101] It may be mentioned as a sort of irony that there occurs a remarkable similarity to Coleridge's aesthetic ideas, which Carlyle

Carlyle and German Romanticism

philosophical contents of Richter's books, again his belief in immortality is mentioned with deep approval. Carlyle is silent about his older idea that Richter was the only exception among the German writers, as he probably had discovered Goethe's belief. He stresses more than before that Richter's philosophy yields as its fairest product a noble system of morality and the firmest conviction of Religion.[102] He tries to refute the surmise that Richter is an atheist and quotes for this purpose a sentence from the disconnected notes (which are nothing more than a string of aphorisms) to "Schmelzles Reise,"[103] which considers all the different forms of religious worship as so many "Ethnic Forecourts of the Invisible Temple and its Holy of Holies."[104] And again Carlyle dwells upon the fundamental sincerity, honesty and tenderness of Richter's human character, which, for Carlyle, gives the final assurance of the seriousness, height and force of his art.

Although the third and by far the longest essay on Jean Paul (*Foreign Review*, 1830) does not bring any marked change of attitude, it is still necessary to comment briefly upon it. In its style it approximates *Sartor*, and in the formulation it is certainly the most personal, the most characteristically Carlylean of the three. The value of the essay is somewhat diminished by its frequent

---

used to reject so violently, but which in this case is explainable by the common source. Cf. the chapters, "On the distinctions of the Witty, the Droll, the Odd, and the Humorous," "The Nature and Constituents of Humour—Rabelais—Swift—Sterne" in *Miscellanies* (Bohn Library, 1885), p. 121, previously in the 2nd volume of the *Literary Remains* and also in the popular editions of the *Lectures and Notes* (e.g. Everyman's Library, p. 258) as the ninth lecture of the 1818 course.

[102] *Essays*, I, 22.
[103] Translation in *German Romance*, I, 58n.   [104] *Essays*, I, 22.

Carlyle and German Romanticism

and extensive quotations from the older articles, which are quoted as the writings of some other English critic, and by the profuse specimens of translations. The selection is quite interesting in itself. Carlyle translates a passage from the *Vorschule der Aesthetik*,[105] in which Jean Paul characterizes the style of the most important German writers, and then, of course, two passages from *Quintus Fixlein*, which he could take from his own translation;[106] he then gives, as a specimen of Jean Paul's humor, his praise of the old spinster, "Extrablatt über töchtervolle Häuser,"[107] the concluding sentences from the Preface to the first edition of *Hesperus*[108] and finally, the famous dream from the first "Blumenstück" to *Siebenkäs*. The essay is burdened with a recital of Richter's life, drawn from the three little volumes of *Wahrheit aus Jean Pauls Leben* (1826-27-28); and, as a supplement to this history of his youth, we get some scanty information taken from Döring, which is sometimes incorrect or vague, e.g. in regard to the confused chronology of Jean Paul's stay in Weimar. The retelling of the life is nevertheless not without charm, as it succeeds in condensing the long-winded autobiography rather well and still manages to reproduce its most vivacious scenes. But all this is of little importance compared to the new phrasing which Carlyle gave to his love and admiration for Jean Paul. In him, "Philosophy and Poetry are not only reconciled, but blended together into a purer essence, into Religion,"[109] a formula which could have been devised to sum up Carlyle's own ambition. Even more prominently, the purely human interest in his

[105] *Vorschule*, pp. 604-606. [106] *German Romance*, II, 287.
[107] *Hesperus*, 3rd edition (Berlin, 1819), II, 196-200.
[108] *Ibid.*, 1st edition, I, 31-32. [109] *Essays*, II, 100.

Carlyle and German Romanticism

subject prompts him to a eulogy on biography and the life of Jean Paul Richter. His life is heroic and pure, it is one long victory over poverty, a stirring example of old-Grecian stoicism (the shadows of Socrates and Diogenes are called up), which overcame the heavy bonds of stifling poverty and stuffy narrowness of rococo Germany; he emerged as a victor over his surroundings and the enemy in his own heart, as a victor who did not lose his own soul of kindness and love. Jean Paul is to him a true philosopher and poet who reveals the "Divine Idea of the World" (Fichte), who is not simply a "Sweet-singer," a mechanistic cause-and-effect philosopher, but a messenger of the Invisible in the Visible, a true prophet of God. As in the older essays, Richter's intellectual and literary character is to him merely the counterpart and image of his practical (in the Kantian sense) and moral character.[110] Carlyle's idea about his historical position has become more concrete: he sees especially his feud with Schiller, which he proves by a quotation from the *Correspondence between Goethe and Schiller*, which had been published in 1828-29.[111] He thinks that the relation with Goethe was cold and restrained and is as yet unable to see the deep conflict which separated the two antipodes. Carlyle, on the other hand, sees the close connection with Herder and Jacobi. He quotes again the rhapsody on Herder from *Vorschule der Aesthetik*.[112] We find here also his final formulas on Jean Paul's characters. In the preceding essays he commented upon the lack of true vitality in Jean Paul's tragic figures, but now he passes over their defects in

[110] *Ibid.*, p. 142.
[111] *Ibid.*, p. 138. Carlyle wrote a long essay about it which was published soon after the "Richter" in *Fraser's Magazine*, 1831.
[112] *Essays*, II, 138; cf. with *Vorschule*, p. 1024.

silence. He divides his humorous figures into two groups: one exemplified by the more idyllic, such as Fixlein, Schmelzle and Fibel, and the other by the grotesque, as Vult in *Die Flegeljahre*, Leibgeber in *Siebenkäs* and Schoppe in *Titan*.[113] He characterizes one of them as "a madcap humourist, honest at bottom, but bursting out on all hands with the strangest explosions speculative and practical."[114] This sounds like a description of the hero of *Sartor Resartus*, the strange philosopher with the strange name, Diogenes Teufelsdröckh.

It would be superfluous for our purpose to list in detail all the other passages where Carlyle refers to Jean Paul. No other author except Goethe is quoted so frequently in his private letters and in prominent points of his writings, as at the end of the *Lectures on the Periods of European Literature*[115] on June 11, 1838, or at the end of the lecture on "The Hero as a Man of Letters" or at the end of the Essay on Novalis.[116] Of all writers, only Jean Paul appears in person in *Sartor Resartus*.[117] Carlyle's love for Jean Paul never changed, though, of course, with the passing years his influence became slighter and slighter. But from his frequent allusions to Jean Paul we can to a certain extent supplement the *Essays*. In the Essay on Goethe,[118] he includes him among the subjectivists, who always can depict themselves better than a strange object, and in the introduction to his translation of Jean Paul's review of Madame de Staël's *De l'Allemagne*,[119] he characterizes

---

[113] *Essays*, II, 151. [114] *Ibid.*, p. 129n.
[115] Ed. J. Reay Greene (New York, 1892), pp. 221f.
[116] *Essays*, II, 54-55. [117] Book I, ch. IV, pp. 25-26.
[118] *Essays*, I, 245.
[119] *Fraser's Magazine*, 1830, and *Essays*, I, 476. Richter's essay was published in *Kleine Bücherschau* (Breslau, 1825), I, 56ff.

Carlyle and German Romanticism

him again very pointedly as "a huge mass of intellect, with the strangest shape and structure, yet with thews and sinews like a real Son of Anak." This rather unknown review is, by the way, quite important for Carlyle's imagery. From it are derived the strange "ästhetische Springwurzeln" of Professor Sauerteig in the article on "Biography"[120] and the image of the light-chafers in Surinam.[121] Once Carlyle prefers Jean Paul expressly to Goethe,[122] but he recanted this heresy again in the *Lectures on the Periods of European Literature*.[123] Even as late as in an essay on Varnhagen's *Denkwürdigkeiten* he translates Varnhagen's long report on his visit to Jean Paul in Bayreuth.[124] With special gratification he repeats Varnhagen's reassuring testimony as to the sincerity, truthfulness and nobility of the man Jean Paul and contrasts his simple civic life "with the poetic Shandean, Shakespearean and even Dantesque that grew from it as its public outcome."[125]

It should now be easy to draw a parallel between Carlyle and this picture of Jean Paul as Carlyle described him. It would frequently be sufficient just to transcribe his words on Jean Paul and apply them to himself. We spoke at length about the style and its similarities; the impression "baroque," or rather "in the tradition of the seventeenth century," is here predominant. We can add a few words on the actual literary influence. It seems mainly confined to technical tricks: I think there cannot

---

[120] *Essays*, III, 49; cf. I, 486.
[121] At the end of the lecture, "The Hero as a Man of Letters," in the letter to Thomas Ballantyne (May 11, 1840), D. A. Wilson, *Carlyle on Cromwell and Others* (New York, 1925), p. 89; cf. with *Essays*, I, 491 and *Kleine Bücherschau*, I, 68.
[122] *Essays*, II, 438.   [123] See note 115 above.
[124] In the year 1808, *Essays*, IV, 94-97.   [125] *Ibid.*, p. 97.

Carlyle and German Romanticism

be much doubt that the framework of *Sartor* is modeled on the pattern of Jean Paul. It reminds us especially of the frame of the *Leben Fibels*—there the author finds the biography he is telling successively on little paper notes, screwed paper bags, rags, bodices—similar to the elaborate procedure with which the author of *Sartor Resartus* pretended to have become the owner and user of Teufelsdröckh's philosophy and biography. A device similar to Professor Teufelsdröckh's watch-tower, from which he looks into the destinies of man, is the pillar on which Giannozzo lives,[126] or the bell-tower in which Flitte resides.[127] There are some analogies to the mysterious birth of Carlyle's hero in Jean Paul (in addition to those in *Fibel*). At the end of the *Palingenesien* there is a scene not unlike that of the garden-house, where Teufelsdröckh finds his Blumine, and the meeting in the mountains could be paralleled both in *Wilhelm Meisters Wanderjahre* and in *Des Luftschiffers Giannozzos Seebuch*. The method of the "Catechism of Dandyism" resembles in its methods the "Statuten des kritischen Fraisgerichts" in the second volume of *Titan*. But by far the most conspicuous analogy between any passage in Jean Paul and Carlyle is the close parallel between Jean Paul's account of his sudden illumination, which takes the form of an inner vision, "Ich bin ein Ich,"[128] with the most powerful scene of *Sartor Resartus* at the end of the "Everlasting No" in the Rue Saint-Thomas de l'Enfer. No doubt it would be foolish to deny the fact of this inner illumination and the intimate reality

---

[126] In the 2nd "Belustigung" from the *Biographische Belustigungen unter der Gehirnschale einer Riesin*.
[127] In *Die Flegeljahre*.
[128] In *Wahrheit aus Jean Paul's Leben*, translated by Carlyle in *Essays*, II, 111.

Carlyle and German Romanticism

of this very same experience for Carlyle. But as there are no contemporary references to a scene corresponding to the end of the "Everlasting No," we may be allowed at least to conjecture that Carlyle condensed a slow development into the dramatic form which was foreshadowed in Jean Paul's quieter account.

The epic skeleton of *Sartor* is strongly determined by Jean Paul's technique. Carlyle never invented any story himself; the epic core of the *Sartor* is simply autobiographical (as it was in *Wotton Reinfred*, an earlier attempt at a fictionalized autobiography), the frame patched together from devices borrowed partly from every tradition of novel-writing and partly from Jean Paul. Also, the figure of Diogenes shows unmistakable signs of Richter's influence. I cannot understand the usual hypothesis, which makes Teufelsdröckh an image of Kant, for there is obviously no similarity between his wild flights of fancy and his clumsy and yet mercurial vivacity as opposed to Kant's regulated and sober life of an abstract thinker. Nor can I see the similarity with the private personality of Jean Paul, especially since he appears in *Sartor Resartus* as a different character. But the similarity with a certain type of Jean Paul's heroes is striking. The grotesque figures enumerated by Carlyle[129] belong to this category, especially the Leibgeber of *Siebenkäs*. Like Teufelsdröckh, he is a model of bizarre ugliness. But in order to leave no room for a prejudiced description, I quote the sketch by Harich, which reads like a description of Teufelsdröckh: "Wie eine Naturgewalt stürmt Leibgeber durchs Leben. Keine menschliche Institution vermag ihn zu fesseln. Er verachtet Frauen und Liebe, kommt und geht wie ein Gewitter.

[129] Vult, Giannozzo, Leibgeber and Schoppe, *Essays*, II, 151.

Carlyle and German Romanticism

Er hat nie recht jung ausgesehen, sein Gang ist hinkend, sein Herz schlägt unter einer zottigen Bärenbrust. Frei, namenlos, unbekannt, muss er leben."[130] This Leibgeber should have appeared again in *Titan*—"Er sollte sich im Titan in die Lüfte schwingen, um von der riesigen Luftperspektive aus auf das kleine Menschengewühl herunterzuschauen—"[131] just like Teufelsdröckh from his turret in "Wahngasse." The figure which ultimately was carried over into *Titan* under the new name of Schoppe is even more similar to Diogenes. "Der Fichteanismus ist der Angelpunkt Schoppes. Sein unbedingtes Freiheitsbedürfnis hängt aufs engste mit Fichtes Ichphilosophie zusammen. Und auch der Humor dieses von jeder Bindung mit der Welt selbstherrlich losgelösten Menschen ist nur die Frucht des unbedingten In-sich-selber-Ruhens." "Auch er ist ein Zyniker, aber im veredelten Sinne des Diogenes."[132] This is the character of Schoppe as drawn by a German Jean Paul specialist, who does not even mention Carlyle. Of course, this parallel cannot be called an influence in the old mechanical sense, as there is simply the inner homogeneousness of the two men which leads to similar results. Such a conclusion is much more interesting than the mere fact of borrowing.

But even more important than these analogies is the fact that Carlyle is also in his whole thought remarkably close to Jean Paul and not to Fichte, or Kant, or even Goethe as is usually maintained. He went through a similar development from the original religiousness of his paternal home through a materialistic crisis under the influence of eighteenth-century skepticism (in Jean Paul it found its expression in his early, intolerably chilly

---

[130] Walther Harich, *Jean Paul* (Leipzig, 1925), p. 547.
[131] *Ibid.*   [132] *Ibid.*, p. 586.

Carlyle and German Romanticism

satires) to a new faith. Jean Paul arrived—just as Carlyle—at an attitude of modern Protestantism, which sacrifices the dogmas of the Church and at the same time clings steadfastly to the great ethical convictions of Christianity.[133] And especially the relation to the chief movements of the eighteenth-century thought is essentially the same. Jean Paul's mental origins are just like Carlyle's in Protestantism as it was handed down in the country and as it survived there comparatively unchanged by the onslaught of eighteenth-century rationalism. We could even say that the most glaring differences between Carlyle and Jean Paul can almost be reduced to the differences between the backgrounds: between the German pietism and the Scotch presbyterianism. Jean Paul, just as Carlyle, saw in the ethical deed, in the practice of life, the whole meaning of life and the whole aim of philosophy. And just as Carlyle, he fought, after his conversion, the rationalistic philosophy of his times (as Carlyle realizes when he quotes him in this sense as an ally against a common foe). And like Carlyle, Jean Paul took essentially a negative attitude toward the philosophy of German idealism, with which he has—like Carlyle—some fundamental ideas in common. Especially through Herder's influence he came into opposition to Kant; he attacked Fichte, though Fichte is much more congenial to Jean Paul, just as he was for Carlyle the most comprehensible and sympathetic philosopher among the great Kantian lineage; he attacked Schelling, in whom he scented the Catholic obscurantist, and Hegel, whom he simply termed the "dialectic vampire." He had little sympathy with the "philosophische Herde"[134] and stuck more or less

[133] Cf. Harich's summary, p. 870.   [134] Harich, p. 475.

Carlyle and German Romanticism

closely to the philosophy of Jacobi and Herder, who were not philosophers in the professional sense but who represent in every respect a pre-Kantian way of speculation. Carlyle himself read Jacobi[135] and recommends him for the depth of his thoughts[136] and his doctrine on the immortality of the soul.[137] Just as in the most important dissertation on German idealism which Carlyle ever wrote,[138] he quotes him on the difference of "Verstand" and "Vernunft" with a clear conscience that he is not a Kantian. Carlyle's whole position agrees with Jean Paul's and these thinkers substantially. Jacobi is, like Carlyle, a typical dualist; he defends chiefly the doctrine that any purely conceptional, i.e. monistic, philosophy must inevitably lead to Spinozism, or rather, to what he thought Spinoza stood for: to atheism, mechanism and materialism. We can—according to Jacobi—escape this danger only by a "salto mortale" into faith, or rather the direct evidence of the feeling, which does not need any proofs.[139] Jacobi sees in the *Critique of Pure Reason* only its negative side, the destruction of the old metaphysical systems, without much regarding Kant's own attempts at a solution. He sees Kant simply as the liberator who again made the road free for faith; and he does not want to admit that in this destruction anything like his own philosophy would be involved as well. Kant's adverse criticism of Herder's *Ideen zu einer Philosophie der Geschichte der Menschheit* shows clearly how much he

---

[135] Cf. *German Romance*, I, 3, and the letter of June 24, 1825, quoted in D. A. Wilson, *Carlyle till Marriage* (New York, 1923), p. 387.

[136] *Essays*, I, 49.   [137] *German Romance*, II, 126.

[138] In the essay on Novalis, II, 27.

[139] Cf. for this whole exposition and interpretation his famous conversation with Lessing in 1780. Jacobi's *Werke* (Leipzig, 1812-24), IV, 51-74.

Carlyle and German Romanticism

was opposed to compromises (or what he regarded as compromises) of the sort of Herder's compromise between Christianity and philosophy. This new faith, which Jacobi hails as the liberator, is called by Carlyle "Vernunft"; its activity is apparent mostly in the practical ideas, in God, in freedom and immortality. How gross a misinterpretation of Kant is here involved can be only hinted at. Jean Paul saw, like Carlyle, the Messiah of these ideas in Fichte, though Jean Paul believed, in accordance with his early pietistic training, in morality as a natural and fundamental instinct of our soul.

Carlyle stands at the same point in the history of thought, at the transition from the Christian philosophy of the eighteenth century to new idealistic theories. He could not avoid using some of the terminology of the new philosophy. But fundamentally, he never even penetrated into the precincts of their thought. This explains the whole wavering attitude of Carlyle, which was not a wavering in his own mind, but is an impression conveyed essentially by his eclectic use of terminology which gives a false appearance of his community in spirit with minds and souls so different as those of the great speculative philosophers. Carlyle is a typical example of a thinker who is in the very depth of his being a Christian— and not only a Christian but also a puritan, who seeks to reconcile his faith by new formulas to a new time. But also in form he shows the signs of his time: the constant wavering between the lucidity and simplicity of the "Enlightenment" and the biblical oratory of the protestant preachers and rhapsodists on the one hand, and the first signs of Romanticism, the humor of Sterne and the vision and humor of Jean Paul, on the other. Carlyle is

Carlyle and German Romanticism

in this respect the most extraordinary mixture in this great crisis of Europe's philosophical and artistic development. The deepest roots are in the Reformation, the battle is fought with the "Enlightenment," and there evolves something like an approach to Romanticism. But probably the strangest thing about Carlyle is that the man who battled with the problems of the late eighteenth century lived until the time of the Franco-Prussian War and determined in many ways the thought and the art of the English nineteenth century. Intellectually he stands before the time of the real English and German Romanticism and chronologically after the tide of the Romantics—a striking illustration of the survival of cultural strata in the lower classes of society and the more outlying provinces, an example which illuminates with the force of a unique personality both the roots of English Romanticism and its dying hours. We confront the head of a Janus, with one face looking far back into the past of England's and our intellectual history, and the other viewing courageously the problems of a new industrial and commercial civilization.

CHAPTER THREE

Carlyle and the Philosophy of History*

In recent years two books have been published devoted solely to a detailed examination of the fundamental historical concepts of Carlyle. Mrs. Louise Merwin Young's *Thomas Carlyle and the Art of History* (Philadelphia: The University of Pennsylvania Press, 1939) is a defense of Carlyle's achievement as a historian and an argument that Carlyle developed a coherent and valid philosophy of history and theory of historiography. Mrs. Young thinks that Carlyle's views should not be judged merely on the basis of his theory of heroes. Carlyle's "real concern as a historian was with the fate of social groups and not of individuals."[1] In conclusion Wilhelm Windelband, the German Neo-Kantian historian of philosophy, is quoted as a star-witness: "The essence of the historical view of the world has been by no one so deeply grasped . . . and warmly set forth as by Carlyle."[2]

Mr. Hill Shine, in his *Carlyle and the Saint-Simonians: The Concept of Historical Periodicity* (Baltimore: The Johns Hopkins Press, 1941) has then selected a central concept of the philosophy of the history, that of historical

---

* Originally in *Philological Quarterly*, XXIII (January, 1944), pp. 55-76.
[1] Page 86.
[2] Page 91, quoted from Wilhelm Windelband, *A History of Philosophy* (New York, 1898), translated by J. H. Tufts, p. 640.

Carlyle and the Philosophy of History

periodicity, by which he means "historical development conceived as a periodic alternation of (1) eras of advance and (2) eras of recession,"[3] and has shown that Carlyle arrived at his own view of an alternation of "organic" and "critical" periods under the influence of his reading in the Saint-Simonian writings during the years 1830-31. Mr. Shine has taken considerable trouble to examine the very rare pamphlets and newspapers of the Saint-Simonians which were sent to Carlyle during these years by procuring microfilm copies in Paris, and he has gone through all of Carlyle's writings in an endeavor to discover echoes and applications of these ideas. He has also investigated the fragment of Carlyle's manuscript, *History of German Literature*, which has been acquired by the Library of Yale University. An introductory section shows that Carlyle had not arrived at his concept of periodicity before coming into contact with the Saint-Simonian ideas. He might have known Goethe's remark about an alternation of periods of belief and unbelief in a note to the *Westöstlicher Divan*,[4] but that seems unlikely as Carlyle began to quote and refer to the passage only in 1832. Mr. Shine's careful argument has proved, beyond doubt, that at least the particular formula of Carlyle's concept of periodicity is derived from the writings of the Saint-Simonians.

Both Mrs. Young's claims for Carlyle's theory and practice of history and Mr. Shine's new alignment of Carlyle with French thought deserve discussion, since they would change considerably the received view of Carlyle as a historian and of his intellectual affiliations. Besides,

[3] Page 1n.
[4] "Israel in der Wüste," Goethe, *Werke*, Weimarer Ausgabe, VII, 157.

Carlyle and the Philosophy of History

the two books raise many important questions of nineteenth-century intellectual history, of the history of historiography and literary historiography, of the provenience and nature of the "historical sense," of the concept of historical development, individuality, and the like. They thus may serve as a starting-point for a discussion which may throw light on these fundamental problems of intellectual history.

Before returning to the conclusions reached by Mrs. Young, we should raise and settle two questions, arising out of Mr. Shine's elaborate and meticulous source-study. Is there, we may ask, a fundamental affinity between Carlyle's theory of history and that of the Saint-Simonians? What is Carlyle's intellectual ancestry in questions of historiography? The answer to the first question must, it seems to me, be wholly negative. In spite of the similarity of the formulas of periodicity, there is an unbridgeable gulf between the philosophy of history of the Saint-Simonians and that of Carlyle. Saint-Simon and his disciples were naturalists (in spite of their philanthropic "New Christianity"). They were and prided themselves in being descendants of the eighteenth-century philosophers of history, of Condorcet and Turgot, and they anticipated Comte (who himself had been a disciple of Saint-Simon for a time) and the whole positivistic philosophy of history on almost every point. This could be demonstrated in detail, but need hardly be, as it is confirmed by all competent students of Saint-Simonianism.[5]

[5] Cf. especially Georges Dumas, "Saint-Simon, père du positivisme," in *Revue philosophique*, LVII (1904), 136-57, 263-87. Also the discussions in Robert Flint, *Historical Philosophy in France* (Edinburgh, 1893), pp. 394-408; J. B. Bury, *The Idea of Progress* (New York, 1932), pp. 282-89; Ernst Troeltsch, *Der Historismus und seine Probleme* (Tübingen, 1922), pp. 383-90; George Boas, *French Philos-*

Carlyle and the Philosophy of History

Thus there is no intellectual and philosophical affinity between Carlyle, the great foe of eighteenth-century naturalism, and the Saint-Simonians. Mr. Shine—unconsciously, of course—misinterprets Carlyle when he speaks of him as arriving at a "sociological" method or even at a "Nineteenth Century sociological, or *a posteriori* methodology in history."[6] Mrs. Young is similarly mistaken when, in Carlyle, she finds "the abstract law—the generic concept of change in time—which emphasized not the individual form but the social life and its historical development from the point of view of modern scientific developments."[7] Such terminology and its implications are quite misleading, for Carlyle's concept of historical development differs radically from that of Saint-Simon and modern positivism. Carlyle never tried to establish laws of historical evolution as Saint-Simon and Comte attempted. He never thought of a detailed prediction of the future, he had no concept of the aim of history, he rejected the usual causal and genetic methods of explanation, and he could not, of course, have thought, as the Saint-Simonians did, that history is a physical science or that mental action and historical evolution are both physiological functions. Neither Carlyle's impatience with metaphysics nor even his contemptuous references to Schiller's "blarney about history"[8] and Mill's philosophy of history[9] prove any sympathy with naturalistic positivism. Carlyle could very

---

ophies of the Romantic Period (Baltimore, 1925), pp. 263-76; and the monographs by Georges Weill, *Saint-Simon et son œuvre* (Paris, 1894); and *L'École Saint-Simonienne* (Paris, 1896).

[6] Pages 88 and 105n.   [7] Page 91.

[8] *Two Note-books*, ed. C. E. Norton (New York, 1898), p. 36.

[9] Reported by Henry James, in *Literary Remains* (Boston, 1885), p. 426.

Carlyle and the Philosophy of History

well object to what he thought vain speculations about ultimate metaphysical questions or about epistemology (a subject which remained always obscure to him) while still disapproving of a naturalistic approach to the philosophy of history. The elder Henry James, in the conversation about Mill just referred to, reports that Carlyle objected precisely to Mill's concept of a predictable future in history, a thought which Mill shares with Comte and Saint-Simon.[10] Carlyle's own conception of development was consciously unscientific and even antiscientific. The whole misunderstanding of both Mr. Shine and Mrs. Young is based on their false assumption that the *a posteriori*, sociological, "modern" method is necessarily the only alternative to *a priori* German metaphysical construction. There was, however, besides the *a priori* schemes of such philosophers as Fichte, Schelling and Hegel a large body of thought on history both in England and in Germany which was neither naturalistic nor idealistic (in the sense of post-Kantian metaphysics). This trend has been variously labeled as "historism," or "organology," and one of its branches has been called the "historical school," but it is a widespread point of view which arose in England and Scotland during the eighteenth century, got some succor from France, flourished in German "Classicism" (Herder and Goethe) and Romanticism, and was thence reexported into France, England, and most other European countries. It cannot be always neatly isolated from ideas which could be called rationalist or naturalistic, nor from the speculations of the German dialectical metaphysicians. But clearly, here

---

[10] "As if any man could ever know the road he is going, once he gets astride such a distracted beast as that" (*loc. cit.*).

Carlyle and the Philosophy of History

were Carlyle's affiliations and ancestry and not in the French rationalists.

I cannot attempt to characterize this body of historical thought in detail. It has been studied well by many students of the history of historiography such as Fueter, Dilthey, Troeltsch, Rothacker, and Meinecke.[11] It may be sufficient for our purposes to point to some of its main distinguishing features: 1) The stress on individuality which remains ultimately *ineffabile*. Under individuality the characteristic uniqueness of a nation or a period or any other collective force is also included. 2) The concept of development which is, however, very different from earlier and later naturalistic evolutionary concepts: it is an unpredictable development with no definite goal in history; its stages or periods are not mere steppingstones toward the end of evolution, but have their own unique position and individual value. And finally 3) its method which is not causal, scientific, aiming at generalizations and even laws, but interpretative, intuitive and even divinatory. This little summary alone brings out the similarity with Carlyle's main conceptions. He also constantly stresses individuality, the mystery of the Individual, his physiognomy, mental and physical, the national character of a literature or the differences among the ages.[12] Carlyle's concept of development is

[11] Eduard Fueter, *Geschichte der neueren Historiographie* (München, 1911); Wilhelm Dilthey, "Das achtzehnte Jahrhundert und die geschichtliche Welt," in *Gesammelte Schriften* (Leipzig, 1927), III, 210-68; E. Troeltsch, *loc. cit.;* E. Rothacker, *Einleitung in die Geisteswissenschaft* (Tübingen, 1920); F. Meinecke, *Die Entstehung des Historismus* (München, 1936), 2 vols.

[12] "Mystery of the Individual," e.g. *Two Note-books*, p. 125; on physiognomy, see letter to David Laing, May 3, 1857, on the Project of a National Exhibition of Scottish Portraits, in *Miscellanies* (Centenary Edition, New York, 1899), IV, 404-405; National physiognomy

also similar to that of the "historical school": its stages have no absolute uniformity and its goal is vague and uncertain.[13] Carlyle's method is also consciously non-rational, opposed to causal explanation, divinatory, or, as he says, a "blazing, radiant insight into fact."[14]

We can give some more detailed indications of the prehistory of some of Carlyle's main historical concepts. On the question of periodicity, Mr. Shine considers only the one passage in Goethe and in a note he refers to similarities to the speculations on the course of history in Fichte's *Grundzüge des gegenwärtigen Zeitalters*. This is a highly abstract *a priori* scheme which is, I think rightly, dismissed by Mr. Shine as unimportant for Carlyle.[15] But if we take up one very striking feature of Carlyle's concept of historical evolution, the idea of "palingenesis," we easily leave the charmed circle of Goethe, Fichte and the Saint-Simonians, in which Mr. Shine's book is moving. Mr. Shine recognizes, of course, that the term "palingenesis" was known before the Saint-Simonians and gives a rather full list of the older users, which includes Bonnet, Jean Paul, and Coleridge.[16] But the term was, primarily, used very frequently and prominently by Herder, a name missing from Mr. Shine's list. The whole fifth book of the *Ideen zu einer Philosophie der*

---

of a literature, see note 43; differences among the ages, see *Cromwell*, ed. S. C. Lomas (London, 1904), I, 73.

[13] See below, note 64.

[14] Quoted in J. A. Froude, *Thomas Carlyle: A History of his Life in London* (New York, 1884), I, 197.

[15] Page 104n. Two German books, Paul Hensel's *Thomas Carlyle* (Stuttgart, 1901) and A. Ströle, *Thomas Carlyles Anschauung von Fortschritt in der Geschichte* (Gütersloh, 1909), make much of this supposed connection. Cf. the sober discussion in C. F. Harrold, *Carlyle and German Thought* (New Haven, 1934), pp. 171-73.

[16] Page 75n.

Carlyle and the Philosophy of History

Geschichte der Menschheit is devoted to it, and there is a special article "Palingenesien" in *Zerstreute Blätter* as well as many references and discussions elsewhere in Herder's voluminous works.[17] Carlyle in 1823, long before he read the Saint-Simonians, copied into his notebook two passages from Herder: one on sleep and death from *Zerstreute Blätter*,[18] the other, the final passage of the fifth book of the *Ideen*, which celebrates, both in prose and verse, the hope of a new birth on another planet, the "palingenesis" of the human soul.[19] In Herder's writings on the philosophy of history, Carlyle could have found the conception of a dynamic evolution of alternating periods, which Herder calls "contrarities," the idea of a balance or "maximum" of every period, the stress on such concepts, older, of course, than Herder, as the spirit of the age or of a nation, the idea of a national physiognomy, and many more.[20] It is not necessary to assert that Carlyle derived these ideas from Herder nor is it surprising that Carlyle disapproved of many naturalistic and theological features of Herder's philosophy of

[17] See Rudolf Unger, "Herder und der Palingenesiegedanke" in *Herder, Novalis, und Kleist* (Frankfurt, 1922), pp. 1-23, for full discussion.
[18] *Two Note-books*, pp. 33-34. Cf. with Herder, *Werke*, ed. B. Suphan, xv, 457-58. Carlyle refers the passage to "Nemesis." But it is in the section "Wie die Alten den Tod gebildet" which follows "Nemesis."
[19] *Two Note-books*, pp. 34-36. Cf. with Herder, *op. cit.*, xiii, 200. Carlyle took the trouble to translate two stanzas of Herder's verse into clumsy English verse. The German quotation of the verse seems misplaced in Norton's edition of the *Note-books*.
[20] There is a large literature on Herder's philosophy of history. Meinecke, *op. cit.*, ii, 383-479, is especially good. Herder as a literary historian is treated well in Sigmund von Lempicki, *Geschichte der deutschen Literaturwissenschaft bis zum Ende des achtzehnten Jahrhunderts* (Göttingen, 1920), pp. 360-414.

Carlyle and the Philosophy of History

history.[21] He did not like his determinism, his close association between nature, life and mind, and he was doubtful about the ideal of humanity. But Carlyle found many of Herder's ideas on the philosophy of history, variously combined or reshaped, in Goethe, in the German Romantics, and in the German and English literary historians he had read during his formative years. In Goethe, besides the passage on Belief and Unbelief, the concept of alternating periods is common: it appears as a struggle between positive historical religion and deism in his reflections on the history of religion; it underlies as a conflict of crude empiricism and airy rationalism the basic scheme of the *Geschichte der Farbenlehre*; and it is implicit in the famous discussion of German literary history in the seventh book of *Dichtung und Wahrheit*.[22] The very terms "diastole" and "systole" used by Carlyle when repeating the idea of an alternation of periods of faith and denial in *Sartor Resartus*[23] are physiological terms which were favorites of Goethe's and occur again and again in his writings.[24]

Among the German Romantics, Carlyle's ideas on history can be most closely paralleled in Novalis. It is no chance that Novalis was closest to Herder among the Romantics, a connection noticed by Carlyle and proved

---

[21] *Two Note-books*, pp. 72-73. Also the criticism directed against "genetical schemes" in the manuscript *History of German Literature*, quoted by Mr. Shine, p. 11n, must refer to Herder who uses the term "genetisches Prinzip" frequently.

[22] On Goethe, see Meinecke, *op. cit.*, II, 480-631; Ewald A. Boucke, *Goethes Weltanschauung* (Stuttgart, 1906), pp. 402-10; E. Cassirer, *Goethe und die geschichtliche Welt* (Berlin, 1932).

[23] *Sartor Resartus*, ed. C. F. Harrold (New York, 1937), p. 112.

[24] These terms occur also in Herder's "Von Geiste der Ebräischen Poesie," in *Werke*, ed. B. Suphan, XII, 20, where they are, however, used in reference to meter.

Carlyle and the Philosophy of History

elaborately by modern German literary scholarship.[25] Novalis' paper "Christenheit oder Europa" (1799), which was known to Carlyle and from which he quoted at the conclusion of his essay on Voltaire,[26] contains a passage which sounds almost like a summary of Carlyle's early ideas on the philosophy of history. "Is not an oscillation, a change of contrary movements essential?" speculates Novalis. "Is not a limited period peculiar to them, is not growth and decay their nature? But is not also resurrection, a rejuvenation, in a new, healthy form, to be expected from them with certainty? Progressive, always more and more increasing evolutions are the matter of history."[27] Novalis then characterizes the Middle Ages as the ages of faith, the eighteenth century as a period of unbelief, and expects and longs for a second reformation, a time of resurrection and regeneration, a new history, a new golden age, which would arise in the near future, especially in Germany. Carlyle, no doubt, could not approve of the Catholic leanings of Novalis nor could he share his sanguine optimism as to the near future; but the main scheme of divisions in history is the same in both Carlyle and Novalis, and the concept of development in Novalis implies an alternation of periods as well as a rebirth, a "palingenesis," two points which also make up the most striking similarity between the Saint-Simonians and Carlyle. Carlyle could have met other, more speculative and more highly elaborated versions of similar schemes in Fichte's *Grundzüge des gegenwärtigen*

---

[25] Carlyle's essay on Novalis in *Miscellanies*, II, 44; Rudolf Unger, "Novalis' Hymnen an die Nacht, Herder, und Goethe," *op. cit.*, pp. 24-61.

[26] "Voltaire" in *Miscellanies*, I, 465-67; cf. with Novalis, *Schriften*, ed. R. Samuel and P. Kluckhohn (Leipzig, 1929), II, 75.

[27] *Op. cit.*, p. 70.

Carlyle and the Philosophy of History

Zeitalters, in Schelling's *Vorlesungen über das akademische Studium*, or in Friedrich Schlegel's *Philosophie der Geschichte*, if he ever had the patience to read them.[28] But it is quite unnecessary to press these parallels, since Carlyle lumped the German philosophy of history together without being interested in individual shades of presentation: he only eliminated anything which seemed to him too farfetched metaphysics or repelled him because of its Roman Catholic tendencies. Carlyle's attitude on this point was exactly the same as his attitude toward German philosophy in general. I have shown elsewhere in detail how Kant, Fichte and Schelling coalesced in his mind to almost one figure and how narrowly his use of German philosophy was confined to a few key ideas.[29]

It is unlikely that Carlyle would have met these ideas only in the context of strict philosophies of history. He found them rather scattered and diluted in many German histories and literary histories of the time, where they lent themselves to immediate use, for Carlyle, in his early career, wrote much on general and literary history himself. Mr. Shine presses the very vague and tenuous similarities of Carlyle's discussion of concrete historical phenomena with the Saint-Simonian theories, but he never raises the question, whether these ideas, as many of them concern literature, could not be derived quite as well from literary histories and general histories of the time. An investigation of such books as the *Universal History* of Johannes Müller or of German textbooks of literature,

---

[28] Carlyle refers to a passage on the French in Schelling's *Methode des akademischen Studium*. See "State of German Literature" (1827) in *Miscellanies*, 1, 83. I am not aware of any evidence that Carlyle knew these particular books of Fichte or Friedrich Schlegel.

[29] See my *Immanuel Kant in England* (Princeton, 1931), pp. 183-202.

Carlyle and the Philosophy of History

such as Eichhorn, Bouterwek, Wachler, Horn, and others might repay the trouble.[30] Certainly Friedrich Schlegel's *Geschichte der alten und neuen Literatur* (1815) is similar both in general scheme and even in individual judgments to Carlyle's *Lectures on the History of Literature* (1838). Carlyle had quoted Schlegel's book as early as 1827,[31] and there are many agreements between his scattered critical pronouncements and those of Schlegel. I might give a few examples drawn from several of Carlyle's writings which are purposely limited to passages quoted by Mr. Shine for comparison with Saint-Simonian ideas. Like Carlyle, Schlegel considers Euripides decadent;[32] he describes chivalry, like Carlyle, as a synthesis of Germanic valor and Christian humility,[33] he argues, as does Carlyle, that the Renaissance begins properly with

[30] Carlyle knew Johannes von Müller's *Vierundzwanzig Bücher Allgemeiner Geschichten* (1810): cf. *Two Note-books*, p. 290; *Love-Letters of Carlyle and Jane Welsh*, 2 vols. (London, 1909), I, 89; *Letters to J. S. Mill* . . . (London, 1923), p. 163. Carlyle quotes Müller on Homer twice in *Lectures on the History of Literature*, ed. J. R. Greene (New York, 1892), pp. 17, 20, from the *Universal History*, Book I, Chapter 13. Werner Leopold, first in *Die religiöse Wurzel von Carlyles literarischer Wirksamkeit* (Halle, 1922) and then in "Thomas Carlyle and Franz Horn," *JEGP*, XXVIII (1929), 215-19, and "Carlyle's Handbooks on the History of German Literature" in C. F. Harrold's *Carlyle and German Thought*, pp. 238-47, has shown how fruitful such an investigation may prove; e.g. the terms "Everlasting Yea and No" come from Horn.

[31] In the "State of German Literature" (1827), *Miscellanies*, I, 80; Carlyle in the *Edinburgh Review* refers to "Schlegel's view," but in the reprint of 1839 changed this to "August Wilhelm Schlegel's verdict." Actually the passage comes from Friedrich Schlegel's *Geschichte der alten und neuen Literatur* (Vienna, 1816), II, 224. This has been noted first by Leopold, *op. cit.*, p. 59n.

[32] Carlyle's *Lectures, op. cit.*, p. 31; cf. F. Schlegel, in *Sämmtliche Werke* (Vienna, 1846), I, 60.

[33] MS *History of German Literature*, quoted by H. Shine, *op. cit.*, p. 15; cf. Schlegel, *op. cit.*, II, 7.

Carlyle and the Philosophy of History

Charlemagne;[34] he thinks, like Carlyle, that Shakespeare was fundamentally Catholic;[35] and like Carlyle, he associates the youth of a nation with lyrical poetry.[36] No pretense, of course, can be made that Schlegel is the only source of these frequently very widespread notions. Carlyle himself refers on the last point to Ludwig Tieck's *Minnelieder aus dem schwäbischen Zeitalter*,[37] and Tieck could have derived this idea from his friend Friedrich Schlegel or from Herder. But these ideas and the general schemes of the history of world literature and of the main periods of German literature were no doubt common among the German antiquaries and literary historians Carlyle consulted. We need not even go outside England to find a great many similar conceptions, imported and elaborated by the Germans and reimported by Carlyle. For instance, Carlyle's unfinished *History of German Literature* was planned on the basis of a fundamentally psychological sequence of the ages of Fancy, Understanding and Reason, a scheme which must remind us of the plan underlying Thomas Warton's *History of English Poetry* (1774-1781). Warton's *History* was well known to Carlyle, not only because it was the standard book of the time, but because he wanted himself to write a rival history of English literature which would use Warton "as a help, though not as a model."[38] Warton uses a scheme

---

[34] MS *History*, quoted by Shine, p. 13; cf. Schlegel, *op. cit.*, I, 204.
[35] *French Revolution*, Centenary Ed. I, 10; cf. Schlegel, *op. cit.*, II, 94.
[36] MS *History*, quoted in Shine, p. 17; cf. with Schlegel, *op. cit.*, I, 214.
[37] Shine, pp. 16-17 from MS *History*. Tieck's Preface in Ludwig Tieck's *Kritische Schriften* (Leipzig, 1848), I, 185-214.
[38] *Two Note-books*, pp. 119-20, sometime shortly after February 1827.

Carlyle and the Philosophy of History

which could be briefly described as a sequence of an age of Imagination, followed by an age of a synthesis of Reason and Imagination, followed by an age of Reason. Similar schemes were, under Warton's influence, common in the many sketches of the history of English literature, published between Warton and Carlyle's plan. Warton's scheme underlies the books of George Alves, George Ellis, whom Carlyle knew and "esteemed," Thomas Campbell and Nathan Drake. Hazlitt in his *Lectures on the English Poets* (1818) varies Warton's scheme slightly, designing a sequence of ages from imagination, represented by the Elizabethans, to the fancy of the metaphysical poets and hence to the wit of the Restoration and the paradox and commonplace of the eighteenth century.[39]

Also the idea of an alternation of periods was widely diffused in English literary historiography of the time. Joseph Berington's *Literary History of the Middle Ages* (1814) uses a scheme which presupposes a constant alternation of periods of degeneracy and ignorance with periods of advancement and enlightenment within a general scheme of progress. Robert Southey in the preface to his *Specimens of the Later English Poets* (1807) distinguished periods of the rise, progress, decline and new revival of English poetry. The idea of an alternation of periods in English literature seems to have become particularly com-

[39] For Warton, see my *Rise of English Literary History* (Chapel Hill, 1941), p. 193; George Alves, *Sketches of a History of Literature* (Edinburgh, 1794); George Ellis, "The Rise and Progress of the English Poetry and Language" in *Specimens of the Early English Poets*, 3 vols. (London, 1801). Cf. Carlyle, *Two Note-books*, p. 127: "Ellis I have read and partly esteemed" (after January 1828); Thomas Campbell, "An Essay on English Poetry" in *Specimens of the British Poets*, 7 vols. (London, 1819); Nathan Drake, *Shakespeare and his Times*, 2 vols. (London, 1817); Hazlitt in *Complete Works*, ed. P. P. Howe (London, 1930), VI, 83.

mon during the thirties, after Carlyle's reading of the Saint-Simonians. But it seems very unlikely that this would have been the effect of Carlyle's scattered pronouncements in anonymous articles on German literature or of direct Saint-Simonian influence. Southey in the "Sketches of the Progress of English Poetry from Chaucer to Cowper" which introduce his *Life of Cowper* (1833) conceives English literature as a "succession of heresies" against the gospel of nature with intervals of correct orthodoxy in the Elizabethan age and his own. He speaks of "fashions in literature which supply a real or supposed defect; and in both cases the spirit of antagonism has generally given rise to the opposite error."[40] Even a popular book which pretends only to be a "textbook for those lectures on English literature, which are given in so many institutions for mechanics and others," Robert Chambers's *History of English Language and Literature* (1836), contains the argument that "in the progress of literature, it would almost seem a fixed law that an age of vigorous writing and an age of imitation and repetition should regularly follow each other."[41] Like Carlyle and the Saint-Simonians, De Quincey, then, in his essay on *Style* (1840), speaks of an alternation of creative and reflective ages of literature, but refers to a classical source for the concept of periodicity—to Velleius Paterculus's *Historia Romana*.[42] These examples, which could be easily augmented, only prove that the ideas were in the "air" and that their particular formulation by Carlyle can hardly be derived from one model.

[40] Quoted from William Cowper, *Works* (London, 1836), vol. II, ch. 12, p. 123.

[41] Edinburgh, 1836, p. 190.

[42] De Quincey, *Collected Writings*, ed. David Masson (Edinburgh, 1889-90), XX, 186ff., especially 200, 202.

Carlyle and the Philosophy of History

Besides, for Carlyle as a literary historian, the occasional use of speculations on periodicity can scarcely be considered very central. Carlyle speaks of an alternation of imaginative and didactic periods of literature in the two essays on the *Nibelungenlied* and on *Reineke Fuchs*, which he seems to have taken from his manuscript *History of German Literature*. But these essays, purely descriptive accounts of little critical importance, are among Carlyle's least distinguished work. Carlyle's achievement as a literary historian and critic is surely rather in his portraits of Goethe, Schiller, and Jean Paul, and in the essays on Boswell and Burns than in any wider historical schemes. If any theoretical pronouncement on literary history in Carlyle is important, it should be sought for in his early advocacy of literary history as the history of the national mind. In his scathing review of William Taylor's of Norwich *Historic Survey of German Poetry* (1831) Carlyle expresses his ideal of literary history: "The history of a nation's poetry is the essence of its history, political, scientific, religious. With all these the complete Historian of Poetry will be familiar: the national physiognomy, in its finest traits, and through its successive stages of growth, will be clear to him; he will discern the grand spiritual tendency of every epoch, which was the highest Aim and Enthusiasm of mankind in each, and how one epoch evolved itself from the other. He has to record the highest aim of a nation, in its successive directions and developments; for by this the Poetry of the nation modulates itself: this *is* the Poetry of the nation. Such were the primary essence of a true history of poetry."[43] Every one of these ideas could be traced to German literary histori-

[43] *Miscellanies*, II, 341-42.

Carlyle and the Philosophy of History

ans, who in turn drew on ideas developed by English and Scottish writers of the eighteenth century. Friedrich Schlegel formulates that "literature is the essence *(Inbegriff)* of the intellectual life of a nation," in the preface to his *Lectures on Ancient and Modern Literature,* mentioned before.[44] "National physiognomy" is a term used by Herder—the great preacher of literary nationalism—who elaborates on the spirit of an age and an epoch.[45] Nationalism in literary history had been faint and scarcely self-conscious in England, but it began to be voiced strongly at the beginning of the nineteenth century, largely in the context of folk-poetry. But Southey, for instance, objected strongly to Pope's and Thomas Gray's scheme for a history of English literature because they ignored the fact that the English have a "costume and character of their own." He speaks of the "homegrowth" of English verse and calls English literature "coloured by the national character, as wine of different soils has its raciness."[46] Carlyle, in the passage quoted, formulates this ideal of literary history more clearly and more fully than anyone before him in England. This conception for a long time determined the ideals of literary history, in England and elsewhere: it permeates the books of Henry Morley, which tell the history of English literature as a story of national ethics. And even W. J. Courthope's *History of English Poetry* (1895-1910), though very un-Carlylean in its critical views, is governed by the idea of a history of literature as that of the national

[44] Schlegel, *op. cit.,* p. xviii.
[45] "Nationalphysiognomie" in Herder, *Werke, op. cit.,* XIII, 365; cf. XIX, 148, "Nationalseele," e.g. III, 30. See Lempicki, *loc. cit.*
[46] Southey, *op. cit.,* p. 126.

Carlyle and the Philosophy of History

mind, which he conceives as most clearly expressed in its political ideas and institutions. There is here no occasion to discuss the obvious dangers of these conceptions of literary history: their stress on nationalism to the exclusion of the common tradition of Western European literature, or the preoccupation with the ideological implications of literature to the exclusion of its artistic function and development. Carlyle only formulated an ideal program which he cannot be said to have attempted to carry out himself on any scale.

These indications about the earlier history of some of Carlyle's historical concepts have been, I hope, full enough to show that Carlyle's philosophy of history has nothing to do with the "sociological," fundamentally naturalistic speculations of Saint-Simon or Comte. Nothing is changed in this conclusion by Mr. Shine's convincing demonstration that Carlyle took up the Saint-Simonian formula of an alternation of organic and critical periods. It must have struck Carlyle as a corroboration of ideas he already held and had met with in the Germans. Carlyle, it is true, generously acknowledged his debt, on this point, to the Saint-Simonians.[47] But in a private letter it was natural to stress agreement; and Carlyle, we may surmise, might not himself have realized quite clearly how deeply his own conceptions differed from those of the Saint-Simonians. The gulf between Carlyle and the French group would become even more obvious if we could examine their basic religious and social beliefs. Mr. Shine promises a full discussion of this point which hitherto has not been handled very com-

[47] Letter to Gustave d'Eichthal, May 17, 1831. In *New Quarterly*, II (1909), 285, quoted by Shine, p. 67.

petently.⁴⁸ *Carlyle and the Saint-Simonians*, in spite of all the care and acumen in the treatment of details, is marred by the excessive isolation of its theme. The book demonstrates again the old truth that the history of even a single concept of a single writer must be investigated in a larger context.

In the light of these results we may take up the question of Carlyle's position and importance as a historian with much greater assurance. Undoubtedly, Mrs. Young's defense of Carlyle as a philosopher of history and historian scores some important points. Too much stress has been laid hitherto on such sayings as that "Universal History is at bottom the History of Great Men."⁴⁹ Carlyle's great men and heroes must not be misinterpreted: they are not Nietzschean supermen, outside the moral order, beyond good and evil, but rather instruments of God's will, executors of a decree which is not of their choosing and does not serve their individual purposes. His heroes are always "representative men," the "synopsis and epitome" of their age,⁵⁰ not egotists and titans.

But the theory of heroes is only one aspect of his theory of history, which is, otherwise, not at all individualistic and atomistic. Carlyle conceives of society as a whole, as a "collective individual," and a theory of history based on such social conceptions must take account of the silent workings of collective forces as well as of the

---

⁴⁸ D. B. Cofer, *Saint-Simonism in the Radicalism of Thomas Carlyle* (College Station, Texas, 1931) is quite uncritical. Ella M. Murphy, "Carlyle and the Saint-Simonians," *Studies in Philology*, XXXIII (1936), 93-118, is more critical, but poorly informed.

⁴⁹ *Of Heroes, Hero-worship and the Heroic in History*, p. 1.

⁵⁰ *Miscellanies*, III, 90 ("Boswell").

Carlyle and the Philosophy of History

deeds of great men. The article on "History" (1830) actually centers on the argument that "battles and war-tumults pass away like tavern-brawls" and that the real history is made by "all the forgotten train of artists and artisans" who have shaped the "inventions and traditions and daily habits that regulate and support our existence." At that time, at least, Carlyle disapproved of histories which stress only diplomacy and politics and recommended the writing of histories of religion and beliefs, of inventions, of philosophy and literature, which alone could be the basis of a future philosophy of history.[51] Some history-books are criticized by Carlyle expressly for neglecting the real "Life of Man." He censures Robertson's *History of Scotland* in almost the same terms as he had censured earlier Scott's *Tales of a Grandfather*, because these books care only for the "amours of a wanton young queen," for a "series of palace intrigues and butcheries and battles," and neglect to answer the main question: "By whom, and by what means, when and how, was this fair Scotland, with its Arts and Manufactures, Temples, Schools, Institutions, Poetry, Spirit, National Character, created, and made arable, verdant, peculiar, great?"[52] Such an ideal cultural and spiritual history implies and demands the concept of slow and continuous development and even progress. Occasionally we find that Carlyle pronounced the view that "in all times, the happiness and greatness of mankind at large have been continually progressive" and that "doubtless this age is also advancing."[53] Even an aim of

[51] *Ibid.*, II, 86-87.
[52] *Two Note-books*, 168-69 (after June 1830) on Scott, and *Miscellanies*, III, 81-83 ("Boswell").
[53] *Miscellanies*, II, 80.

Carlyle and the Philosophy of History

history in a "higher, heavenly freedom" seems dimly envisaged.[54]

The process of development itself is conceived of frequently on the age-old analogy of human life and its ages. "Society has," also for Carlyle, "its periods of sickness and vigour, of youth, manhood, decrepitude, dissolution and new birth."[55] The transition from period to period must necessarily be slow and almost as imperceptible as the biological changes in our life. "Our clock strikes when there is a change from hour to hour; but no hammer in the Horologe of Time peals through the universe when there is a change from Era to Era."[56] "The weightiest causes," he recognizes, "may be the most silent." As the process of history is an "ever-living, ever-working Chaos of Being," the historian, with his narrative method, is at a disadvantage; our "chains" and "chainlets," our "causes and effects," make "narrative *linear*," while all "action is *solid*." It is "extended in breadth and depth, as well as in length . . . it spreads abroad on all hands, modifying and modified; as well as advances towards completion."[57] This "mighty tide of thought and action" is ultimately mysterious and, because of its mysterious reality, worthy of reverence and acceptance. Carlyle goes so far as to say that "whatsoever has existed has had its value: without some truth and worth lying in it, the thing could not have hung together."[58] The awe of the mere fact that something was once real and true, inspires much of Carlyle's distrust of fiction and reverence for history. "King Lackland," comments Carlyle on a passage in the chronicle of Jocelin of Brakelond, "was there, verily he; and did leave these

[54] *Ibid.*, 82.   [55] *Ibid.*, III, 13.   [56] *Ibid.*, II, 88.
[57] *Ibid.*, II, 89.   [58] *Ibid.*, III, 100.

Carlyle and the Philosophy of History

tredecim sterlingii ... and did live and look in one way or the other, and the whole world was living and looking along with him. There, we say, is the grand peculiarity; the immeasurable one; distinguishing, to a really infinite degree, the poorest historical fact, from all Fiction whatsoever."[59] The unique fact of the past event, the slow, continuous development of great collective forces—these are the two central concepts of a historical view of the world which the young Carlyle had adopted and scattered about in casual pronouncements in many essays.

But do these pronouncements which we have reduced to some logical order make Carlyle a great philosopher of history? Was he a second Hegel or Comte? Mrs. Young is surely mistaken when she speaks of Carlyle's philosophy of history as "Hegelian" or, more carefully, of his conception of social institutions as a "mingling of Hegelian and Herderian elements."[60] There is no evidence that Carlyle, at least in the early years, knew more of Hegel than his bare name; but apart from the question of actual historical relationship, Carlyle cannot be called even remotely a Hegelian, for there is a deep difference between the development of the concrete Idea in Hegel's philosophy of history and Carlyle's irrational tide of thought and action. Carlyle knows no end of history and could not see its fulfillment in its own time as Hegel did. Carlyle's own prophecy of the future does not amount to more than a fear of imminent upheavals and revolutions, which, he seems to hope, might after two centuries of violence lead to a new age of faith and stabilization.[61] Nor is Carlyle a Comte, who tried to es-

[59] *Past and Present*, p. 46.
[60] *Loc. cit.*, p. 68.
[61] *French Revolution*, I, 133.

Carlyle and the Philosophy of History

tablish a science of social change and painted the establishment of perfect humanity as the goal of the beginning positive stage.

But if Carlyle is neither a Hegel nor a Comte, is it even true that he holds consistently to the historical point of view? Is it not rather that the views which we have expounded occur at a particular period, around 1830, and then recede into the background? And are they not, frequently even from the very beginning, combined with other conflicting and contradictory views which have far deeper roots in Carlyle's mind and past? What about his practice? Has he written history according to the theory which he seems to have held with such conviction? It seems undeniable that Carlyle was never able to keep consistently to the historical point of view, that he always introduced a set of ethical standards which are not derived from history itself and which prevent him from judging the individuality of a man or time by its own inherent criteria. Carlyle is an absolutist, an ethical rigorist, who applies a standard of truth, sincerity and faith to each and every event or person or epoch with which he is confronted. When Carlyle seems to apply a metaphysical criterion of reality versus illusion, he is also pronouncing a thinly disguised ethical judgment: illusion means to him sham, insincerity, falseness, while reality is truth, sincerity, goodness. Carlyle surely has nothing of the historian's feeling for the individuality of an epoch which Ranke, echoing Herder, had described as being "unmittelbar zu Gott."[62] Carlyle said so him-

---

[62] Leopold Ranke, *Über die Epochen der neueren Geschichte.* Cf. Herder, *Werke* (ed. Suphan, v, 527): "Kein Ding im ganzen Reich Gottes . . . ist allein Mittel—alles Mittel und Zweck zugleich, und so gewiss auch diese Jahrhunderte."

Carlyle and the Philosophy of History

self: in speaking of the seventeenth century in England he declared that "thus do the two centuries stand related to me—the seventeenth *worthless* except precisely in so far as it can be made the *nineteenth*."[63] Not only is history considered by Carlyle as *magister vitae*, but the only worthwhile history seems to him that which is preoccupied with what is "alive and frondent for us." To hear of what "reaches no longer to the surface, never to send forth leaves and fruit for mankind anymore," is to him "an affliction," the task only of "Pedants and Dullards and disastrous malefactors."[64] Lack of interest in the past in itself could not be formulated more sharply: this passage with its stress on the durable and present is surely in flat contradiction to the passage on John Lackland quoted earlier, as Lackland precisely will never return again and has been there at Bury St. Edmunds only once.

But it is not only ethical and utilitarian preoccupations which make Carlyle ignore or neglect the pastness of history. It is also a metaphysical conviction of the fundamental unreality of time which makes for a static view of the world. No other teaching, or rather supposed teaching of Kant's—for Kant never thought that Time is an illusion—made such an impression on Carlyle as his argument in favor of the phenomenality of space and time. To Carlyle, Time becomes "lying Time" and "illusory Appearance," the "grand anti-magician and universal wonder-hider." In a late entry in his journal Carlyle testified again to the deep impression which the theory of the ideality of Time and space had made on

[63] *Correspondence of Thomas Carlyle and R. W. Emerson* (Boston, 1888), II, 10-11 (letter, dated August 29, 1842).
[64] *Cromwell's Letters and Speeches*, ed. Lomas, I, 6.

Carlyle and the Philosophy of History

him. "I have felt greatly oppressed in thinking of the long duration of Time past and Kant offered a relief in the suggestion that Time may be something altogether different from what we imagine."[65] Carlyle did not want to transfer himself to another time, as the historian does; he wanted to sweep away the illusion of Time, to rend it asunder, to "pierce the Time-element and glance into the Eternal."[66]

Also, his conception of development has one marked feature which sets it off sharply from that of the "historical school." Certainly Carlyle avoided the pitfalls of the rigid constructions of both Hegel and Comte: he knows no dialectics nor three stages of progress. But only occasionally does he understand the concept of slow and continuous development. Most frequently Carlyle thinks of history as interrupted by convulsions and catastrophes, revolutions rather than evolutions, out of which society arises anew, completely newmade, like a Phoenix.[67] The psychological affinity to the individual need for conversion, for a sudden illumination such as Teufelsdröckh experiences in the Rue Saint-Thomas de l'Enfer, may have helped Carlyle to see the need and the fact of such catastrophes in history, much as contemporary geology found them also in the history of the earth.

If we glance at Carlyle's actual practice of history writing our observations will be confirmed many times

---

[65] *Sartor Resartus* (ed. C. F. Harrold, New York, 1937), p. 262; Journal, dated April 1851, quoted in D. A. Wilson, *Carlyle at his Zenith* (London, 1927), p. 374; also in W. Allingham, *Diary* (London, 1908), p. 273. Entry dated Feb. 5, 1879.

[66] *Sartor*, ed. Harrold, p. 261.

[67] *Sartor*, III, Ch. v, "Phoenix," (ed. Harrold, pp. 231-38). Cf. also p. 268.

Carlyle and the Philosophy of History

over.⁶⁸ In her investigation of Carlyle's practice as a historian Mrs. Young scarcely goes beyond *The French Revolution* and dwells far too much on a justification of narrative and dramatic history, a technique which Carlyle shares with most historians before the time of archive research. The actual question to be answered is whether Carlyle carried out his collectivistic and developmental theories in practice. In spite of some of the arguments which can be brought forward in mitigation of a negative answer, one has to conclude that Carlyle almost completely neglected institutions, inventions, economics, social forces—all of which he demanded of Robertson's *History of Scotland*. He certainly neglected origins and continuities, transitions from epoch to epoch. Mrs. Young never touches on the arguments which have been brought forth against the validity of Carlyle's conception of the French Revolution or his excessive underestimation of the constitutional struggle between Parliament and Crown during the English Civil Wars or his neglect of the administrative work of Frederick the Great in favor of personalities and battle pictures. The French Revolution is conceived in Carlyle as an outbreak of the daemonic element in man, a struggle

⁶⁸ For considered views on Carlyle as a historian, see, H. Taine, *History of English Literature*, Book IV, Ch. V (translated H. van Laun, Edinburgh, 1872, II, 467-76); F. Harrison, "Histories of the French Revolution," in *The Choice of Books* (London, 1886), especially pp. 408-14; G. M. Trevelyan, "Carlyle as an Historian" in *Living Age*, vol. 223 (1899), 366-75; C. H. Firth, introduction to Mrs. S. C. Lomas's ed. of *Cromwell's Letters and Speeches* (London, 1904, 3 vols.); E. Fueter, *Geschichte der neueren Historiographie* (München, 1911); A. Aulard, "Carlyle, Historien de la Révolution Française" in *La Révolution Française*, LXII (1912), 193-205; G. P. Gooch, *History and Historians in the Nineteenth Century* (London, 1913), pp. 323-32; J. W. Thompson, *A History of Historical Writing* (New York, 1942), II, 301-303, is disappointingly brief and thin.

of God and the Devil, a constant illustration of the law of retribution, of Nemesis, as an exemplification of God's particular providence.[69] Whole epochs—among them the eighteenth century—are condemned as purely negative, as sham, illusion, even nonexistent; they are never understood as valid in themselves or even as functioning in a series. Each of Carlyle's historical books serves a definite timely purpose: *The French Revolution* seems written to warn the England of its time and exhort it to social responsibility, the *Cromwell* surely paints the picture of the desired leader, the account of Jocelin of Brakelond in *Past and Present* evokes a social utopia, and even Frederick the Great is held up as a model-king and ruler.

The question of Carlyle's "historical sense" and position as a historian cannot be decided by arguments which show that Carlyle took great trouble to study his sources and was, according to the standards of the time, an accurate scholar. Mr. Harrold has shown how skillfully and conscientiously Carlyle combined and used the French memoirs and *Moniteurs* for *The French Revolution*;[70] and Mr. Richard A. E. Brooks, in his edition of a hitherto unpublished journal of a *Journey to Germany: Autumn 1858*,[71] has proved how carefully Carlyle studied the topography on the spot for his battle-scenes in *Frederick the Great* and how impartially he weighed the written evidence available to him. We need

---

[69] *French Revolution*, I, 48, 65, etc. J. A. Froude, *Thomas Carlyle: Life in London*, II, 394, quotes a late entry in the journal (December 1869): "I find lying deep in me withal some confused but ineradicable flicker of belief that there is a 'particular providence.'"

[70] C. F. Harrold, "Carlyle's General Method in the *French Revolution*," PMLA, XLIII (1928), 1150-69.

[71] New Haven, Yale University Press, 1940.

Carlyle and the Philosophy of History

not argue against this by pointing to Carlyle's strange omissions, ruthless interpolations and rewritings in *Cromwell's Letters and Speeches* or to his complete neglect of manuscript sources.[72] The whole question is not one of scholarly ethics, nor of Carlyle's personal veracity and sincerity, which I think should be granted to so earnest a man. The lack of historical sense in Carlyle comes out far more clearly in the deplorable affair of the Squire papers (which is never even alluded to by Mrs. Young) in which Carlyle showed not only an almost unbelievable naïveté confronted with a hoaxer, but also an utter lack of sense for the style and atmosphere of the seventeenth century. He was taken in by the crudest forgeries of letters written supposedly by an ancestor of Mr. Squire and constantly repeated his complete confidence in their undeniable authenticity.[73] Carlyle's lack of historical insight appears perhaps most glaringly in his misinterpretations of the motives and the character of Frederick the Great, whom he absurdly exalted to a Carlylean hero of truthfulness and faith.[74] On the whole, Carlyle's sense of individuality and human personality seems grossly exaggerated by his enthusiasts. It is true that Carlyle's irrational psychology which recognizes that man's actions are not solely determined by reason and personal happiness, and his divinatory method, which spurned causal explanations and "motive-grind-

---

[72] On Cromwell, see Reginald F. D. Palgrave, "Carlyle, the 'Pious Editor' of Cromwell's Speeches," in *National Review*, VIII (1887), 588-605, and C. H. Firth, *loc. cit.*

[73] Firth, *loc. cit.* All the documents are reprinted in W. Aldis Wright, "The Squire Papers," *English Historical Review*, I (1886), 311-48.

[74] Norwood Young, *Carlyle: His Rise and Fall* (London, 1927), is frequently unfair, but his criticism of *Frederick* is valid.

Carlyle and the Philosophy of History

ing," saved him from the mistakes of much eighteenth-century historiography which found everywhere conscious intentions and calculations and hence fraud and trickery. But Carlyle rarely enters a man's mind sympathetically: he frequently is content with sketching his external physiognomy, with a "flame-picture" or, at his worst, with the lurid light of the theater or the grimace of a caricature. His portraits of Coleridge or Lamb are the achievements of a superb caricaturist, his sneering condemnations of Shelley, Keats, Hazlitt, or August Wilhelm Schlegel mere ventings of prejudice and spite.[75] Carlyle's narrow range of sympathy is in itself a contradiction of the true "historical spirit" and must account for the most repulsive traits of his adoration of mere power, which comes out in his attitude to the Irish or Polish question, to the Negroes or the Czechs.[76] Henry James the elder,

[75] On Coleridge, see *Life of Sterling*, Ch. VIII. On Lamb, see *Reminiscences*, ed. C. E. Norton (Boston, 1887), I, 94; cf. *Two Note-books* (New York, 1898), p. 218. On Shelley, *Reminiscences*, II, 292-93; Letter to Browning in *Letters to Mill, Sterling and R. Browning* (London, 1923), p. 292; W. Allingham, *Diary* (London, 1908), p. 242; Sir Charles G. Duffy, *Conversations with Carlyle* (London, 1892), pp. 63-64; T. Wemyss Reid, *Life of Richard Monckton Milnes, Lord Houghton*, 2 vols. (London, 1890), I, 435-36. On Keats, see Reid, *loc. cit.*, and W. Allingham, *op. cit.*, pp. 41, 205, 310. On Hazlitt, *Two Note-books*, p. 213; *Letters, 1826-1836*, ed. C. E. Norton, 2 vols. (Boston, 1888), I, 171; *Letters to Mill, Sterling . . .*, ed. cit., pp. 28-29. On Schlegel, see *Two Note-books*, p. 258, and D. A. Wilson, *Carlyle on the French Revolution* (London, 1924), p. 284.

[76] On Irish question, see *Cromwell*, ed. Lomas (I, 459-62, 472-73; II, 58-60); "Reminiscences of my Irish Journey in 1849," *Century Magazine*, XXIV (1882). Cf. also a letter approving Froude's views in Herbert Paul, *Life of James A. Froude* (London, 1905), p. 224, and a letter on Daniel O'Connell in *Correspondence of Thomas Carlyle and R. W. Emerson* (Boston, 1883), I, 143. On Polish question, see approval of partitions in *Frederick* (VIII, 44, 55, 59, 120, 123-24). On Negro question, see "Occasional Discourse on the Nigger Question" in *Fraser's Magazine*, XL (1849) and "Ilias Americana in Nuce" in *Macmillan's Magazine*, VIII (1863). On Czechs, see *Journey to Germany: Autumn 1858*, ed. cit., pp. 71-92.

Carlyle and the Philosophy of History

in an essay little known today, put, I believe, the finger on the spot: "The main intellectual disqualification, then, of Carlyle, in my opinion, was the absoluteness with which he asserted the moral principle in the human bosom, or the finality which his grim imagination lent to the conflict of good and evil in men's experience."[77]

The attempts, then, to claim for Carlyle a deep comprehension of the historical point of view or even an anticipation of a modern sociological conception of the laws of history are doomed to failure. No doubt, for a time and in certain contexts, Carlyle adopted some of the main tenets of the historical creed: its stress on individuality and development. But these ideas remained in Carlyle unassimilated next to contradictory and far more deeply rooted unhistorical presuppositions. These largely moralistic, dualistic conceptions of history as a battlefield of God and the Devil gained completely the upper hand in Carlyle's later writings and were never absent from his actual practice. There was, of course, some merit in Carlyle's early pronouncements of the historical point of view; but his own writing of history cannot be said to exemplify this theory of history. Carlyle adopted many of these ideas merely as welcome weapons against the common foe of eighteenth-century rationalism. He himself never assimilated them in his practice, just as he never wrote literary history according to his recipe of a history of the national mind. In his very depth of being Carlyle remained a Calvinistic Christian, who tried by new formulas to reconcile his faith to a new time. His deepest roots are in the creed of his ancestors, which had survived almost unchanged in the country and region of his birth. Carlyle's position in a

[77] *Literary Remains*, ed. William James (Boston, 1885), p. 457.

Carlyle and the Philosophy of History

history of the philosophy of history is thus amazingly similar to his position in a general history of thought: again he only *seems* to proclaim the new German idealism, but in reality he has seized only a few key ideas with which to fight the eighteenth century. Both in philosophy and in the theory of history Carlyle approximated the new German point of view only for a short time. But just as in philosophy, where his affiliations were with an irrationalistic undercurrent rather than with the great dialectical philosophers—with Jacobi and Jean Paul rather than with Kant, Fichte or Hegel—[78] so also his interest in the ideas of German philosophy of history was limited to Herder and the Romantics in preference to the speculative systems of Fichte, Schelling or Hegel. In his heart of hearts Carlyle refused to accept either the new idealistic monism or the historical point of view as it had been defined in Germany at the turn of the century. This may disqualify Carlyle as a philosopher in a technical sense or as a historian, especially as he could not oppose the new creed with any complete and coherent view of his own. But there may be something laudable and possibly important and great in Carlyle's ultimate refusal to accept these viewpoints. We have seen too much of the dangers of excessive "historicism" not to know that it may lead to a complete anarchy of values, to the "worst of absolutes, absolute relativism."[79] There is an old and deep insight in Carlyle's rigid moralism and even dualism which cannot

---

[78] I repeat here the conclusion on Carlyle's relations to German philosophy reached in my paper "Carlyle and German Romanticism" (1929), printed above, pp. 34-81 and in the section on Carlyle in my *Immanuel Kant in England* (Princeton, 1931), pp. 183-202.

[79] An expression used by Norman Foerster.

overlook the "daemonic" element in man and history. Evolution, slow, continuous evolution was and is, no doubt, one of the central tools and criteria of modern historiography. But the dogma of the continuity of evolution or the absolute regularity of cycles of growth and decay has far too frequently led to a blind trust in progress or an equally blind pessimistic fatalism in the style of Spengler. Modern biology, which has come to accept such concepts as "mutations" and "sports," may suggest that there is something even in the idea of a "Phoenix" or a "palingenesis" of society. Recent history must have taught the most obtuse that there are catastrophes and cataclysms, that the old saying *natura non facit saltum* could be changed into *historia facit saltum*. Though Carlyle as a historian must be found wanting in many essential qualifications, his insight into some features of the historical process may be deeper than that of the professional historians of the nineteenth century. But this is a question which a paper concerned with Carlyle's historical position is scarcely obliged to answer.

CHAPTER FOUR

De Quincey's Status in the History of Ideas*

✸ In recent years, at least among literary scholars, a great deal of attention has been devoted to De Quincey. There have been three new biographies,[1] a collection of new letters, a German book on his historical and religious thought,[2] numbers of scattered articles on many aspects of his life and work;[3] and now a large volume discussing his theory of literature has been published by the University of Michigan.[4] Its author, Sigmund K. Proctor, died in 1938, but the book has been carefully edited by Professors Clarence D. Thorpe and Paul Mueschke. Professor Thorpe has added a long section, "Addenda, and a Comment on De Quincey's Re-

* Originally in *Philological Quarterly*, XXIII (July 1944), pp. 248-72.

[1] Edward Sackville-West, *A Flame in Sunlight; the Life and Work of Thomas De Quincey* (London, 1936); Horace Ainsworth Eaton, *Thomas De Quincey: A Biography* (New York, 1936); John Calvin Metcalf, *De Quincey: A Portrait* (Cambridge, Mass., 1940). Since then, John E. Jordan, *Thomas De Quincey Literary Critic. His Method and Achievement* (Berkeley, Calif., 1952), gave a judicious sympathetic analysis.

[2] *De Quincey at Work: As Seen in One Hundred Thirty New and Newly Edited Letters*, collected and edited by Willard H. Bonner (Buffalo, 1936); E. T. Sehrt, *Geschichtliches und religiöses Denken bei Thomas De Quincey* (Berlin, 1936).

[3] A list of sixteen items in Appendix to Mr. Proctor's book, p. 276n.

[4] Sigmund K. Proctor, *Thomas De Quincey's Theory of Literature* (University of Michigan Publications: Language and Literature, Vol. XIX [Ann Arbor, The University of Michigan Press, 1943], viii + 311 pp).

De Quincey and the History of Ideas

lation to German Literature." Mr. Proctor has collected all of De Quincey's views which can be said to concern the theory of literature, has analyzed and explained them minutely, arranged them in a systematic order, and given us a reasoned judgment. Though he is by no means uncritical and uncovers contradictions and incongruities, he puts forward large claims for De Quincey's importance in a history of literary theory and even in the construction of a literary theory. Mr. Proctor's competence in assembling and analyzing his materials is beyond doubt. His general method seems, however, more disputable, and I shall try to demonstrate that his critical evaluation of De Quincey's thought is quite mistaken. The discussion of Mr. Proctor's book will, I hope, serve as occasion for an examination of De Quincey's status in the history of ideas and of methods used in the study of the history of ideas.

Mr. Proctor's book is based on the assumption that he can extract a coherent scheme of ideas from the multifarious and confessedly casual utterances of De Quincey. An inner logic, an ideal system in De Quincey's mind is presupposed and frequently alluded to.[5] Mr. Proctor not only assumes that he can uncover this inner logic, but that he knows De Quincey's mind better than De Quincey himself. He tells us, e.g. that De Quincey "has got off the track of his real thought," or that he "must have had in mind" this or that idea.[6] Mr. Proctor actually wants both to reconstruct De Quincey's theory and to construct his own on the basis of suggestions furnished by De Quincey. The method is dangerous, especially as Mr. Proctor is not always clear whether he

---

[5] E.g. pp. 192, 212.   [6] Pages 176, 249.

115

De Quincey and the History of Ideas

is merely uncovering the pattern of De Quincey's system as it was actually in his mind but not completely articulated by him, or whether he is repairing a defect of De Quincey's system, tidying up, finishing a job which was left undone. Such awe-struck phrases as "De Quincey has vouchsafed us only a few direct hints"[7] seem to imply the former alternative; but elsewhere Mr. Proctor is frankly correcting De Quincey. The "primary concern" and even the "most general result" of Mr. Proctor's study is the discovery of a fundamental contradiction;[8] and references to discrepancies, inconsistencies and confusions are rather frequent.[9] Mr. Proctor unfortunately never discusses his methodological assumptions and never really takes into consideration the possibility that De Quincey was, on critical questions, a strictly "occasional" writer who wrote, over a long period of years, miscellaneous articles with specific purposes, in special moods, with little unity beyond that of his temperament and style. Only the conclusion that De Quincey was a systematic and original thinker could justify Mr. Proctor's method of approach. Thus, before we return to the question of method, it will be best to examine the pretensions of De Quincey as a thinker and the claims made by Mr. Proctor for his theories.

Mr. Proctor begins, very properly, with a discussion of De Quincey's philosophy, for which his relations to Kant are central, as Kant was the one author about whom he wrote frequently. The treatment of this relation in my *Immanuel Kant in England*[10] comes in for

[7] Page 54.   [8] Pages 138, 264.
[9] Pages 191, 210, 249, 251, 252, 253, 257—"confused," pp. 191, 200, 201, 206, 236n. Cf. also "his absent-minded moments" (p. 258).
[10] Princeton, 1931, pp. 171-80.

De Quincey and the History of Ideas

sharp criticism. My view that De Quincey's personal experience with Kant "remained only skin-deep, the expression of a mood, a moment's despair and tedium" is dismissed as "too absurd to require refutation."[11] And the conclusion that De Quincey was ignorant of the true Kantian position is called "scarcely less tenable than the one that his disappointment was only superficial."[12] But Mr. Proctor himself has to admit that "De Quincey's writings do not contain even the most sketchy elucidation of Kant's ideas"[13] (though an exception is made for the chapter on "German Studies and Kant in Particular"), and that he gives a "patently false characterization of Kant and his philosophy."[14] One passage, says Mr. Proctor, "judged by itself, might seem proof positive that De Quincey did not understand" the philosophy of Kant.[15] In the Appendix, Mr. C. D. Thorpe seems to confirm my own judgment, without expressly mentioning Mr. Proctor's view or mine. He speaks even of the "humbug of defense mechanism" in De Quincey's explanation of Kant and asks whether we may "not believe that De Quincey had himself found the Kantian theory a bit too elusive for his full grasp and shrank from committing himself to elucidating its mysteries."[16] Mr. Thorpe quotes Mr. Eaton to the effect that De Quincey "plays with Kant's minor works or unessential ideas," and Mr. Dunn to the effect that "he failed to penetrate the essential core of speculation that constitutes the work of Kant."[17] James Hutchison Stir-

---

[11] *Ibid.*, p. 180; Proctor, p. 29.
[12] *Ibid.*, p. 29.   [13] *Ibid.*, p. 17.   [14] *Ibid.*, p. 32.
[15] *Ibid.*, p. 30. It is difficult to see why the passage should not be judged by itself.
[16] *Ibid.*, pp. 296-97.
[17] *Ibid.*, p. 290, quoting Eaton, *op. cit.*, p. 312; *ibid.*, p. 294, quot-

De Quincey and the History of Ideas

ling, who knew something of German philosophy, had come to similar conclusions even more sharply expressed.[18]

But there is no need to fortify my position by the authority of the only other close students of the question. It is sufficient to point to the texts in which De Quincey confuses "transcendent" and "transcendental," "transcendental" and *a priori*; speaks of the categories as "large ideas"; describes Kant as an "Appolyon mind" who propounds a "Ghoulish creed," was "something of a brute," "never read a book in his life," and "lied" to his King.[19] Besides, the element of bluff and downright charlatanry in De Quincey's constant promises of elucidation, announcements of profound understanding, and disparagements of all other commentators, seems to me undeniable. De Quincey calmly declares that he has read "many hundreds" of commentators, but that none had "succeeded in throwing a moonlight radiance upon Kant's philosophy," while he, of course, by one explanation will put "the reader in possession of Kant's system, as far as he [the reader] could understand it without an express and toilsome study." De Quincey then announces an explanation of the meaning of Kant's claim to a Copernican revolution, boasting that "no student of Kant . . . can have known heretofore what consistent, what rational, interpretation to give to it: and, in candour, he ought to own himself my debtor for the light

---

ing William A. Dunn, *Thomas De Quincey's Relation to German Literature and Philosophy* (Strassburg, 1900), p. 115.
[18] "De Quincey and Coleridge upon Kant" in *Jerrold, Tennyson and Macaulay, with other critical Essays* (Edinburgh, 1868), pp. 172-224.
[19] *Collected Writings*, ed. Masson, I, 98-99, 155; VIII, 90, 93, 104.

De Quincey and the History of Ideas

he will now receive."[20] These boisterous promises and declamations which are never followed by any commensurate accomplishment are sufficient to throw doubts on the enormous importance and depth which Mr. Proctor ascribes to De Quincey's experience of Kant. Mr. Proctor's argument that I give credit to Heinrich von Kleist for a "sincere reaction of pain and complaint" to Kant,[21] which I deny to De Quincey, does not prove any inconsistency on my part. In Kleist we can trace the agonizing results of the clash with Kant, while De Quincey made nothing even of his misinterpretations beyond vague hints at mysteries and professions of profound understanding.

De Quincey's relations to other philosophers were hardly more fruitful. Plato is attacked for the "Otaheitian carnival of licentious appetite" which he proposed for the guardians of the *Republic*; he is criticized for "mysticism" and "vagueness of purpose"; and his philosophy is surprisingly called "by no means remarkable for its opulence in ideas."[22] De Quincey "hated" Hobbes, disliked Locke, and tried to refute Hume on miracles. His references to Bacon, Spinoza and Descartes are quite perfunctory. Of Leibniz he seems to have known more.[23] Fichte is mentioned several times; and the

[20] *Ibid.*, II, 87, 93, 96, 97.

[21] Proctor, p. 29. On Kleist and Kant, see, e.g., E. Cassirer, *Kleist und die kantische Philosophie* (Berlin, 1919) and I. S. Stamm's "A note on Kleist and Kant" in *Studies in Honor of John Albrecht Walz* (Lancaster, Pa., 1941, pp. 31-40).

[22] Masson, VIII, 46, 47, 81.

[23] Hobbes, *Posthumous Works*, I, 101; Locke, Masson, X, 28ff.; III, 130; II, 76; Hume, *ibid.*, VIII, 157ff.; Bacon, *ibid.*, II, 93. Spinoza, *ibid.*, IV, 135. Descartes, *ibid.*, VIII, 262. Leibniz, *ibid.*, VIII, 92; X, 16. A copy of the *Théodicée* in German translation (ed. J. C. Gottsched, Hannover, 1763) is in the Yale University Library. It belonged to

De Quincey and the History of Ideas

Essay on War relies heavily on the bellicose arguments of Fichte's *Begriff eines wahrhaften Krieges*.[24] It was apparently pure chance that De Quincey discovered some of Coleridge's plagiarisms from Schelling in a volume of *Philosophical Writings* which had been lent to him for a few hours. Hegel is only "the great master of the impenetrable."[25] But all these references do not prove any real study of the German idealist philosophers, nor do the writings of De Quincey show any traces of their influence, beyond the one borrowing from Fichte.

De Quincey knew something of traditional logic. His papers on Sir William Hamilton show certainly a detailed acquaintance with logical conundrums, such as "Achilles and the tortoise." He refers to Hamilton's quantification of the predicate and tells us there of his intention to translate and adapt for English readers Lambert's *New Organon*.[26] Lambert, who was a precursor of Kant, a mediator between Locke and Wolff,[27] is a

---

De Quincey and bears his notation to the effect that Coleridge had borrowed it from him, entered some marginalia and returned it with only 80 pages cut.

[24] Fichte, Masson, II, 146; III, 397; X, 430. According to Sehrt, *op. cit.*, 39n., the postscript to the "Essay on War" (Masson, VIII, 393), contains disguised quotations from Fichte and "The Philosophy of Roman History" uses them again in a simplified form (*ibid.*, VI, 429f.).

[25] Schelling, Masson, II, 145, and later note II, 226-28. The volume of Schelling is called *Philosophische Schriften* (Landshut, 1809), not *Kleine Philosophische Werke*. See my *Immanuel Kant in England*, pp. 96ff.; Hegel, Masson, IV, 314; XI, 399. The further mention (*ibid.*, p. 464) is in the "Note on Tieck" which certainly is not by De Quincey, but by Julius Hare (see Hans Galinsky, "Is Thomas De Quincey the Author of the Love-Charm?" *MLN*, LII [1937], 389-94).

[26] Masson, V, 338, 339.

[27] On Lambert, see Otto Baensch, *Johann Heinrich Lamberts Philosophie und seine Stellung zu Kant* (Tübingen, 1902), and E.

De Quincey and the History of Ideas

rare name to meet in English, but as nothing came of De Quincey's plan, we cannot tell how he would have solved his problem. As De Quincey has "left us not so much as one essay of original speculation," we must conclude, with Mr. Proctor, that he was "no philosopher."[28] Nor did he, it seems to me, give any evidence of close knowledge of any one philosopher or of the history of philosophy. His whole work in the field is that of a popularizer and disseminator of mostly peripheral ideas of the great philosophers.

But, Mr. Proctor argues, De Quincey had a view of the world: he accepted a "Christian moral mysticism" which implied "an antiintellectualist solution to the problem of knowledge" by stressing the evidence of the "understanding heart."[29] No doubt, De Quincey was by training and conviction a believing and practicing Anglican. Atheists and deists aroused his hatred, and dissenters, Roman Catholics and Greek and Roman polytheists, his pity or contempt.[30] But it is difficult to see why his position in a history of theology should be described as "Christian moral mysticism." There is nothing mystical in the religion of the heart, nor in an argument for miracles as actual happenings of Biblical times, nor even in a defense of *credo quia absurdum est*.[31] De Quincey's religious beliefs are colored by his upbringing in an Evangelical environment. He knew, disliked and satirized Mrs. Hannah More, but though he reacted

---

Cassirer, *Das Erkenntnisproblem in der Philosophie und Wissenschaft der neueren Zeit* (Berlin, 1922), II, 534ff.

[28] Pages 14, 17.

[29] Proctor, pp. 43, 46, 50.

[30] On deism cf. Masson, XI, 82f.; or judgment on Thomas Paine, V, 79.

[31] *Ibid.*, VIII, 157; VII, 178.

De Quincey and the History of Ideas

against Evangelicalism, he preserved considerable regard for the whole revival of piety brought about by the movement.[32] De Quincey showed some, though distant and cautious, interest in Edward Irving,[33] but obviously, in religious questions, he was most strongly influenced by Coleridge. Like Coleridge and many other contemporaries, he argued against the literal inspiration of the Bible.[34] This and his stress on the Church as a social institution separated him more and more from the Evangelicals. But he does not seem to have approved the Broad Church movement either, for he was critical of Dr. Arnold and was violently attacked by Julius Hare.[35] His bolder speculations which speak of Christianity as "advancing forever," of its "infinite development," put him in the neighborhood of Newman, whose argument in the *Essay on the Development of Christian Doctrine* he accepted, though otherwise he does not show any sympathy with the Tractarian movement.[36] His strongest religious experiences seem to flow from the contemplation of the infinities of space and time, but his stress on the Church seems to have largely social and political reasons. He belongs to the Romantic conservatives such as Southey and Coleridge, who hoped for an ultimate establishment of a theocracy on earth.

Christianity is viewed by De Quincey as an "organ of political movement" which might even lead, "if Christianity shall have traversed the earth and reorganized the structure of society,"[37] to the abolition of war. At

---

[32] *Ibid.*, XIV, 94-131; II, 129; V, 24-31.
[33] *Ibid.*, II, 121-25.   [34] *Ibid.*, VIII, 264-66.
[35] *Ibid.*, XI, 101f.; III, 243. Julius Hare, "S. T. Coleridge and the English Opium-eater," *British Magazine*, VII (1835), 15-27.
[36] Masson, VIII, 208, 309, 289-90.
[37] *Ibid.*, VII, 236, 369-97.

De Quincey and the History of Ideas

the same time, De Quincey is an enthusiastic defender of war in the present age, especially if it is waged as a crusade against the forces of darkness or in the interest of the British Empire, for De Quincey the torchbearer of Christianity.[88] De Quincey's political views are obviously in agreement with those of Burke, whom he admired as the greatest mind of the eighteenth century,[89] and the Romantic conservatives, with whom he hated the ideas of the French Revolution, exulted in the fall of Napoleon as in the restoration of Christianity, and *in concreto* approved of most Tory politics including even the Peterloo massacre.[40] But De Quincey more strongly than Coleridge has faith in progress; he refutes the view that "the human race is on the downgrade," lauds even railroads among the "increased possibilities of sympathy in the present age" and generally shares its social optimism even though he knows that Christianity is "but in its infant stages" and that "a long time will be needed before we see God."[41] Any one of these ideas is commonplace enough. But the whole position is rather peculiar precisely because De Quincey, on the one hand, keeps away from the speculative implications of Coleridge's political philosophy and, on the other, manages to hold a good many progressivist notions. Most surprising is his sincere belief in Ricardo's theory of political economy which De Quincey expounded as the ulti-

---

[88] E.g. "the power constitutes the title" (VII, 429) about the English in India. Praise of "Carnage, God's Daughter," VIII, 392. "The True Justification of War" in *Posthumous Works*, I, 135f.

[39] On Burke, Masson, XI, 35-40; X, 114.

[40] For details, see Sehrt, *op. cit.*, and Charles Pollitt, *De Quincey's Editorship of the Westmoreland Gazette* (Kendal, 1890).

[41] "Is the Human Race on the Downgrade?" *Posthumous Works*, I, 180ff.; "Increased Possibilities of Sympathy in the Present Age," *ibid.*, I, 165ff., 170; II, 228.

De Quincey and the History of Ideas

mate truth, a solution "deduced from the understanding itself, standing upon an eternal basis."[42] De Quincey disparaged Southey, Wordsworth and Coleridge for their views on economics[43] without apparently sensing the materialistic and liberalistic (in the sense of *laissez faire*) implications of Ricardo's theories. This is possibly another fundamental contradiction in De Quincey, but I think it is more correctly described as further evidence of how loosely De Quincey held his opinions, how rarely he saw through their implications and how little system there was in his agile and nimble mind.

His attitude toward nature seems to put him again in the neighborhood of the Romantic metaphysicians. Mr. Proctor finds De Quincey's meaning "puzzling, whenever he introduces his favorite notion of hieroglyphics."[44] But there is nothing more commonplace and widespread at that time than the idea of nature as a language of symbols. We find it in Coleridge, in Carlyle and Emerson; it permeates the German Romanticists such as Novalis, Jean Paul, Schelling; and it could be traced back in various forms to the eighteenth century, to Schiller, Herder, Hamann, Hemsterhuis, Saint-Martin, and, of course, Swedenborg, Berkeley, Sir Thomas Browne and Böhme. It must be derived ultimately from the Neo-Platonic nature philosophy of the Renaissance and even from the Pre-Socratics.[45] It is not very clear

---

[42] Masson, II, 340; III, 432ff.; IX, *passim*.

[43] *Ibid.*, II, 341, 344-45; V, 189.

[44] Page 70.

[45] On hieroglyphics in nature cf. Novalis, *Schriften*, ed. P. Kluckhohm (Leipzig, 1928), I, 7, 22, 30, 31; III, 170; Charles F. Harrold, *Carlyle and German Thought* (New Haven, 1934), pp. 106-107; J. Warren Beach, *The Concept of Nature in Nineteenth-Century Poetry* (New York, 1936), pp. 302, 308; A. Gode von Aesch, *Natural Science in German Romanticism* (New York, 1941), p. 219. Karl

De Quincey and the History of Ideas

how firmly De Quincey himself believed in this "great alphabet of nature." The essay on "Modern Superstition" (1840) which refers to the "interesting speculations" of Novalis on this subject, considers its literal interpretation a superstition which De Quincey labels "Ovidian," but other passages such as the fanciful interpretation of the nebula Orion leave hardly any doubt that De Quincey held that "universal signs are diffused through nature," that nature, in the sense of Berkeley, is the "visual language of God."[46] Thus, De Quincey's ideas on philosophy, theology and natural philosophy cannot be described as original: De Quincey rather mirrors different tendencies of his time. He has no original view of his own and certainly cannot be called an originator of philosophical ideas.[47]

But, of course, the main claims made for De Quincey's thought refer to his theory of literature. On some points Mr. Proctor is modest enough in his demands. He recognizes that De Quincey "contributed nothing whatever" to the theory of Imagination and that it is "impossible to credit De Quincey with much originality in his theory of style." He knows that little is original in De Quincey's pronouncements on genius, though surprisingly enough he makes an exception for "the striking concept that in genius the whole man is speaking."[48] Surely the

---

Joel, *Der Ursprung der Naturphilosophie aus dem Geiste der Mystik* (Jena, 1906), traces the idea back to antiquity. De Quincey knew an ardent Swedenborgian, the Rev. John Clowes, in his youth (cf. Masson, II, 118). Since: Liselotte Dieckmann, "The Metaphor of Hieroglyphics in German Romanticism," in *Comparative Literature*, VII (1955), 306-12.

[46] Masson, VIII, 410, 411, 18-20.

[47] Recently, J. Hillis Miller, in *The Disappearance of God* (Cambridge, Mass., 1963) has reinterpreted De Quincey's experience of death and of the absence of God in existential terms.

[48] Pages 158, 164, 226.

De Quincey and the History of Ideas

idea that genius is the whole man, while talent is partial, is one of the commonplaces of the long trend of European speculations on genius. If we open Jean Paul's *Vorschule der Aesthetik*, a book highly praised by De Quincey,[49] and read the chapter on genius, we get little else but an elaboration of the view propounded by De Quincey. "In Genius all powers of the soul stand in bloom," while "talent is only partial," announces Jean Paul, and draws a contrast between genius similar to an Aeolian harp and talent similar to one string on a clavichord.[50]

If we trace this old idea back in the history of German thought, we find Baumgarten defining *ingenium* as "determinata facultatum cognoscitivarum proportio inter se in aliquo" as early as 1739.[51] Goethe, in *Dichtung und Wahrheit* sums up the teaching of Hamann: "Aber was der Mensch zu leisten unternimmt ... muss aus sämtlichen vereinigten Kräften entspringen; alles Vereinzelte ist verwerflich." Goethe's fervent praise of Winckelmann several times singles out the perfect harmony of his faculties.[52] The sixth letter of Schiller's *Briefe über die aesthetische Erziehung des Menschen* (1793) culminates in the concept of a "Totalität der Kräfte" and De Quincey even quoted this crucial discussion.[53] Kant's concept of genius in the *Critique of Judgement* is that of a union of all mental faculties, a consensus and harmony of imagination and understand-

---

[49] Masson, XI, 267, 270.
[50] *Vorschule der Aesthetik, Sämmtliche Werke* (Berlin, 1841), XVIII, 48, 56.
[51] *Metaphysica* (Halle, 1739), p. 648.
[52] *Sämtliche Werke*, Jubiläumsausgabe, XXIV, 81, and XXXIV, 11-12, 17.
[53] Masson, X, 452-54n.

De Quincey and the History of Ideas

ing. Adelung, a good commonplace rationalist, speaks of genius as "man in which all kinds of both of the lower and the higher powers of the soul are together in an equally high degree."[54] More loosely, the conception of genius as the whole man is connected with the Renaissance *uomo universale*. Certainly, De Quincey did not tell us anything new about genius.

But the most interesting and novel claims are put forward for De Quincey as a literary historian or rather as a theorist of literary history. Mr. Proctor ascribes to him "a profound grasp of what may be called the organic conception of literature," and says that "it is De Quincey's distinction to have enunciated more forcibly and consistently than any of his contemporaries the general principle of the organic relation between the literature of any nation and period and the culture and society of which it is an expression." De Quincey's general conception is, according to Mr. Proctor, "well advanced for his day, modern and scientific."

Specifically, his theory of the difference between pagan and Christian literature "remains a highly interesting application of the organic principle, and perhaps the most original aspect of his theory of literature."[55] To substantiate these claims, Mr. Proctor relies mainly on two passages: one from the "Poetry of Pope" (1848) which asserts that there is a social evolution, which is inevitable and necessary and which is mirrored in the history of literature as it passed from dealing with elementary affections and passions to depicting society and

---

[54] *Critique of Judgement*, paragraph 49. Kant, *Werke* (Akademieausgabe) v, 316-17. Adelung, quoted in Grimm's *Wörterbuch*, p. 3422 (under *Genie*). Cf. also Alfred Bäumler, *Kants Kritik der Urteilskraft*, vol. 1 (no more published) (Halle, 1923).
[55] Pages 167-68, 176.

De Quincey and the History of Ideas

manners. The other passage comes from the *Autobiography* (from a section first printed in 1835). There De Quincey argues against the distinction of Classical and Romantic literature, which he wants to replace by one between ancient and Christian. De Quincey sees the main distinction between antiquity and Christianity in the differing attitudes toward death. The pagan is full of gloomy uncertainties and thus tries to veil and disguise the idea of death; the Christian faces its horrors firmly because he believes in resurrection. De Quincey claims that he has "ascertained the two great and opposite laws under which the Grecian and the English tragedy has each separately developed itself," and fortifies his contrast by calling Greek tragedy "sculpturesque" and English tragedy "picturesque."[56]

All this "we have heard before." The idea of a contrast between picturesque modern literature and sculpturesque Greek literature occurs in Coleridge, who derived it from August Wilhelm Schlegel, who, in turn, acknowledges indebtedness to the forgotten eighteenth-century Dutch Platonist Hemsterhuis.[57] The twist De Quincey gives to the distinction between Romantic and Classical by stressing the Christian element in modern literature is also nothing new. It is rather surprising that De Quincey disparages both Schlegels systematically and, in this very context, merely acknowledges that they have "barely indicated" the distinction of Classical and Romantic but are "not entitled to credit for any discov-

---

[56] Masson, XI, 60-62; II, 72-4; X, 315.

[57] Coleridge, *Shakespearean Criticism*, ed. T. M. Raysor, I, 176, 222; II, 159, 262; A. W. Schlegel, *Über dramatische Kunst und Literatur* (Heidelberg, 1808), I, 13-16. On Hemsterhuis and Schlegel, see O. Walzel, *Wechselseitige Erhellung der Künste* (Berlin, 1917), pp. 32-33.

De Quincey and the History of Ideas

ery at all." "Beyond this, neither the German nor the French disputers on the subject have talked to any profitable purpose" and "no one step has been made in advance, up to this day"[58] in the whole dispute. But De Quincey's account of the views of the Schlegels is surely quite misleading and greatly exaggerates the difference between his views and theirs, on this point. Both in August Wilhelm and in Friedrich Schlegel, Christianity is made to be the distinguishing sign of Romantic literature, and in both series of lectures there are full discussions of the influence of Christianity in marking the main break in the history of civilization and literature.[59] The idea that the distinction between Romantic and Classical is caused by the introduction of Christianity is so obvious and so general that it would be difficult to find anybody who discussed the question and ignored it. Still, De Quincey must be aiming at some difference from the usual view. I venture the theory that he took over the discussion of the question in Jean Paul's *Vorschule der Aesthetik*. There, in the first edition, Jean Paul had said that "the origin and character of the whole modern poetry can be derived so easily from Christianity, that one could call romantic poetry just as well Christian,"[60] and had proceeded to contrast the sensuous finite world of antiquity with the spiritual infinity of Christianity. In the second edition, Jean Paul shows that the distinction between Romantic and Classical is not a formal one. As Bouterwek had argued in his *Aesthetik*, the Greek spirit can express itself in irregular forms. Neither does

---
[58] Masson, II, 73-74; IV, 417, 428; VIII, 92; X, 42-44, 122, 127, 350; XI, 160-63, 227.

[59] A. W. Schlegel, *op. cit.*, I, 13; Friedrich Schlegel, *Geschichte der alten und neuen Literatur, Sämmtliche Werke* (Wien, 1846), II, 6ff.

[60] Jean Paul, *op. cit.*, pp. 94, 101.

De Quincey and the History of Ideas

the Romantic consist in the mixture of the serious or even tragic with the comic: such a mixture can be found in Aristophanes.[61] De Quincey thus apparently identified the Schlegels (whose main books had, of course, appeared only since the first edition of Jean Paul's and Bouterwek's *Aesthetik*) with Bouterwek's view of a purely formal distinction and used Jean Paul's argument against Bouterwek as if it were directed against the Schlegels. He elsewhere denies to antiquity a sense of the infinities and "what is worse the moral infinities."[62] But whatever the exact derivation of De Quincey's ideas, the association of Christian and Romantic was firmly established in German discussions and cannot be claimed as original for De Quincey.

There remains, however, the use De Quincey makes of the different attitudes toward death of Classical antiquity and Christianity which seems so original to Mr. Proctor.[63] Jean Paul refers to it only in passing when he says that "on German coffins one would have never painted the merry, exuberant groups of the ancient urns and sarcophagi as the Greeks and even the gloomy Etruscans did."[64] But in Jean Paul this is only a distant echo of a long and

---

[61] *Ibid.*, p. 95; Friedrich Bouterwek in his *Aesthetik* (Leipzig, 1806, II, 244) calls romantic art originally enthusiastic ("schwärmerisch") and overloaded with what is called style ("und überladen mit dem, was Styl heisst"). He disapproves of attempts to reduce the whole history of literature to a contrast of the Greek and the Romantic and opposes a revival of the Romantic. All modern art is, according to him, "classical Romanticism," a synthesis of the Greek and the Medieval (pp. 239-40). The text is completely changed in the second edition (Göttingen, 1815, pp. 226-33). It now contains no trace of the formalism with which Bouterwek was charged by Jean Paul. The new discussion includes the statement that "die Seele der romantischen Kunstschönheit ist das Christenthum" (p. 230).

[62] *Posthumous Works*, I, 279.

[63] Page 176. [64] Jean Paul, *op. cit.*, p. 105.

De Quincey and the History of Ideas

very prominent debate. Lessing and Herder wrote papers with the title "Wie die Alten den Tod gebildet," and their results reverberate in poems of Goethe and Novalis and even Mrs. Browning and Gautier.[65] With arguments based on a study of sarcophagi, Lessing elaborately refuted the view that the skeleton was the classical symbol of death, the view propounded by Spence in *Polymetis* and supported by Lessing's main enemy Klotz. Lessing shows that either a genius putting out a torch or Sleep and Death as twin brothers appear on ancient tombs, and hopes that Christians will give up the terrible skeleton.[66] Herder gave a psychological interpretation of the classical conception which is identical with De Quincey's view: "The ancients did not want to imagine death but wanted to prevent us from thinking of him."[67] Schiller's poem "Die Götter Griechenlands" (1788), in its nostalgic glorification of classical mythology, then sentimentalizes the ancient conception:

> Damals [i.e. in antiquity] trat kein
> grässliches Gerippe
> Vor das Bett des Sterbenden. Ein Kuss
> Nahm das letzte Leben von der Lippe!

[65] Lessing, "Wie die Alten den Tod gebildet" (1769) in *Werke*, ed. J. Petersen and W. v. Oshausen (Leipzig, n. d.), XVII, 309-57; Herder, "Wie die Alten den Tod gebildet" (1786) in *Werke* (ed. B. Suphan), XV, 429ff.; Schiller, "Die Götter Griechenlands" (1788); Goethe, "Die Geschwister," *Werke* (Weimarer Ausgabe), 11, 124, and "Venetianische Epigramme," No. 1, *ibid.*, p. 307; Novalis, fifth "Hymne an die Nacht," *Schriften, loc. cit.*, I, 59-64; Mrs. Browning, "The Dead Pan" (1844), and Théophile Gautier, "Bûchers et Tombeaux" in *Émaux et Camées* (1852). On Germans, see Walther Rehm, *Der Todesgedanke in der deutschen Dichtung vom Mittelalter bis zur Romantik* (Halle, 1928), esp. p. 375n.
[66] *Op. cit.*, pp. 356-57.
[67] *Op. cit.*, p. 450.

De Quincey and the History of Ideas

Still und traurig senkt' ein Genius
Seine Fackel.[68]

Obviously De Quincey knew of this debate. He himself translated *Laokoon*, which in a note contained a first sketch of Lessing's view.[69] He says that "he found Schiller and Goethe applauding the better taste of the ancients" and that he had heard Coleridge approving of this German sentiment, an obvious allusion to Schiller's poem and to Goethe's enthusiastic praise of Lessing's argument in *Dichtung und Wahrheit*.[70] De Quincey's individual contribution seems then to be reduced to his judging differently of the value of the two symbols. In contrast to Lessing, Schiller and Goethe, he disapproves of the ancient view and praises the Christian who could face the corruptions and other "dishonors"[71] of the grave in serene hope. There is, I think, no reason why he could not have arrived at his conclusion independently, given his Christian outlook and his whole strong anti-Hellenism apparent in his discussions of Greek religion and literature, throughout his writings. But it is striking that the fifth *Hymne an die Nacht* of Novalis, whom De Quincey had read, contains an answer to Schiller's poem in terms very similar to De Quincey's thought. The ancients, Novalis says, suffered from the fear of death for which there was

[68] *Werke*, Säkularausgabe, ed. E. von der Hellen, I, 158. I quote the first version. The 1803 version replaces the last two lines by: "seine Fackel senkt' ein Genius."

[69] Lessing, *Werke*, loc. cit., IV, 346n. De Quincey's translation leaves out section X completely. His section X (Masson, XI, 204) corresponds to Lessing's XII.

[70] Masson, II, 73; Goethe, *Dichtung und Wahrheit*, 8th book, *Werke* (Weimarer Ausgabe), Erste Abteilung, vol. 27, pp. 165-66.

[71] Masson, II, 73.

De Quincey and the History of Ideas

no consolation, while Christ revealed eternal Life in Death, is himself Death and makes us whole.[72]

Thus, even here, De Quincey was completely anticipated by the German Romanticists—or rather a certain group among them—who reacted like De Quincey against the glorification of pagan antiquity. In Germany where —with Winckelmann, Schiller, Goethe and Hölderlin— pagan antiquity had become a fervid cult, this reaction was extremely sharp. An anti-Hellenism arose which exalted medieval Christianity at the expense of antiquity, or gave to Greek antiquity a Christian interpretation which stressed its mystical, Oriental elements and saw in Sophocles an anticipation of Christ. We can trace this development even in such an ardent Grecian as Friedrich Schlegel, who, reacting against his early enthusiasm, stressed more and more the insufficiency and even falsity of the Greek view of nature and God, the destiny of man and the origin of the world, and later came to see only the dark sides of Greek life and the lack of hope in Greek religion.[73] Others like Adam Müller criticized the Greek drama for its lack of reconciliation and victory over death or any real transfiguration of the hero, as only Christ broke the power of death.[74] The painter Phillip Otto Runge contrasted the Sistine Madonna of Raphael with a head of Jupiter in order to show that Love and Life came into the world only through Christianity.[75] Classical

---

[72] *Schriften, loc. cit.*, I, 60-62.

[73] Friedrich Schlegel, *Sämmtliche Werke, loc. cit.*, I, 44, 50; XIII, 232-34.

[74] Adam Müller, "Vom religiösen Charakter der griechischen Bühne" (1808) in *Vermischte Schriften über Staat, Philosophie und Kunst*, 2nd ed. (Vienna, 1817), 2. Theil, pp. 141-213.

[75] Quoted, *ibid.*, from *Ausgewählte Briefe* (Berlin, 1913).

De Quincey and the History of Ideas

philology and archeology began to support these views. Even such an extremely sober and technical scholar as Phillip August Boeckh in his *Public Economy of Athens*, a book known to De Quincey, came to the conclusion that "with the exception of a few great spirits who lived in a world of their own, the mass [of the Athenian people] were deprived of love and comfort which only a purer religion has infused into the hearts of men."[76] A complete reinterpretation of classical antiquity was also attempted. Symbolic mythology represented by Creuzer and the rising Oriental philology began to discover a priestly, religious, archaic Greece: the interest in the Eleusinian mysteries was widespread and deep and reached even Schelling and Hegel. The way was being paved for the tragic Dionysiac conception of Greece which we know best from Nietzsche's fervid exposition.[77]

The history of English nineteenth-century Hellenism and anti-Hellenism is less clear, partly because it has not been explored in all its aspects.[78] Hellenism never reached the fever heat nor commanded the influence it had in

---

[76] Masson, I, 180n.; VI, 60. *Posthumous Works*, I, 259. *Die Staatshaushaltung der Athener* (Berlin, 1817), II, 159. An English translation by George Cornwallis Lewis, 2 vols. (London, 1828).

[77] Cf. Rehm, *Griechentum und Goethezeit, loc. cit.*, pp. 512-15. Hegel as a young man wrote a poem, "Eleusis." The brother of Novalis, Karl von Hardenberg, is the author of a novel *Die Pilgrimschaft nach Eleusis* (1804). Schelling's *Über die Gottheiten von Samothrace* (1815) was used by Coleridge (cf. W. K. Pfeiler, "Coleridge and Schelling's Treatise on the Samothracian Deities," in *MLN*, LII [1937], 162-65).

[78] Douglas Bush, *Mythology and the Romantic Tradition* (Cambridge, Mass., 1936) and Stephen A. Larrabee, *English Bards and Grecian Marbles* (New York, 1943) discuss aspects of the problem very fully. Hedwig Luise Glücksmann, *Die Gegenüberstellung von Antike-Christentum in der englischen Literatur des 19. Jahrhunderts* (Hanover, 1932) concerns Swinburne and Pater. De Quincey is not mentioned.

De Quincey and the History of Ideas

Germany, though we must not forget that there was a nostalgic Hellenism in the eighteenth century, which culminated in Landor, Byron, Shelley, and Keats. But even when these poets were anti-Christian, their opposition to Christianity was rarely definitely Greek and pagan as in Germany. Thus, anti-Hellenism never assumed or needed to assume the violence of the German reaction. When there were objections to the cult of antiquity, they were either inspired by motives which could be called pietistic, as in Mrs. Browning's "Dead Pan," conceived as an answer to Schiller's "Götter Griechenlands," or by fervent admiration of modern progress as in Hazlitt and Macaulay. English medievalism was either picturesque and antiquarian as in Scott or political and social as in Carlyle and Ruskin, who glorified the stability and organic order of the medieval system. Also, the Tractarian movement can scarcely be described as motivated by special hostility to Hellenism. De Quincey, in the fury and violence of his anti-Hellenism, is, it seems, exceptional in the English context, and much of his fervor may be explained by his thinking frequently in terms of dislike for German Hellenism. Paganism also was associated for him with eighteenth-century materialism and the cult of antiquity during the French Revolution. His position is therefore, on this point, parallel to that of Chateaubriand, who in his *Génie du Christianisme* wrote a whole poetics of Christianity, arguing for the superiority of Christian to Classical poetry. But De Quincey names Chateaubriand as an "elegant sentimentalist" only in passing, and then in the same breath with Florian,[79] and was on the whole so unsympathetic to French literature

---

[79] Masson, X, 121.

De Quincey and the History of Ideas

that one cannot assume any closer acquaintance with the parallel development in France which also there led to a Christian anti-Hellenism or a growing stress on the irrational and Romantic elements of antiquity, e.g. in Maurice de Guérin.[80]

De Quincey's fury is directed against the classical gods, and the implications of Greek religion. According to him, the Greek gods inspired only blind terror and were feared as "public nuisances" and "rattlesnakes." The gods were mortal and had a dark murderous nature. Greek religion was a degrading influence. Beyond its ritual, there was nothing at all. All the moral theories of antiquity (and De Quincey admired Stoicism as next best to Christianity) were utterly disjoined from religion. The ancients thus never prayed properly, penitential feelings were unknown to them; in short, they could not conceive of spirituality, or even of ordinary charity.[81] The Greek tragic poets were the only rays of moral light in the pagan darkness. But their tragedies are conceived of by De Quincey as almost statuesque *tableaux vivants* which show no real struggle and represent "a life within life: a life sequestered into some far-off slumbering state having the severe tranquillity of Hades; a life symbolized by the marble life of sculpture: but utterly out of all symmetry and proportion to the realities of that human life which we moderns take up as the basis of our Tragic

---

[80] René Canat, *La Renaissance de la Grèce antique (1820-1850)* (Paris, 1911). Cf. the excellent comments and the further literature on French Hellenism in Henri Peyre, *L'Influence des littératures antiques sur la littérature française moderne* (New Haven, 1941). Some late manuscript notes by De Quincey on French drama were published in *More Books*, XIV (1939), 347-52.

[81] Masson, VIII, 210, 213, 214, 217, 218, 222, 227, 302.

De Quincey and the History of Ideas

drama."[82] De Quincey, in his writings on the Greek drama, carries the Schlegelian parallel between Greek sculpture and Greek drama to fantastic lengths. Also, in his conception of Greek religion he is bound by an unhistorical assumption of a complete gulf between pre-Christian religion and Christianity. This explains his perverse essay on the Essenes whose very existence as a sect separate from Christianity is denied, and his attitude to the ancient mysteries such as the Eleusinian, which he calls "humbug" and "mean hoaxes."[83] The scholarly artillery for these arguments is drawn from contemporary German mythologists: especially from Lobeck and Otfried Müller. Lobeck was a rationalist who attacked the Romantic symbolistic interpretation of Greek mythology; Otfried Müller expounded the idea of the rise of Greek mythology from local legends, on the analogy of folklore in Germany.[84]

In every way, De Quincey's view of Greek religion was unhistorical, as it denied a continuity between religions and the universality of the religious experience. His views on other questions of classical philology were equally anti-romantic, e.g. his attack on the Wolfian

[82] *Ibid.*, VIII, 59; X, 359. The whole "Theory of Greek Tragedy" (1840) of which De Quincey claims that "no man has attempted the solution" (x, 344), is little more than a paraphrase of the third lecture of A. W. Schlegel's *Von dramatischer Kunst und Literatur*. The view that Greek drama is purely sculpturesque is also expounded in the paper on *Antigone* (x, 360-88), which contains the surprising assertion that the whole subject of Greek drama is *"res integra*, almost unbroken ground" (x, 371n.).

[83] "The Essenes" (1840) in *ibid.*, VII, 101-72; VIII, 191ff.

[84] Masson, I, 372; VII, 45, 199, 252. For a discussion of contemporary research in Greek mythology, see Otto Gruppe, *Geschichte der klassischen Mythologie und Religionsgeschichte* (Leipzig, 1921). On Lobeck, pp. 150f. On Müller, pp. 157ff.

De Quincey and the History of Ideas

theory of the collective authorship of the Homeric epics. There he again depended on ammunition from German scholars: from Voss, Ilgen, and especially Nitzsch.[85]

Even though De Quincey thought of himself as the "second Greek scholar in the country" (Coleridge apparently being the first) and never shook off the fascination of antiquity, he really represents an extreme Christian reaction which wanted to widen the gulf between classical antiquity.

We still have left untouched De Quincey's ideas on social evolution in relation to literature and the necessary passage from a poetry of passion to a literature of manners. Its derivation is very different from the passage on Christian versus Classical poetry. De Quincey's interpretation of the Classical-Christian contrast associates him with conservative, Christian Romanticism, though some of the anti-Classical arguments seem strongly tinctured by rationalism. His scheme of social evolution is, however, merely an echo of eighteenth-century speculations on the development of society and literature. The idea that poetry developed from an age in which it expressed elemental passions to an age in which it reflected society and manners is one of the hoariest commonplaces of eighteenth-century criticism. It is part and parcel of the viewpoint which we are accustomed to label primitivism. Diderot, for instance, declaimed: "plus de verve chez les peuples barbares que chez les peuples policés. . . . Partout décadence de la verve et de la poésie, à mesure

---

[85] "Homer and the Homercidae" in Masson, VI, 7-95. Most of the arguments seem to come from Gregor Wilhelm Nitzsch's (1790-1861) contributions to the *Allgemeine Encyclopadedie* (see Masson, VI, 16). De Quincey knew also Karl Ilgen's edition of the Homeric hymns (*ibid.*, VI, 30-32). Some account of these scholars is in J. E. Sandys, *History of Classical Scholarship* (Cambridge, 1908), III, 63-64, 105, etc.

De Quincey and the History of Ideas

que l'esprit philosophique a fait des progrès."[86] Condillac, in his *Traité sur l'Art d'écrire*, contrasts the age of vivid impression and imagination with the modern age of analysis, taste and criticism.[87] In England, Bishop Hurd took up the view in his dialogue *Of the Golden Age of Queen Elizabeth*; and Thomas Warton's *History of English Poetry*, the standard book even in De Quincey's time, is permeated by such a psychological assumption, that the growth of the reasoning power dries up the sources of imagination.[88] Warton was extremely influential, and his outline was taken over practically by every writer on the history of English literature who preceded De Quincey.[89] To quote only one example: Hazlitt's *Lectures on the English Poets* and on the *English Comic Writers* are constructed around a similar scheme which distinguishes, e.g. the imaginative comedy of Shakespeare from the comedy of manners of the Restoration.[90] De Quincey's special wrath against the term "French school" in English literature is also nothing new. The term "school of France" was used by Thomas Gray in his scheme of a History of English Poetry, and was frequently attacked, e.g. by Southey, who in his *Specimens of the Later English Poets* (1807) objected to the classification of the English poets into alien schools because it implied that "we

---

[86] *Œuvres Complètes*, ed. Assézat-Tourneux (Paris, 1875-79), XI, 131.

[87] See Gustave Lanson, "Les idées littéraires de Condillac" in *Études d'histoire littéraire* (Paris, 1929), pp. 210-23.

[88] Cf. my *Rise of English Literary History* (Chapel Hill, 1941), pp. 191, 194.

[89] Cf. my "Carlyle and the Philosophy of History," *PQ*, XXIII, 63-64 (January 1944). See above pp. 94-95.

[90] Hazlitt, *Works*, ed. P. P. Howe, V, 82; VI, 37. De Quincey quotes Hazlitt's *Lectures on the English Comic Writers* on Horace Walpole's *Castle of Otranto*, Masson, V, 150n.

De Quincey and the History of Ideas

have no school of our own."[91] Southey, motivated like De Quincey by patriotism and a dislike for the French strengthened by the Napoleonic wars, argued for a "costume and character of our own," for the "homegrowth" of English poetry, though he did not go to the length of denying French influence on the Restoration and the eighteenth century as De Quincey did.[92]

The idea of close relationships between the evolution of literature and society is, of course, old and dates back at least to Classical antiquity, to discussions like those in Longinus on the influence of liberty on letters, which were revived by Milton and Shaftesbury and were common in the eighteenth century. Also the conception that this evolution is somehow fatal and necessary is by no means modern: it is implied in the old analogy of the evolution of society on the pattern of an individual's development from youth through maturity to old age. We find this idea, e.g. in Florus, and in Aristotle's *Poetics* there is the suggestion of a necessary evolution of a genre: tragedy grows and reaches a certain stage of perfection.[93] The idea of cyclical progress also was well known to antiquity.[94] De Quincey refers to Velleius Paterculus, whom even Ascham had quoted long ago in this context. Hume formulated the theory most clearly: "When the arts and sciences come to perfection in any state, from that mo-

[91] *Specimens of the Later English Poets* (1806), I, xvii.

[92] William Cowper, *Works*, ed. R. Southey (1836), II, 116, 126.

[93] Florus, *Epitome of Roman History*, I, 1 (Loeb ed., 1929, pp. 6-8). Aristotle, *Poetics*, ch. IV.

[94] On cyclical progress cf. Clara Marburg, *Sir William Temple* (New Haven, 1922), pp. 43ff.; E. Spranger, "Die Kulturzyklentheorie und das Problem des Kulturverfalls" in *Sitzungsberichte der preussischen Akademie der Wissenschaften* (Berlin, 1926); F. J. Teggart, "A Problem in the History of Ideas," *Journal of the History of Ideas*, I (1940), 494ff.

De Quincey and the History of Ideas

ment they naturally, or rather necessarily decline, and seldom or never revive in that nation, where they formerly flourished."[95] De Quincey also knows an alternation of productive and incubative periods: the idea of an oscillation which was very widespread at that time. We find it in Goethe, in Carlyle, in the Saint-Simonians and in many English authors.[96]

De Quincey's ideas seem to me merely echoes of widely known developmental schemes of the eighteenth century, which are basically rationalistic and *a priori* in their mechanical rigidity and abstractness. One striking example may fortify this conclusion. In 1818 William Roscoe, known to De Quincey personally, delivered the opening discourse of the Liverpool Royal Institution, "On the Origin and Vicissitudes of Literature, Science, and Art, and their Influence on the Present State of Society." This is a ponderous oration of a man steeped in eighteenth-century ideas, who does not pretend to originality but rather tries to survey accepted opinions. He refuses to admit theories either of a continual decline or progress. He rejects the widespread theory of the decisive influence of climate. He argues elaborately against the idea of necessary cycles, which seems to him merely a statement of fact which leaves the question of causal explanation untouched. His solution is the influence of society, the "unceasing operation of moral causes." In practice he then discusses the effects of government and ends with

---

[95] Velleius Paterculus, *Historiae Romanae*, Lib. I, xvii, 6 (Loeb ed., 1924), p. 44; R. Ascham, *Scholemaster* in *English Works*, ed. W. A. Wright (London, 1904), p. 256; D. Hume, "Essay on the Rise and Progress of the Arts and Sciences," in *Essays* (eds. Green and Grose), I, 195.

[96] Masson, X, 196ff., 202. Cf. "Carlyle and the Philosophy of History," *PQ*, XXXIII (1944), 63-65. See above pp. 83, 88-90, 95-96.

De Quincey and the History of Ideas

recommending "rational liberty, the continuance of public tranquillity, successful industry and national prosperity," as the circumstances which will bring about continuous improvements in literature. There, in a small compass, the theories of the time are surveyed: the relations between literature and society, the idea of a necessary development which is either decline or progress or cyclical progress. No German is ever alluded to, though Tiraboschi, Andrés, Dubos, and Hume are named and quoted.[97] There is thus no reason to describe this group of ideas as the "organic conception of literature" and to call it "the principal flower of German romantic criticism" and, almost in the same breath, to praise it as "well advanced for De Quincey's day, modern and scientific."[98] What has been called the "organology" of German Romanticism has distinct features which set it off from eighteenth-century ideas of development: its concept of evolution is very different from that of the eighteenth century, or that of positivistic sociology. It is not a complex of complications of psychological processes, but the evolution of individualities and individual totalities which have a single center, the *Volksgeist*.[99] In De Quincey no use is made of these ideas, and whenever he encounters some of their implications, such as the interpre-

---

[97] Roscoe's oration in *The Pamphleteer*, XI (1818), 508-35; De Quincey on Roscoe, Masson, II, 127-29.

[98] Pages 167-68.

[99] For German historiography, ideas of development, etc., cf. E. Rothacker, *Einleitung in die Geisteswissenschaften* (Tübingen, 1920); E. Troeltsch, *Der Historismus und seine Probleme* (Tübingen, 1922); and F. Meinecke, *Die Entstehung des Historismus*, 2 vols. (Munich, 1936). Since, see my essay "The Concept of Evolution in Literary History" in *Concepts of Criticism* (New Haven, 1963), first published in 1956; and J. Kamerbeek, "Legatum Velleianum" in *Creative Wedijver* (Amsterdam, 1962).

De Quincey and the History of Ideas

tation of the Homeric epics in Wolfian terms, he rejects them violently. To call any and all interpretation of literature in connection with social development "organic" is a blurring of distinctions which does not serve any good purpose. Nor is the "organic" conception particularly modern and scientific. Its lineal descendant, the German *Geistesgeschichte*, is open to very grave objections.[100] De Quincey shows precisely no grasp of organic unity as we get it in Coleridge and, for a certain time, in Carlyle. He is rather echoing schematic, rationalistic formulas of the universal history as it was constructed in the eighteenth century.

This analysis can be corroborated by one further argument. In a note Mr. Proctor refers to Shelley's *Defence of Poetry* and states that there "the influence of German romantic criticism is particularly apparent."[101] It seems unlikely that Shelley, who knew very little German, could have had any direct acquaintance with the German critics, though he read Schlegel (probably August Wilhelm Schlegel's *Lectures on the Drama* in John Black's translation [1815]) aloud to his two female companions on his trip to Italy in 1818.[102] August Wilhelm Schlegel is the most rationalistic of the German Romanticists, a trait which may explain his great success in the West. But more important than any possible external evidence is an examination of the text of the *Defence*, in which Shelley sketches the history of man and of poetry quite in the approved and common naturalistic manner of the

---

[100] Cf. my "Parallelism between Literature and the Fine Arts" in *English Institute Annual, 1941* (New York, 1942), pp. 29-63.

[101] Page 167n.

[102] Mary Shelley's Journal, March 16, 19, 21, 1818, quoted in E. Dowden, *Life of P. B. Shelley* (London, 1886), II, 187-88. I cannot find any reference to Schlegel in Shelley's works.

De Quincey and the History of Ideas

eighteenth century. Poetry is connate with the origin of man: the savage first expressed his passions about surrounding objects, then man in society became the object of his passions. In the youth of the world every man was a poet, men danced and sang and spoke a language "vitally metaphorical." Poets were legislators and prophets. The progress of poetry is closely bound up with moral progress.[103] The whole sketch derives from eighteenth-century discussions on the origin of poetry, of the original union of poet and legislator for which hundreds of parallels could be found. For example, a book by John Brown is full of these ideas, though Shelley probably derived his speculations about history rather from French sources.[104] That Shelley does not draw from the Germans is obvious from one little detail: he speaks of the "Celtic" conquerors of the Roman Empire and the predominance of the Celtic nations after the fall of Rome.[105] Such a confusion of Celtic and Teutonic occurs, e.g. in Paul-Henri Mallet and in the *celtomanes* of the eighteenth century, but could scarcely be found in Germany.[106] Shelley's *Defence* is, in his historical sections, an echo of the eighteenth-century speculations on his-

[103] "The Defence of Poetry" in *Shelley's Literary Criticism* (ed. Shawcross, London, 1909), pp. 122-24.

[104] Speculations on origins of poetry, the metaphorical character of early language, etc., discussed in my *Rise of English Literary History*, loc. cit., pp. 74-80, 87-89.

[105] Shelley, op. cit., pp. 142-43.

[106] Paul Henri Mallet's *Introduction à l'histoire du Danemarck* (1755) was translated by Thomas Percy as *Northern Antiquities* (1770) with an introduction pointing out the confusion of Celtic and Teutonic in Mallet. Shelley ordered Percy's translation from his bookseller in August 1817. See Shelley, *Complete Works*, Julian ed. IX, 237. On *Celtomanie*, etc., cf. Thor J. Beck, *Northern Antiquities in French Learning and Literature (1755-1855)*, 2 vols. (New York, 1934-35), esp., I, 10-12.

De Quincey and the History of Ideas

tory, just as is De Quincey's argument. There is nothing organic or German about it, though I recognize, of course, that in the theoretical part, the *Defence* draws on Plato and on Sidney, and thus transcends the limitations of most eighteenth-century views.[107]

There remain, then, as contributions of De Quincey to literary theory only two points: his distinction between the literature of power and the literature of knowledge, and the definition of rhetoric as mind-play. The first distinction (for which De Quincey cites Wordsworth as a source)[108] is, at first sight, a mere reformulation of the distinction between poetry and science made by Wordsworth and Coleridge. "Literature of power" allowed De Quincey to subsume imaginative lyrical prose under this term and thus avoid the implications of fiction by grouping together what the Germans call "Dichtung" irrespective of meter. "Power" in De Quincey means emotional impact and is surely allied to similar distinctions drawn by Hazlitt[109] and possibly even to Herder's attempt to make "power" the central concept of poetry when, in the first *Kritisches Wäldchen* (1769), he tried to refute Lessing's *Laokoon*. De Quincey had translated the *Laokoon*, in part, with comments, and had written a

[107] See Lucas Verkoren, *A Study of Shelley's Defence of Poetry: Its Origin, Textual History, Sources and Significance*, Amsterdam, 1937. There nothing is said on German sources nor is much attention given to Shelley's sketch of history.

[108] Masson, x, 48n.

[109] *Complete Works*, ed. Howe (London, 1930), XVIII, 8. "Science depends on the discursive or *extensive*—art on the intuitive and *intensive* power of the mind.... In fact, we judge of science by the number of effects produced—of art by the energy which produces them. The one is knowledge—the other power." An article in *The Morning Chronicle*, 1814. First pointed out by Elizabeth Schneider, *The Aesthetics of William Hazlitt* (Philadelphia, 1933), p. 45n.

brief account of Herder.[110] But De Quincey seems not to have been aware of the German debate and may rather have drawn on the eighteenth-century discussions of the sublime. He himself somewhat shifted in his use of the distinction between power and knowledge. The early passage (1823) emphasizes the difference between "power" and "pleasure" and sees the function of literature in the exciting of unawakened feelings. "I say, when these inert and sleeping forms *are* organized, when these possibilities *are* actualized, is this conscious and living possession of mine *power*, or what is it? . . . when I am thus suddenly startled into a feeling of the infinity of the world within me, is this power, or what may I call it?"[111] But later (1848) De Quincey defines the distinction differently: literature of power speaks to the human *spirit*, literature of knowledge to the meager *understanding*.[112] Power is even called "deep sympathy with truth," "exercise and expansion to your latent capacity of sympathy with the infinite." It lives in relation "to the great *moral* capacities of man." It is identified with "the *understanding heart*," with intuitive knowledge; "peace" and "repose"[113] are proclaimed to be essential to great works of art—an attempt to counteract the merely affective, overpowering implications of the early use of "power." Like Longinus, De Quincey tries to keep both "ekstasis" and "katharsis." But the term "literature of power" has not survived in criticism because "power" does not clearly

[110] See Masson, XI, 156-221, and IV, 380-94. De Quincey's piece on Herder is little more than a patchwork of quotations from Jean Paul and Caroline Herder's *Life*.
[111] Masson, X, 48-49.
[112] *Ibid.*, IV, 308.
[113] *Ibid.*, XI, 55-56. Cf. V, 106; X, 45n.

De Quincey and the History of Ideas

suggest emotional impact and because "knowledge," in a well-known saying, is power.

As for De Quincey's curious theory of rhetoric, it scarcely merits the high praise which Mr. Proctor bestows on it. Forgetting that he has called the distinction between Classical and Christian De Quincey's most original contribution, he now says that the "Rhetoric" is De Quincey's "most original contribution to criticism" and that "it is possible to argue that De Quincey's theory of rhetoric as mind-play represents his most substantial specific contribution to critical theory." On the very next page, De Quincey's definition is called "at once brilliant and impossible—a valuable half-truth."[114] It is, however, difficult to see what is achieved by distinguishing oratory and rhetoric and by giving rhetoric a new meaning which is not justified by the history of the term. There is no special importance in the commonplace observation that there is such a mind-play and that we take pleasure in it. The actual history of rhetoric sketched by De Quincey is not even in close agreement with his conception of rhetoric as "thinking for thinking's sake." Seneca, Tertullian, Donne, Sir Thomas Browne, Jeremy Taylor and Burke come in for most praise and attention.[115] A power of fanciful metaphor as a criterion of rhetoric thus seems frequently more prominent in De Quincey's mind than sheer delight in mental pyrotechnics. The fact that De Quincey has wrenched an accepted term into a new meaning, does not make him "almost certainly the most original philosopher of rhetoric since Aristotle."[116] De Quincey's use of rhetoric is rightly forgotten.

[114] Pages 259-60, 273.
[115] Masson, x, 95, 96, 100-101, 104, 114.
[116] Page 261.

De Quincey and the History of Ideas

All this may sound like a general disparagement of De Quincey. But it is only a protest against his pretensions and the claims made recently for his importance as a thinker on literature. It leaves his status as a writer of ornate prose, as a spinner of elaborate dreams and fancies quite untouched. Besides, there are the charm and interest of his autobiographical sketches and reminiscences of contemporaries. There is still his practical criticism: the lively portraits, the scattered observations and judgments. His recognition of Donne, Jeremy Taylor and Sir Thomas Browne, his praise of Wordsworth, Landor and Lamb, his somewhat ambiguous essays on Pope, his brilliant *jeu d'esprit* "On the Knocking at the Gate in Macbeth" show flashes of insight or rare meetings of sympathy. But even as a practical critic, De Quincey was hopelessly erratic and eccentric: witness some of his absurdities on Greek, French, and even German literature. I am objecting not so much to his highly amusing moralizing on *Wilhelm Meister*, as to the shallow and ignorant articles on Goethe and Schiller in the *Encyclopaedia Brittanica*, for which the sympathetic pages on Jean Paul are the only compensation. I thus cannot agree with Mr. Thorpe's conclusion[117] that De Quincey's work on German literature has an importance exceeding that of Carlyle's on the ground that he was more critical of German literature. De Quincey shows only a very limited knowledge of Goethe and Schiller: he dismisses, e.g. *Faust* as "unintelligible" and ignores Goethe's lyrics. He does not even mention any work of Schiller's later than *Wallenstein* and neglects his prose and poetry. De Quincey thought Goethe "far inferior to Coleridge in

[117] Proctor, p. 297.

De Quincey and the History of Ideas

power and intellect" and prophesied that "posterity will wonder at the subverted idol, whose basis, being hollow and unsound, will leave the worship of their fathers an enigma to their descendants."[118] The papers on Herder and Lessing are made up largely of quotations from Caroline von Herder, Jean Paul and Friedrich Schlegel. The pages on Jean Paul are good, but slight in comparison with Carlyle's essays. The paper on Tieck, which overrates him extravagantly, is not by De Quincey but by Hare.[119] De Quincey wrote on no other German literary figures; and his sketch of German literary history preceding Schiller[120] is very thin. His criticism of German literature echoes only current objections to its morality and to the "Gothic" style of writing. Carlyle's essays contain substantial information on medieval German literature, and give vivid, however one-sided, portraits of German authors (Goethe, Schiller, Jean Paul, Novalis, Zacharias Werner). His effect and prestige were, of course, also very much greater than De Quincey's.[121]

De Quincey's contributions to philosophy, theology, politics, and the theory of literature have, no doubt, their own interest for the student of the diffusion of ideas of the period. De Quincey's mind is illuminated even by the oddities and vagaries of his highly inaccurate miscellaneous scholarship and his wavering attitude toward the main streams of current thought. He represents a piquant

---

[118] Masson, IV, 418; II, 120, 225. There is now a fuller discussion which comes to the same conclusion by Peter Michelsen, "De Quincey und Goethe," in *Euphorion*, L (1956), 86-125.

[119] Cf. note 25 above.

[120] Masson, IV, 422-31.

[121] See the preceding essays on Carlyle, the pages on Carlyle in my *Immanuel Kant in England*, and the chapter in *A History of Modern Criticism*, vol. III.

De Quincey and the History of Ideas

and odd mixture of eighteenth-century rationalism, Christian pietism and Romanticism of a conservative type.

We are now ready to return to our initial question of method. Mr. Proctor's book illustrates the difficulties of our current study of ideas. A falsely intellectualistic approach imposes a conceptual scheme on a writer of artistic temperament and, at any price, extracts a system from *obiter dicta*. That these ideas were pronounced in different decades of the writer's life, in specific polemical situations, in certain moods and for certain purposes is forgotten. The individuality of the writer is distorted and misrepresented: what was living and acceptable in a certain context becomes the mere dry bones of a museum preparation. If rigid philosophical standards of judgment are then applied to this construed system, it will necessarily appear illogical, self-contradictory and even foolish. This must be the effect of Mr. Proctor's book on a critical reader, and my own exposition of De Quincey's thought and ideas, though it differs widely on the estimation of De Quincey as a thinker, will only strengthen this impression.

But we must have doubts whether it is fair to a writer whose powers lie elsewhere to take his opinions as a citizen, member of a church or profession, and put them to the test of coherence, sense and originality in the light of modern scholarship. Undoubtedly, De Quincey himself had great pretensions of scholarship and intellect, but we are certainly mistaken if we take them at their face value. There is in all of us a lingering belief in the *poeta vates*, in the superior wisdom of the poet concerning all questions he touches. Whatever truth there may be in the belief that poetry is or was prophecy, De Quincey belongs to the age and tribe of specialists. He was a vir-

De Quincey and the History of Ideas

tuoso of the dream-fugue: he was also a gentleman-scholar who had read widely and delivered his opinions on all subjects—from the Toilette of the Hebrew Lady or the Opium Question with China to the Logic of Political Economy or the *Critique of Pure Reason*. His display of omniscience, the pontifical tone, the constant self-congratulations, the mysterious hints at enormous hidden knowledge on faraway subjects (and things German and Kantian were faraway then), the heavy-handed jocularities are not only temperamental failings, but must be explained by conformity to the tone of the magazines for which De Quincey wrote and the hopes which he had to raise in editors and readers. But modern scholarship has taken these potboilers (to call many of these articles by their true name) far too seriously, has inflated the ideas and impressions which were, after all, even for De Quincey himself only of peripheral importance.

It all resolves itself into a lack of perspective. A balanced view of De Quincey's many writings would make such an overelaboration and inflation impossible. But no such view can be taken unless the student has a power of distinguishing between the original and the echo, unless he can expertly survey the intricate currents of modern thought. We should remember and confess candidly that many of our scholarly publications (and Mr. Proctor's is far from being the worst) are but good apprentice-work, displays of reading and exercises in method. It has become one of the tasks of criticism to restore the upset balance, to remove the accretions accumulated by farfetched hypotheses, to reject the many pseudo-problems raised and to rediscover what had been known long ago. Otherwise the landmarks on our map of literature will be obliterated by a flood of immature scholarly contributions. But we need not deplore the fact that much of literary scholarship (as a good part of this paper) has become polemical. Knowledge advances through refutation, thought is incited by opposition, the whole history of scholarship (and not only of scholarship) is one of thesis: antithesis and a temporary or faraway synthesis.

CHAPTER FIVE

The Minor Transcendentalists and German Philosophy*

✱ The relations between New England Transcendentalism and German philosophy have never been studied in any detail. Most discussions are content to assume the influence of German philosophy, referring in general terms to Kant, Schelling and Fichte, or try to dismiss the influence altogether.[1] There are many suggestive remarks in books and articles, but we have no systematic study which would examine this relationship in the light of all the evidence, on the background of a thorough knowledge of the German philosophers. In this paper little more can be attempted than the first outlines of such an investigation. As an excuse for presenting it, I shall only plead that I have not met such a survey elsewhere and that possibly my earlier studies in Kant and

---

* Originally in *The New England Quarterly*, xv (No. 4, 1942), pp. 652-80.

[1] There are no discussions of the relations of Alcott, Parker, Brownson, Miss Fuller, Follen or Hedge to the German thinkers, except references in biographies and general studies of Transcendentalism (Frothingham, Goddard, Riley, Girard, Muirhead, Townsend). There is, however, a recent paper, "George Ripley: Unitarian, Transcendentalist or Infidel?" by Arthur R. Schultz and Henry A. Pochmann, in *American Literature*, xiv (1942), 1-19, which discusses Ripley's relations to German philosophy.

Since this paper was written, Henry A. Pochmann, in his *German Culture in America* (Madison, Wis., 1957), has accumulated much new material, and Stanley M. Vogel, in *German Literary Influences on the American Transcendentalists* (New Haven, 1955), has touched on the problem in a wider context.

153

Minor Transcendentalists

his influence in England[2] have given me a starting point and some initial scheme of reference.

In approaching the question of the relations between New England Transcendentalism and German philosophy, it will be necessary to touch first on a subordinate subject: the exact beginnings of this influence and the way in which German thought was imported into this country. I touch on it only because there are two widely held views on this point which seem to me mistaken. One theory ascribes the importation of German thought to the return of American students such as Ticknor and Bancroft from Germany; the other assumes that German philosophy reached America first, and only, through Coleridge and Carlyle.

It has been shown convincingly that intellectual relations between America and Germany were by no means nonexistent even in the seventeenth century, and that the general lack of German books or of the knowledge of the German language in America has been exaggerated.[3] Especially toward the end of the eighteenth century there was considerable interest in German *belles lettres*: John Quincy Adams, for instance, translated Wieland's *Oberon* into good verse, and the Reverend William Bentley, pastor at Salem, collected German books which included the works of Klopstock and Schiller and many others. In the periodical literature there appear even scattered mentions of the recent German philosophers. An issue of the Philadelphia *Monthly Magazine* for 1798 included a note on Kant based on a German source, which speaks

[2] *Immanuel Kant in England, 1793-1838* (Princeton, 1931).
[3] Harold S. Jantz, "German Thought and Literature in New England, 1620-1820," *Journal of English and Germanic Philology*, XLI (1942), 1-45.

Minor Transcendentalists

of the *Criterion* [sic] *of Pure Reason*; and the *Boston Register* of 1801 contains quotations from Fichte refuting the charges of atheism.[4] In Samuel Miller's interesting *Retrospect of the Eighteenth Century* (1803) there is a hostile account of Kant which reproduces a review by William Taylor of Willich's *Elements of Critical Philosophy* (1798) from the London *Monthly Review* of January 1799.[5] Obviously not much can be made out of such scattered notices except to suggest that the names of Kant and Fichte had begun to reach America.

An actual motive for the study of German thought was supplied only by the New England theologians, who became interested in German Biblical scholarship long before the earliest migration of American students to German universities after the end of the Napoleonic wars. As early as 1806, the Reverend Joseph Stevens Buckminster, later pastor of the Brattle Street Church at Cambridge, brought a library of some three thousand German books from Europe and started to lecture on Biblical criticism at Harvard College. Buckminster died young and apparently left few traces of his interests.[6] But Moses Stuart, Professor of Sacred Literature at Andover Theological Seminary, must have been a far more influential figure. In 1812 he encouraged his young friend Edward Everett to translate Herder's *Letters on Theology*; and in 1814, when Everett went on a trip to New

[4] I. W. Riley, *American Thought from Puritanism to Pragmatism and Beyond* (New York, 1923), pp. 232-35; Jantz, "German Thought and Literature in New England," p. 41.

[5] Cf. *Immanuel Kant in England*, pp. 13 and 268. Harold S. Jantz, "Samuel Miller's Survey of German Literature, 1803," *Germanic Review*, XVI (1941), 267-77, notes that Miller owes this section to a "British literary journal," but does not identify the source.

[6] *The Dictionary of American Biography.*

Minor Transcendentalists

York, Stuart asked him to buy German books. He wanted him especially to get a "copy of Kant's philosophy," whatever that may mean, which "would be a great curiosity."[7] He used Rosenmüller and de Wette in his classroom and in 1822 translated from the Latin a book called *The Elements of Interpretation* by the German J. A. Ernesti. In 1825 he underwent investigation for his views by the trustees of his college. The Committee reported that "the unrestrained cultivation of German studies has evidently tended to chill the ardor of piety, to impair belief in the fundamentals of revealed religion, and even to induce, for the time, an approach to universal skepticism."[8] But Stuart continued with his work, and as late as 1841 sent a spirited defense of German Biblical scholarship to the *Christian Review*. The work done by other figures, such as Dr. Convers Francis and James Walker, both students of German theology, still needs exploring.

The strongest argument for the role of Coleridge in transmitting German thought is furnished by the work of James Marsh, President of the University of Vermont from 1826 to 1833. In 1829 he edited *Aids to Reflection* adding a long preliminary discourse expounding the distinctions of German philosophers (such as that between Reason and Understanding) in the interpretation of Coleridge. In a letter to Coleridge, Marsh acknowledged his debt on this point quite specifically: "The German philosophers," he wrote, "Kant and his followers are very little known in this country; and our young men who have visited Germany have paid little attention to

---

[7] O. W. Long, *Literary Pioneers* (Cambridge, 1935; hereinafter, "Long"), 237, note 6.

[8] Daniel Day Williams, *The Andover Liberals* (New York, 1941), p. 17.

Minor Transcendentalists

that department of study while there. I cannot boast of being wiser than others in this respect; for though I have read a part of the works of Kant, it was under many disadvantages, so that I am indebted to your own writings for the ability to understand what I have read of his works, and am waiting with some impatience for that part of your works which will aid more directly in the study of those subjects of which he treats."[9]

But Marsh certainly extended his interest in German thought beyond a secondhand knowledge derived from Coleridge. He read the anthropological and scientific writings of Kant and planned a book on logic designed to follow the textbook of Johann Jacob Fries, who had given an extreme objectivist interpretation to Kant. Nor could Marsh have needed Coleridge's stimulus to translate Herder's *Spirit of Hebrew Poetry* in 1833, or two scholarly German books, the *Geography of the Scriptures* and the *Historical Chronology*. Marsh can be described as a belated Cambridge Platonist, whose interests were primarily theological and educational.[10] Thus, clergymen who studied German Biblical scholarship and Kant appear to have made the first contact with modern German thought.

The role of the American students who returned from Germany has been, it seems to me, extremely overrated, at least for our question. Edward Everett, who was to procure that copy of Kant's philosophy for Moses Stuart, studied classical philology in Göttingen. Everett was President of Harvard from 1846 to 1849, but no interest

[9] Marjorie H. Nicolson, "James Marsh and the Vermont Transcendentalists," *Philosophical Review*, XXXIV (1925), 33.

[10] Nicolson, p. 49. Cf. also John Dewey, "James Marsh and American Philosophy," *Journal of the History of Ideas*, II (1941), 131-50.

Minor Transcendentalists

in German philosophy is recorded in his life except an abortive plan to give an address on "the influence of German thought on the contemporary literature of England and America," in 1837.[11] As early as 1816 George Ticknor came to the conclusion that the present "barrenness" of German literature was to be charged to the philosophy of Kant, which "absorbed and perverted all the talents of the land." It was a vast "Serbonian bog where armies whole have sunk."[12] After his return to Harvard, Ticknor lectured on French and Spanish literature. George Bancroft, who kept up an interest in German *belles lettres* and later wrote several valuable studies, went to hear Hegel in Berlin, but thought the lectures merely a "display of unintelligible words." He admired Schleiermacher, however, whom he heard lecture on education, largely because "he has never suffered himself to be moved by any one of the many systems which have been gaining admirers and losing them successively for thirty years past."[13]

Neither Motley nor Longfellow showed any interest in German philosophy.[14] The one exception among these students was Frederick Henry Hedge, who was, however, in Germany as a boy and developed interest in German philosophy only much later. In 1833 he wrote a review of Coleridge for the *Christian Examiner* which gives a fairly detailed account of German philosophy.[15] Hedge

---

[11] Long, p. 75.   [12] Long, p. 16; letter of February 29, 1816.
[13] Long, p. 248, note 53; letter of December 28, 1820; and p. 133, letter of November 13, 1820.
[14] Long on Motley. On Longfellow, see James Taft Hatfield, *New Light on Longfellow* (Boston, 1933). In 1844 Longfellow read Fichte's *Nature of the Scholar* (Hatfield, p. 110) and in 1848 he read Schelling's essay on Dante, which he translated for *Graham's Magazine* (Hatfield, p. 118).
[15] *The Christian Examiner*, New Series, IX (1833), 108-29.

Minor Transcendentalists

there deplores the meager information on German philosophy in Coleridge and proceeds to explain his own views. They show a knowledge which is quite independent of Coleridge and a firsthand acquaintance with Fichte's *Wissenschaftslehre* and Schelling's *System des transzendentalen Idealismus*. Kant, according to Hedge, "did not himself create a system, but furnished the hints and materials from which all the systems of his followers have been framed." The transcendental point of view is described as that of "interior consciousness." "In the language of the school, it is a free intuition, and can only be attained by a vigorous effort of the will. The object is to discover in every form of finite existence, an infinite and unconditioned as the ground of its existence, or rather the ground of our knowledge of its existence, to refer all phenomena to certain *noumena*, or laws of cognition. It is not a *ratio essendi*, but a *ratio cognoscendi*." This sounds like a description of Kant's procedure. Hedge, however, elaborates the point that the method is "synthetical, proceeding from a given point, the lowest that can be found in our consciousness, and deducing from that point 'the whole world of intelligences, with the whole system of their representations.'" Immediately afterwards this description, which might apply to Schelling, is modified, and an explanation of the "alternation of synthesis and antithesis" in Fichte is followed by a quite technical and literal reproduction of the beginnings of the *Wissenschaftslehre*. But Fichte is criticized as leaning toward skepticism and as "altogether too subjective." Schelling seems to Hedge the most satisfactory of all the Germans. "In him intellectual philosophy is more ripe, more substantial, more promising, and, if we

Minor Transcendentalists

may apply such a term to such speculations, more practical than in any of the others." Hedge describes briefly the main principle of Schelling's natural philosophy as an endeavor to show that "the outward world is of the same essence with the thinking mind, both being different manifestations of the same divine principle." Hedge alludes to Oken's development of Schelling's system and mentions him with Hegel and Fries, apologizing that "our information would not enable us to say much, and our limits forbid us to say anything" about them. Unfortunately Hedge never followed-up the promise held out by these few competent pages. He collaborated in the *Dial*, to which he contributed a translation of Schelling's inaugural lecture at Berlin, and published an anthology of the *Prose Writers of Germany* (1847) which contained translated extracts from Kant's *Critique of Judgment*, Schellings's oration on the fine arts and passages from Friedrich Schlegel's and Hegel's *Philosophies of History* and Fichte's *Destiny of Man*. Late in his life, Hedge became Professor of German at Harvard and wrote papers on Leibniz and Schopenhauer.[16] Hedge was no original thinker, but he had a really good knowledge of German from the time of his schooldays. He could talk on German philosophy with his elders and friends, Emerson and Alcott, and may serve as an indication that America was not confined to secondhand information on German philosophy through either Coleridge or the French eclectics.

The influence of the German immigrants belongs mostly to a later time. Carl Follen, the first instructor and later professor of German at Harvard, is the most

[16] O. W. Long, *F. H. Hedge: A Cosmopolitan Scholar* (Portland, Maine, 1940).

Minor Transcendentalists

important figure among these. He was an enthusiastic German *Corpsstudent*, an admirer of Jahn, the nationalistic gymnastics teacher, and of Theodor Körner, the poet of the Napoleonic wars. But he also studied theology under Channing and in 1830 gave a course on moral philosophy which shows firsthand knowledge of Kant.[17] In the course of a brief history of ethics which discusses the Greeks, the New Testament and Spinoza, we get a fairly full exposition of Kant's philosophy. The description of the *Critique of Pure Reason* is elementary and vitiated by Follen's repeated reference to time, space and categories as "innate ideas": he suspects Kant's system of leading to subjective idealism and skepticism, but then gives an exposition of the moral philosophy which shows far better insight and even critical acumen. Kant is criticized for his mistake of considering man "sometimes entirely as a rational and moral, and sometimes entirely as a sensual or phenomenal being," and some good points are scored against the categorical imperative, which to Follen appears vague and general and merely an advice to search the nature, particularly the rational and moral nature, of man. Kant's religion of reason seems to him "nothing less than an avowal of atheism." His attitude toward Kant is extremely unsympathetic: he criticizes him not from the point of view of later German idealism (which he apparently did not know though he alludes to Fichte), but with empirical arguments which he manages to combine with a philosophy of faith. Nevertheless, in the following year, Follen, in his inaugural discourse as professor of German at Harvard, included a defense of German phi-

---

[17] In Follen's *Works* (5 volumes, Boston, 1841), vol. III. The "Life" by his widow in Vol. I gives date of delivery of the lectures, p. 290.

Minor Transcendentalists

losophy. He argued that its "records, from Leibniz to Kant and his disciples, Fichte, Schelling, Jacobi, and Fries do not exhibit the name of a single materialist or absolute skeptic."[18] Though Follen, in spite of his premature death, did something to foster interest in things German, he can scarcely be described as a propagandist for German idealist philosophy.

The other Germans who wrote on philosophy came later and could not have been of decisive importance. Frederick A. Rauch became President of Marshall College in Pennsylvania and wrote a Hegelian *Psychology: or a View of the Human Soul* (1841). Johann Bernhard Stallo settled in Cincinnati and wrote *General Principles of the Philosophy of Nature* (1848), a book which attracted Emerson's interest sufficiently to warrant long extracts in his *Journals*.[19] The editor of the *Journals* printed so few quotations from Emerson's transcript that it is impossible to judge the nature of his interest in Stallo, but the book may very well have been a source of Emerson's knowledge of Schelling, Oken and Hegel. Since Stallo does little more than give abstracts, it is difficult to lay one's hand on any indebtedness which Emerson might not have incurred from the original texts or from other secondhand accounts.[20] Another German, Emmanuel Vitalis Scherb, tried to instruct Emerson on Hegel in 1849 and 1851, but since the *Journals* do not tell us precisely of what this instruction consisted, we might as well not even begin to guess.[21]

---

[18] "Inaugural Discourse" (September 3, 1831) in Follen's *Works*, vol. v. See especially p. 136.
[19] Emerson, *Journals* (Boston, 1909-1914), December 1849, VIII, 77.
[20] Two possibilities will be suggested in the paper on Emerson.
[21] Emerson, *Journals*, VIII, 69. See also VIII, 246.

Minor Transcendentalists

All this is strictly preliminary, by way of clearing the path to a direct examination of the main figures in the Transcendentalist group. But I cannot suppress a few reflections on the general problem presented by the contact of two great intellectual movements. I avoid the term "influence," which to be used safely needs some closer definition. In discussing such a relation, we must, I think, distinguish carefully several questions which are frequently not kept clearly apart by investigators. First, we must see what was the reputation of German philosophy, the vague secondhand or tenthhand information which was floating about, and distinguish it from actual knowledge of German philosophy, either in more detailed descriptive accounts by English or French writers or in a real firsthand acquaintance with the texts themselves, in translation or in the original. Only when this first problem of the actual knowledge has been settled can we profitably inquire what precisely was the attitude and the opinion that American writers had of the German philosophers. Only after this can we raise the question of actual influence. Even then we have to distinguish between the use of isolated quotations or ideas and a really basic similarity in philosophical outlook or mental evolution. Isolated parallels merely establish the fact of the relation; one can speak of real influence only if the whole system of one man is compared with the whole system of another. ("System," of course, need not imply any systematic exposition in any technical sense, but merely means a personal view of the world.) Even then we ought to know exactly the original features (or at least the peculiar combinations of ideas in the two systems we are comparing) before we can maintain with absolute certainty that we have defined a shaping and determining influence and not merely uncovered a spiritual kinship, possibly explainable by similar intellectual antecedents. In the case of American Transcendentalism, this problem becomes extremely complex, since the ancestry of Transcendentalism includes almost the whole intellectual history of mankind: Plato; the pre-Socratic philosophers known to Emerson and Alcott in fairly detailed accounts; Neo-Platonism, partly available in the recent translations of Thomas Taylor; the English Neo-Platonists of the seventeenth and eighteenth centuries; the great tradition of mysticism represented especially by Jacob Böhme and Swedenborg, not to speak of Swedenborg's disciples in America (Sampson Reed) and France (Oegger); the native tradition of Calvinist and Unitarian theology; the British "moral sense" philosophy of the eighteenth century, represented by Bishop Butler, Price and others; Coleridge, Carlyle and a few other interpreters of Kant, writing in English; and the French eclectic philosophers and the early Utopian socialists, including Madame de Staël, Cousin, Jouffroy, Benjamin Constant, Leroux and Fourier. At a later period Oriental philosophies must be added, and finally, before we mention the actual German philosophers, the many German poets and novelists who, in one or another form, assimilated and transmitted the philosophical thought of the technical philosophers: Goethe, of course, Schiller, Jean Paul, the Schlegels and Novalis. Who has ever clearly defined which idea comes from where? The historian of ideas would almost need a dictionary similar to the *Oxford Dictionary* which would list the first occurrence (subject to correction) of thoughts, giving author and date. And even this would not solve our difficulties, since the his-

Minor Transcendentalists

tory of thought is the history not merely of unit-ideas but of systems and interrelations, new combinations and syntheses. When we look at German philosophy itself, we are also confronted with a difficult problem of distinctions, trends and conflicts within the fold itself. There is Leibniz looming in the background; Kant, still steeped in eighteenth-century rationalism, open to at least three or four widely divergent interpretations, not to speak of the hundred misinterpretations; then Herder, Jacobi and Schleiermacher, who sought the intuitive evidence of religion; then the dialectical philosophy growing out of Kant: Fichte, the early Schelling and later Hegel, all three distinct in their approach and intellectual background—Fichte, a moralist and dualist, Schelling primarily a philosopher of nature with mystical leanings, Hegel a logician and philosopher of history. Lorenz Oken and Henrik Steffens (a Norwegian) are speculative scientists nearest to Schelling; Novalis and Friedrich Schlegel have the closest links with Fichte, Jean Paul with Jacobi, Schiller with Kant, Goethe with Herder and Neo-Platonism. The Transcendentalists knew them all, more or less intimately, without, of course, necessarily understanding their relationships but instinctively looking for congenial ideas in kindred minds. Here is, at least, the suggestion of a convenient and feasible approach. We may take up each important figure in the Transcendental movement and ask several questions. What did he know about German philosophy—what from hearsay and what secondhand and what from actual texts? What did he think of the German philosophers? Which of the German thinkers did he treat with greatest sympathy and understanding? Thus, by empirical methods, we may place every American thinker in the

Minor Transcendentalists

scheme of the much-studied and carefully analyzed development of German philosophy and determine his approximate historical position. We may then make distinctions and lay out at least the ground for a discussion of direct influences.

We may begin with Bronson Alcott, who not only was the oldest in the group, but in his mental make-up represented also the oldest tradition of thought among them. Alcott knew scacrely any German (though he bought books in German when he was in London in 1842, including the mysterious volume called *Vernunft* by Fichte),[22] but early found his way to what appealed to him in German thought, namely, Jacob Böhme, the seventeenth-century cobbler from Silesia who evolved an elaborate system of mystical theosophy that was widely read in English translations during both the seventeenth and the eighteenth centuries. In 1833, when Alcott was in Philadelphia, he read Okely's *Life of Behmen*, and he read and re-read much of Böhme at different times. As late as 1882 he founded a small Mystic Club for the express purpose of discussing and reading Böhme.[23] The few published writings of Alcott contain a little essay on Böhme (first published in *The Radical*, 1870; reprinted in *Concord Days*, 1872). In this Alcott praises his "teeming genius, the genuine mother of numberless theories since delivered."[24] Law, Leibniz, Oken, Schelling, Goethe, and Baader seem all derived from him. Alcott thinks of Böhme as "the subtilest thinker on Genesis

---

[22] Odell Shepard, *Pedlar's Progress* (Boston, 1937), p. 341.

[23] Shepard, *Pedlar's Progress*, pp. 160, 341, 350, and 416; also *The Journals*, Odell Shepard, editor (Boston, 1938), pp. 34, 109, 332, and 530.

[24] *Concord Days* (Boston, 1872), p. 238.

Minor Transcendentalists

since Moses,"[25] though he disagrees with him on the fall of man and the symbolism of the serpent, as mystics are apt to disagree on the details of their allegories and symbols.

In 1849, Alcott read Lorenz Oken, the speculative scientist, whose *Elements of Physiophilosophy* had been translated in England in 1847.[26] Soon afterwards, Alcott had his second "illumination," in which he saw the universe as "one vast spinal column";[27] and all his following speculations on Genesis and the meaning of nature seem to be full of Oken's ideas and terminology, though obviously Alcott drew also from many other sources in the same tradition. To illustrate this, I like to point out a passage in Emerson's essay on Swedenborg,[28] in which he speaks of "a poetic anatomist of our day," obviously referring to Alcott, and then proceeds to reproduce his ideas. These ideas represent a combination of two different authors from whom Alcott seems to have drawn. He speaks first of the mystical quadrant of man (the vertical) and the serpent (the horizontal), an idea derived from Oegger's *True Messiah*, which Emerson had copied in his *Journals* more than twenty years before;[29] and then he paraphrases Oken's curious fancy that the skull is another spine, and that the hands have been transformed into the up-

[25] *Tablets* (Boston, 1868), p. 189.

[26] Translated by Alfred Tulk, member of the Royal College of Surgeons of England; printed for the Ray Society (London, 1847). Cf. Alcott's *Journals*, pp. 211 and 212.

[27] Shepard, *Pedlar's Progress*, p. 439.

[28] Emerson, *Representative Men*, in *Complete Works*, Centenary Edition (Boston, 1903-1904), IV, 107-108.

[29] Emerson, *Journals*, III, 515, from Oegger, *Le Vrai Messie* (Paris, 1829). A partial translation by Elizabeth Peabody was published in Boston in 1835.

per jaw, the feet into the lower.[30] Alcott's precise relations to the German scientists like Oken and von Schubert, and possibly to the theosophist Baader, are quite unexplored and cannot be solved definitely without access to the fifty manuscript volumes of his journals. For our purpose it is sufficient to say that he was strongly attracted by the speculations of the Schellingian philosophy of nature and combined it with Neo-Platonic and generally mystical elements.

But Alcott knew also something of the main German idealistic philosophers. As early as 1833, in Philadelphia, before he had met Emerson or settled at Boston, Alcott read two expositions of Kant written in English by Germans, late in the eighteenth century.[31] One was Willich's *Elements of Critical Philosophy* (1798), in Odell Shepard's life of Alcott ascribed to Wellick. From the other, Friedrich August Nitsch's *View of Kant's Principles* (1796), Alcott copied out some 57 pages, proof, by the way, that he did not need the mediation of either Coleridge or the French to learn something about Kant. But Alcott's own view of Kant was soon decidedly unfavorable: he classed him with Aristotle, Bacon and Locke, and thought that all had "narrowed the range of the human faculties, retarded the progress of discovery by insisting on the supremacy of the senses and shut the soul up in the cave of the Understanding."[32] Alcott here interprets Kant as a skeptic, as a critic of all metaphysics, and uses Kant's own distinction between Reason and

---

[30] Oken, *Elements of Physiophilosophy* (London, 1847): "The Mouth is the stomach in the head, the nose the lung, the jaws the arms and feet" (364).

[31] Shepard, *Pedlar's Progress*, p. 160. Willich and Nitsch are discussed in *Immanuel Kant in England*, pp. 7-15.

[32] Alcott, *Journals*, pp. 38-39.

Minor Transcendentalists

Understanding in a Coleridgean sense to condemn Kant's philosophy as pedestrian and sensual.

Later in his life, Alcott was brought into personal contact with the St. Louis Hegelians. He visited them in 1859 and again in 1866, and became the nominal head of the Concord School of Philosophy, where for years Hegelians like William Torrey Harris expounded their doctrines under Alcott's patronage.[33] At first he was flattered by their admiration and overwhelmed and puzzled by Hegel's *Philosophy of History* and James Hutchinson Stirling's *Secret of Hegel*, which his daughter Louisa had brought from Europe as a present.[34] In the *Tablets* (1868) and the *Concord Days* (1882) there are quotations from Harris and two little essays on speculative philosophy and dialectics.[35] For a time, at least, Alcott expected a new philosophy in New England, "to which the German Hegel shall give impulse and furtherance."[36] But he soon decided that Hegel is not only "dry and crabbed," "strange and unintelligible," but that his own thinking is "ideal, his method analogical rather than logical" and thus "of a subtler and more salient type" than Hegel's, since it "implies an active and sprightly imagination inflaming the reason and divining the truths it seeks."[37] Thus, Alcott defines his own position clearly as an adherent of an imaginative, "analogical" mysticism which rejects as irrelevant the epistemological and logical methods of both Kant and Hegel.

[33] Shepard, *Pedlar's Progress*, pp. 474-76, 480-84, and 507ff. Cf. Austin Warren, "The Concord School of Philosophy," *New England Quarterly*, II (1929), 199-233.
[34] Alcott, *Journals*, pp. 340 and 383; August 1861, and July 1866.
[35] Alcott, *Tablets*, pp. 164-65; *Concord Days*, pp. 73-74; "Speculative Philosophy," pp. 143ff; and "The Dialectic," pp. 156ff.
[36] *Concord Days*, p. 145.
[37] *Journals*, p. 497, July 1879; and p. 536, August 1882.

Minor Transcendentalists

George Ripley and Theodore Parker present a striking contrast to Alcott in their attitude toward German philosophy. Both were Unitarian clergymen who found in German thought additional support for their liberal religious convictions. Ripley was the more timid and also the more orthodox of the two. His early writings praise Herder and Schleiermacher[38]—"the greatest thinker who ever undertook to fathom the philosophy of religion"[39]— and his own thought seems to agree in every way with this professed sympathy. But Ripley knew also something of Kant. As early as 1832 he defended him as a "writer and reasoner from whom the great questions ... have received more light than from any uninspired person, since the brightest days of Grecian philosophy." He contrasts him sharply with Coleridge, describing Kant's "cool, far-reaching, and austere habits of thought," "the severe logic, the imperturbable patience, the mathematical precision, and the passionless exhibition of the results of pure reason."[40] But soon, in a detailed account of Herder's conflict with Kant, Ripley sides with Herder, praising him for having made the system "lower its pretensions, and assume a more modest rank," though he recognizes Herder's incompetence to "do justice to the great merits" of the Kantian system "as an analytical exposition of the grounds of human knowledge."[41] In

[38] Review of James Marsh's translation of Herder's *Spirit of Hebrew Poetry*, in the *Christian Examiner*, XVII (1835), 167-221; "Herder's Theological Opinions and Services," *ibid.*, XIX (1835), 172-204; and "Schleiermacher as a Theologian," *ibid.*, XX (1836), 1-46. Also Ripley's "Letters to a Theological Student" (written in December 1836) in the *Dial*, I (1840), recommends Herder highly (p. 187).

[39] O. B. Frothingham, *George Ripley* (Boston, 1882), p. 229.

[40] Review of Carl Follen's "Inaugural Discourse," *Christian Examiner*, XI (1832), 375.

[41] Review of Marsh's *Spirit of Hebrew Poetry*, in the *Christian Examiner*, XVIII (1835), 209.

Minor Transcendentalists

a later article on Fichte (1846) Ripley criticizes him as having failed to solve "the mighty problems of Divine Providence and Human Destiny" and tries to find in him merely negative virtues. According to Ripley, Fichte has shown the fruitlessness of speculation and thrown man back into "the world of moral emotions," "the instinctive sense of justice," "the interior voice"[42]—that is, precisely the teachings of Herder and Schleiermacher, with whom the historical Fichte had only scant sympathy. Ripley even sees in the study of Fichte a preparation for the acceptance of the doctrines of Fourier, possibly because of Fichte's strong collectivist outlook on social questions.

Ripley's attitude toward German philosophy became more and more hostile. Reviewing Hedge's *Prose Writers*, he asks "to what does [German philosophy] amount";[43] and a review of Stallo's book *Philosophy of Nature* is completely negative. Ripley thinks that its thoughts "offer no points of contact with the American mind." To him now, the study of German philosophy has only historical interest, much as "studying the remains of the Later Platonists or the Oriental philosophers" would have. The German thinkers produce only "wonderful specimens of intellectual gymnastics." They try to "explain the universe or the human soul by the mere force of thought, without the scientific analysis of facts," which is "as absurd as the attempt to leap over one's own head."[44] Later, Ripley also attacked Strauss and Feuerbach and the mid-nineteenth-century materialists like Büchner, and he showed some interest in Eduard Hart-

[42] *Harbinger*, II (1846), 297ff.
[43] *Harbinger*, VI (1848), 107.
[44] *Harbinger*, VI (1848), 110.

mann's *Philosophy of the Unconscious*.[45] But evidence enough has been presented to show that Ripley stands with Herder and Schleiermacher as a philosopher of faith, that he welcomed the German idealists only as far as they seemed, in his interpretation, to make room for such a philosophy, and that later he roundly condemned what he considered their mistaken intellectualism and *a priori* ways of thinking. It would be difficult to say which ideas Ripley could have derived from Germany, because the idea of a "religious sense" could have been found in British and French philosophy too.

Theodore Parker was both a bolder mind and man and a greater scholar than Ripley; but in our context he is nearest to Ripley, though he drifted further from the moorings of the church. Parker early studied German Biblical criticism and theology and translated a two-volume *Introduction to the New Testament* by de Wette, a liberal German theologian who was a follower of Fries and thus remotely of Kant. Parker's learning in German scholarship, theological, historical and literary, was really imposing, though the long strings of indiscriminately jumbled names in an article in defense of the German literature in the *Dial*[46] arouse some suspicions whether his knowledge, at least at that time, was always so thorough and firsthand as it seems. In this long and able article, which is ostensibly a review of Menzel's *History of German Literature*, little is said of German philosophy, though Parker calls Menzel's views on Kant "exceedingly unjust" and recognizes the polit-

---

[45] Frothingham, pp. 230 and 286.
[46] *Dial*, I (1841), 315-39. Reprinted in Parker's *Critical and Miscellaneous Writings*, second edition (New York, 1864), pp. 28-60.

Minor Transcendentalists

ical bias of his attacks on Hegel.[47] The next year, 1843, Parker went to Germany, called on de Wette in Basel and other theologians, and heard Werder, a Hegelian, lecture on logic in Berlin. The performance seemed to him merely ridiculous, as did Schelling, whom he heard lecture on the philosophy of revelation.[48] After his return, Parker became immersed in German theology, jurisprudence, ecclesiastical history, and later, of course, the cause of abolitionism. He thus never returned to German philosophy proper. But in the fine confession of faith which he wrote to his parishioners from Santa Cruz when on his last voyage to Italy in 1859, he confessed his debt to Kant, "one of the profoundest thinkers in the world, though one of the worst writers, even of Germany." "He gave me the true method, and put me on the right road. I found certain primal intuitions of human nature, which depend on no logical process of demonstration, but are rather facts of consciousness given by the instinctive action of human nature itself: the instinctive intuition of the divine, the instinctive intuition of the just and right, the instinctive intuition of the immortal. Here, then, was the foundation of religion, laid in human nature itself."[49] There is little point in stressing that this is a false interpretation of Kant. It is more interesting to note that this interpretation is in perfect harmony with the intuitive philosophy of Jacobi or Schleiermacher, of the French eclectics, and even of the Scottish common-sense school. Parker stands with Ripley, but succeeds in interpreting the *Critique of*

[47] *Dial*, I (1841), 335-36; reprinted as above, pp. 54-55.
[48] H. S. Commager, *Theodore Parker* (Boston, 1936), pp. 95-96.
[49] J. Weiss, *The Life and Correspondence of Theodore Parker* (Boston, 1864), II, 454-55.

Minor Transcendentalists

Practical Reason as support for a philosophy of faith as an instinctive intuition of the human mind.

Orestes Brownson, or rather the early Brownson before his conversion to Roman Catholicism in 1844, who alone can be called a Transcendentalist, is related in outlook and starting point to both Ripley and Parker. Early in life he became an intuitionist, who read, admired and propagated Cousin and the other French eclectics. But Brownson had a stronger philosophical bent than his friends and associates, and a genuine gift for speculation as well as an altogether unusual grasp, in his time and place, of philosophical technicalities. He alone of all the Transcendentalists seems to have been seriously disturbed by the problems of knowledge and truth, and he alone made a close examination of Kant's actual text. This was written down shortly after his conversion, but the point of view there expounded can be found already in the scattered and unsympathetic pronouncements of his preconversion writings. The remarkable consistency and uniformity of his criticism of Kant and Hegel, which extends over a period of some thirty-five years of indefatigable writing, seems to point to a greater coherence and consistency in Brownson's philosophical outlook than is usually allowed by those who see only the shiftings and changes of his religious associations.

As to German philosophy, there is only one marked change of attitude. Brownson had learned to read German in 1834; and in a little book, *New Views of Christianity* (1836), he recommended the German theological movement starting with Herder and culminating in Schleiermacher. Brownson commended the "meeting of inspiration and philosophy" in Schleiermacher and

Minor Transcendentalists

praised him as a man for "remarkable warmth of feeling and coolness of thought," hinting at the similarity between him and Saint-Simon.[50] After the conversion, Brownson condemned Schleiermacher's views, since he makes religion purely subjective and "resolves the church into general society." He even went out of his way to brand Schleiermacher's "pantheistic spiritualism" as worse than rationalism, deism, and even the atheism of D'Holbach.[51]

But no such marked change can be discerned in his relations to Kant, Fichte, Schelling and Hegel. His attitude toward Kant seems to have been defined very early. Brownson had a great admiration precisely for the technical side of Kant's analysis of judgment and categories. In all his writings he was again and again to repeat the view that "Kant has with masterly skill and wonderful exactness, drawn up a complete list of the categories of Reason. His analysis of Reason may be regarded as complete and final."[52] This analysis, Brownson thought, was purely empirical and correct as far as it went. Very early he defended Kant against the charge of transcendentalism. Kant's method, he argued, "was as truly experimental as Bacon's or Locke's." Even when Kant professed to describe *a priori* knowledge, he did so "by experience, by experiment, by a careful analysis of the facts of consciousness, as they actually present themselves to the eye of the psychological observer." If Kant is to be criticized, he should not

---
[50] *Collected Works*, ed. H. F. Brownson (Detroit, 1882-1907), IV, 44-45.
[51] *Collected Works*, III, 45; IV, 519; VIII, 424; and IX, 480; quotations dating from 1850, 1844, 1872 and 1873 respectively.
[52] "Synthetic Philosophy," *Democratic Review* (1842), reprinted in *Works*, I, 165; see also I, 222; II, 299; V, 507; and IX, 263.

Minor Transcendentalists

be charged with leaving the "path of experience" or "rushing off into speculation." Rather, Brownson suggested, Kant fails in a thoroughgoing application of his method because he conceives of experience too narrowly as merely experience of the senses.[53]

But in spite of these frequent acknowledgments of Kant's power as an analyst of thought, Brownson seems never to have been in doubt as to his objections to the main epistemological position of Kant. In a review dating from 1842, Brownson rejected philosophical idealism as clearly and forcefully as he was to reject it for the rest of his life: "The refutation of Kant and Fichte, and therefore of all idealism, egoism, and skepticism, whether atheistic or pantheistic, is in a simple fact . . . that the objective element of thought is always *not me*. The error of Kant, and the error which led astray his whole school and all others, is the assumption that the *me* does or may develop as pure subject, or, in other words, be its own object, and therefore at once subject and object. Kant assumes that the *me* develops itself, without a foreign object, in cognition; hence he infers that all knowledge is purely subjective, and asserts the impotency of reason to carry us out of the sphere of the *me*." In a note, Brownson recognizes that this was not all of Kant's teaching: "We know very well that this was not the real doctrine of Kant, that it was only demonstrated by him to be the result, to which all philosophy must come, that *is based on pure reason*. He himself relied on practical reason, that is to say, on plain common sense, and his purpose of writing critiques of pure reason, was to demonstrate the unsatisfactory character of all purely

[53] "Eclectic Philosophy," *Boston Quarterly* (1839), in *Works*, II, 536-38.

Minor Transcendentalists

metaphysical speculations. A wise man, after all, was that same Emanuel Kant."[54] But this partial retraction, which seems to point to some knowledge of the *Critique of Practical Reason*, did not remain in Brownson's mind. He dismissed Kant's practical reason as nothing else than the common sense of Hume[55] and later was to write his criticisms of Kant without regard to other books than the *Critique of Pure Reason*.

When Brownson, immediately after the conversion, in the "Introduction" to *Brownson's Quarterly*, surveyed his own intellectual development, he could, it seems to me, with reason minimize the importance of German philosophy for his own development and define his attitude toward Kant in terms substantially in agreement with the earlier pronouncements. "The German philosophers," he says, "have afforded me very little satisfaction. It is true, that I have made no profound study of them; but, so far as I know them, I claim no affinity with them. I feel and own, the eminent analytic ability of Kant, but I am forced to regard his philosophy as fundamentally false and mischievous. His *Critic der reinen Vernunft*, if taken in any other light than that of a protest, under the most rigid forms of analysis, against all modern philosophy, is sure to mislead, and to involve the reader in an inextricable maze of error."[56] Strangely enough, Brownson thought it worthwhile to make a careful study of the *Critique of Pure Reason*, apparently in the original, shortly afterwards and to write

[54] "Charles Elwood Reviewed," *Boston Quarterly* (1842), in *Works*, IV, 355.
[55] "The Philosophy of History," *Democratic Review* (1843), in *Works*, IV, 391.
[56] "Introduction," *Brownson's Quarterly Review*, I (1844), 8.

Minor Transcendentalists

three closely reasoned essays on it for the first volume of his new quarterly.[57] There we find his fullest discussion of Kant, which is, however, in its approach and conclusion, completely identical with the preconversion pronouncements. Brownson criticizes Kant's fundamental question. It is "absurd to ask if the human mind be capable of science; for we have only the human mind with which to answer the question." Kant's phenomenalism is completely mistaken. One cannot find the object in the subject. "This simple truism, which is nothing but saying what *is*, is, completely refutes the whole critical philosophy." Brownson drives home this main point with considerable dialectical power. Kant is thus interpreted as the arch-skeptic, who denied the very possibility of knowledge, as the "most masterly defender of Hume." With a flourish of Carlylean rhetoric Brownson depicts the dire consequences of this supposed universal skepticism. "So all science vanishes, all certainty disappears, the sun goes out, the bright stars are extinguished, and we are afloat in the darkness, on the wild and tempest-roused ocean of Universal Doubt and Nescience."[58] Kant, according to Brownson, turned out to be fundamentally a "sensist" and a "materialist." Brownson dismisses Kant's own development of his teachings in the other *Critiques* far too lightly;[59] but he has come, at least, to actual grips with the text of Kant, with his dialectics and logic, as no contemporary in Amer-

---

[57] "Kant's Critic of Pure Reason" (1844), 137-74, 181-309, and 417-99; also in *Works*, I, 130-213.

[58] "Kant's Critic of Pure Reason," 282, 284, 308, and 309; *Works*, I, 162, 163, 184, and 185.

[59] "Kant's Critic of Pure Reason," 309; *Works*, I, 185-186. Here Brownson quotes Heine, in the French translation, ridiculing the *Critique of Practical Reason* as prompted by "fear of the police."

ica did. All the many later pronouncements of Brownson on Kant are merely variations on this point of view. He reiterates again and again his admiration for Kant's analysis of mind, his table of the categories and his negative conclusion which seems to Brownson to have established that "man's own subjective reason alone does not suffice for science."[60] But he also condemns his subjectivism, the views that the categories are mere forms of our mind, the denial of the objectivity of knowledge, and hence the skepticism which seems to him the "hardly disguised" result of Kant's philosophy. Kant thus was a philosopher who asked questions and who gave acute technical discussion of logical and epistemological questions; but his main position was entirely repugnant to Brownson, who early in his life had become an objectivist, an enemy of Cartesianism and all its forms.[61]

It is almost needless to expound Brownson's attitude toward Fichte. He appeared to him early as the *reductio ad absurdum* of idealism. Fichte, he says in an article written before the conversion, "asserted the power of the *me* to be his own object and sought the proof of it in the fact of volition. Hence he fell into the absurdity of representing all ideas as the products of the *me*, and even went so far as to tell his disciples how it is that man makes God." But again, as in the case of Kant, Brownson was aware of the existence of Fichte's later views, which corrected some of his speculative errors.[62] Later, Brownson was to repeat several times that the "egoistic philosophy, so energetically asserted by Fichte, that God

[60] "An Old Quarrel," *Catholic World* (1867), in *Works*, II, 299.
[61] Later passages on Kant, in *Works*, I, 222 and 244-45; II, 47, 295, and 520; V, 507; VI, 106; X, 263; and XIX, 384.
[62] "Charles Elwood Reviewed," *Boston Quarterly* (1842), in *Works*, IV, 355.

Minor Transcendentalists

and the external world are only the soul projecting itself, is only a logical deduction from the Kantian premises," and that Cartesianism leads to Fichtean egoism.[63]

Toward Schelling and his disciples Brownson had at first, during the Emersonian stage of his development, shown some vague though cautious sympathy. He thought that "they give us a magnificent poem, which we believe to be mainly true, but which nevertheless is no philosophy and can in no degree solve the difficulty stated by Hume."[64] But later, Schelling was neglected or put down as an atheist and Spinozist. He "maintains the identity of subject and object, and thus asserts, from the subjective point of view, the Egoism of Fichte and, under the objective point of view, the Pantheism of Spinoza, while under both he denies intuition and even the possibility of science."[65]

From these pronouncements, we can already guess at Brownson's attitude toward Hegel. It was again defined long before the conversion. Brownson first rejects the whole deductive method. He cannot believe that "the system of the universe is only a system of logic," that the "ideal and essential, idea and being," are identical. Hegel's method "claims for man confessedly finite, absolute knowledge, which would imply that he himself is absolute and therefore not finite, but infinite." But "the boast is also in vain, for in the order of knowledge we are obliged to reverse the order of existence. We rise through nature up to nature's God, instead of de-

---

[63] "The Giobertian Philosophy," *Brownson's Quarterly* (1864), in *Works*, II, 250; and "The Cartesian Doubt," *Catholic World* (1867), in *Works*, II, 373.

[64] *Christian Examiner*, XXI (1836), 46.

[65] "The Giobertian Philosophy," *Brownson's Quarterly* (1864), in *Works*, II, 251.

Minor Transcendentalists

scending from God through man to nature. None but God himself can know according to the order of existence, for none but he can know being in itself, and from the absolute knowledge of the cause, have a perfect *a priori* knowledge of the effect." While rejecting the pretensions of Hegel's philosophy to absolute knowledge, the American democrat Brownson cannot help smiling at Hegel's view that "the infinite God and all his works through all the past have been engaged expressly in preparing and founding the Prussian monarchy" and that "his gracious majesty Frederick William" could be "the last word of creation and progress."[66] After the conversion the tone of the objections against Hegel becomes more strident. Hegel's system appears to him, under other forms, "nothing but a reproduction of old French Atheism," his principles appear "unreal and worthless," and his philosophy "really less genuine, less profound, and infinitely less worthy of confidence" than that of Reid.[67] In detail, Brownson pays some attention to Hegel's first triad, in which he sees a false attempt to derive the real from the possible, existence from nothing.[68] He does not admit that Hegel is an ontologist.

[66] "The Philosophy of History," *Democratic Review* (1843), in *Works*, IV, 369 and 384.

[67] "Introduction," *Brownson's Quarterly Review*, I (1844), 8. See also a passage containing the astonishing assertion that Hegel reproduces Holbach's *Système de la Nature* in "Transcendentalism," *Brownson's Quarterly* (1846), in *Works*, VI, 97; "The Refutation of Atheism," in *Brownson's Quarterly* (1873), in *Works*, II, 76; and "The Giobertian Philosophy," in *Brownson's Quarterly* (1864), in *Works*, II, 251.

[68] Repeated frequently, e.g. *Works*, I, 401; II, 38, 71, and 268; VI, 97; VIII, 384; IX, 273; and XI, 229. Brownson refers several times to Hegel's *das Ideen*, a mistake for *Das Ideelle*, which does not inspire confidence in his reading of Hegel or close knowledge of German (cf. *Works*, VIII, 384; and III, 502).

Minor Transcendentalists

To Brownson he is a pure psychologist, who only ostensibly attempts to identify the psychological process with the ontological. Hegel is a subjective idealist who ends in pantheism and atheism, like all the other followers of Kant.[69]

Brownson's criticisms of German philosophy cannot always be justified: he surely overstressed the purely negative critical side of Kant and misunderstood the Hegelian dialectics; but within limits he presented the case against German philosophy forcefully and consistently from the point of view of an objective intuitivism which deplored the whole turn modern philosophy had taken since Descartes. He could even write that "Germany has produced no philosophical system not already exploded and no philosophers to compare with Vico, Galluppi, Rosmini, Gioberti and Balmes."[70] Thus, from his own point of view, Brownson rightly thought Leibniz to have been the "greatest of all modern philosophers" not in the Catholic communion. He could praise his refutation of the Cartesian doctrine that the essence of substance is extension and his rejection of the atomic in favor of a dynamic theory of matter. But even Leibniz is criticized as "the veritable father of German rationalism," and as a believer in the ontological argument and the priority of the possible before the real.[71] Brownson's lifelong sympathies were with an intuitivism and realism which managed finally to reconcile Reid and

---

[69] *Works*, I, 401; II, 268; III, 502 and 504; and XI, 229.

[70] "Spiritual Despotism," *Brownson's Quarterly* (1857), in *Works*, VII, 486.

[71] "Catholicity and Naturalism" (1865), in *Works*, VIII, 352; "Holy Communion—Transubstantiation," *Brownson's Quarterly* (1874), VIII, 268; and "Refutation of Atheism," *Brownson's Quarterly* (1873), II, 38.

Minor Transcendentalists

Gioberti, Catholicism and common-sense philosophy. In spite of his interest in some of the arguments of Kant, German philosophy stood for everything Brownson rejected all his life—subjectivism and pantheism, skepticism and atheism.[72]

Margaret Fuller stands apart from the other Transcendentalists. Her interests were obviously not primarily philosophical and theological, but rather aesthetic and later political. Her study of German led her to Goethe, Jean Paul, Bettina Brentano and, rather incongruously, the sentimental Theodor Körner and the spiritualist Justinus Kerner. Her direct contacts with German philosophy seem rare and not too happy. In Cambridge (presumably some time before 1833) she obtained books by Fichte and Jacobi, and she tells us: "I was much interrupted, but some time and earnest thought I devoted. Fichte I could not understand at all; though the treatise which I read was intended to be popular, and which he says must compel (*bezwingen*) to conviction."[73] She must refer to Fichte's *Sonnenklarer Bericht* (1801), which in its subtitle is called "Ein Versuch, die Leser zum Verstehen zu zwingen."[74] "Jacobi," she continues, "I could understand in details, but not in system. It seemed to me that his mind must have been moulded by some other mind, with which I ought to be acquainted, in order to know him well—perhaps Spi-

---

[72] A fuller discussion of Brownson's intellectual development, with stress on social and political questions, is given in Arthur M. Schlesinger, Jr., *Orestes A. Brownson: A Pilgrim's Progress* (Boston, 1939).

[73] *Memoirs of Margaret Fuller Ossoli*, by R. W. Emerson, W. H. Channing, and J. F. Clarke (Boston, 1881), I, 127.

[74] J. G. Fichte, *Werke* (Berlin, 1845), II, 323. "Bezwingen" in the text of the *Memoirs* is certainly an error, either of the transcriber or printer, for "zu zwingen."

noza's." Later, in the *Dial*, when she wrote a review criticizing Menzel's view of Goethe, she referred to Jacobi as having written "the heart into philosophy as well as he could."[75] Reading the life of Sir James Mackintosh, she was pleased, "after my late chagrin, to find Sir James, with all his metaphysical turn, and ardent desire to penetrate it, puzzling so over the German philosophy, and particularly what I was myself troubled about, at Cambridge,—Jacobi's *Letters to Fichte*."[76] In Groton, when she was planning her abortive "Life of Goethe," she came to the conclusion that she ought to get "some idea of the history of philosophical opinion in Germany" in order to understand its influence on Goethe. She consulted Buhle's and Tennemann's *Histories of Philosophy* and dipped into Brown, Stewart and "that class of books."[77] In the winter 1836-37 she went one evening every week to Dr. Channing and translated for him German theological writings, mainly de Wette and Herder.[78] In 1841, apparently in connection with her "conversations," she translated Schelling's famous lecture "Über das Verhältniss der bildenden Künste zu der Natur," a labor she might have saved had she noticed that Coleridge had paraphrased the very same oration very closely.[79] (The translation by Margaret Fuller has remained in manuscript.) Later, after her arrival in New York, she drifted more and more away from Transcendental contacts and interests. In the last year of her reviewing for the New York *Daily Tribune* (1846), she

[75] *Life Without and Life Within* (Boston, 1859), 15. First appeared in the *Dial*, I (1841), 342.
[76] *Memoirs*, I, 165.   [77] See note 73.   [78] *Memoirs*, I, 175.
[79] Coleridge's lecture "On Poesy or Art" was first printed in *Literary Remains* (Volume I, 1836). Sara Coleridge's edition in *Notes and Lectures* (1849) gives a list of the parallels to Schelling's lecture.

Minor Transcendentalists

wrote a report on William Smith's *Memoirs of J. G. Fichte*, which consists largely of quotations. Still, it shows her obvious pleasure that William Smith brought out "the sunny side" of Fichte's character and gave a "charming account of the sincere, equal, generous and tender relation between him and his wife."[80] In a review of Charles Brockden Brown's *Ormond* and *Wieland*, she interestingly reveals her (and the Transcendentalists') weird conception of Hegelianism. She calls Brown and Godwin "born Hegelians, without the pretensions of science" as "they sought God in their consciousness and found him. The heart, because it saw itself so fearfully and wonderfully made, did not disown its Maker."[81] Sometimes she protests against all analytical philosophy, alluding particularly to Fichte. "I do not wish to *reflect* always, if reflecting must be always about one's identity, whether '*ich*' am the true '*ich*' etc. I wish to arrive at that point where I can trust myself."[82] On the whole, if one can combine these meager and scattered statements, they seem to show that Margaret Fuller cared nothing for what she thought were German technicalities and had only vaguely understood that German philosophy from Jacobi to Hegel justified the religion of the heart. Her point of view therefore seems to be nearest to Ripley's.

Thus, the minor Transcendentalists show only slight contacts with German philosophy proper. Alcott neglected the great German philosophers and found solace and support in the fanciful speculations of Jacob Böhme

[80] New York *Daily Tribune*, July 9, 1846. Listed in Mason Wade's bibliography, *M. Fuller, Writings* (New York, 1941), p. 600.
[81] *Art, Literature and the Drama* (Boston, 1875), p. 323; originally appeared in the New York *Daily Tribune* of July 25, 1846.
[82] *Memoirs*, I, 123.

Minor Transcendentalists

and Lorenz Oken. Ripley and Parker looked for a religion of the heart, a justification of intuitive faith, and found it either in Schleiermacher or in a misinterpreted Kant. Margaret Fuller faintly echoes this view in her writings. In Brownson, the Germans had a formidable critic of their subjectivism and pantheism. But only a full discussion of Emerson's relations to German philosophy will make these distinctions stand out more clearly and allow us to draw general conclusions.

CHAPTER SIX

Emerson and German Philosophy*

✵ Emerson's relations to the German thinkers deserve the fullest attention. The difficulties of the problem are manifold, and it seems hazardous to attempt to distinguish the exact provenience of every idea, since Emerson, as contrasted with the other Transcendentalists, was a remarkable artist who assimilated all foreign ideas into the special ways of his own expression. He was, besides, a fragmentary, though not therefore inconsistent, thinker who disparaged all system, all elaborate chains of reasoning, and the whole method of discursive philosophy. The indirect channels through which German thought could have reached him were especially numerous.[1]

* Originally in *The New England Quarterly*, XVI (no. 1, 1943), pp. 41-62.

[1] Besides general studies of Transcendentalism (Frothingham, Goddard, Riley, Girard, Muirhead, and Townsend) and biographies (especially Cabot), the following discussions of Emerson are useful: John Smith Harrison, *The Teachers of Emerson* (New York, 1910); Henry David Gray, *Emerson, A Study of New England Transcendentalism* (Palo Alto, 1917); Ralph L. Rusk, Introduction to *The Letters of Ralph Waldo Emerson* (New York, 1939), I, xi-lxiv; and Fred B. Wahr, "Emerson and the Germans," *Monatshefte für deutschen Unterricht*, XXXIII (1941), 49-63. G. Runze, "Emerson und Kant," *Kant-studien*, IX (1904), 292-306, is poorly informed and vague.

Since this paper was written, Henry A. Pochmann, in his *German Culture in America* (Madison, Wis., 1957), has reexamined the question thoroughly with results I find excessively schematic. I cannot

187

Emerson and German Philosophy

As early as 1820 Emerson read Drummond's *Academical Questions*, which contains a fairly detailed, extremely hostile account of Kant.[2] In 1823 he read Dugald Stewart's *Dissertation*, which discusses Kant, again in a hostile spirit.[3] Madame de Staël's friendly though vague description of German philosophy follows on Emerson's reading list;[4] and he read Cousin in 1828, Coleridge in 1829, and Carlyle after 1830.[5] The most curious instance of secondhand quoting of Kant occurs in Emerson's early volume *Nature* (1836). There, in the section on Idealism, Emerson says that "the problem of philosophy, according to Plato, is, for all that exists conditionally, to find a ground unconditioned and absolute."[6] There is,

---

agree that there was a distinct Kantian phase (1830-1838) in Emerson's thought (p. 158).

The new complete edition of *The Journals and Miscellaneous Notebooks*, ed. William H. Gilman and Alfred R. Ferguson (Cambridge, Mass., 1960-63) has, with the 3 volumes published, covered the years up to and including 1832. It does not contain any new evidence of importance for that time. Still, in 1832 it lists William Law's Translation of Behmen among Emerson's books (see vol. III, 204), i. e. *The Works of Jacob Behmen*, 4 vols. (London, 1764).

[2] Emerson, *Journals*, I, 76 and 89. On Sir William Drummond, cf. my *Immanuel Kant in England* (Princeton, 1931), pp. 38-40.

[3] *Journals*, I, 289 and 290.

[4] See *Journals*, II, 121, 129, 143, 164, 284, and 387.

[5] Emerson read Cousin's *Cours de Philosophie* in French, first in 1828; see *Letters*, Ralph Rusk, editor (New York, 1939), I, 322. He borrowed the *Biographia Literaria* in November 1826 from the Harvard Library (Kenneth Walter Cameron, *R. W. Emerson's Reading* [Raleigh, North Carolina, 1941], 46). Coleridge's *The Friend* and *Aids to Reflection* followed in December 1829 (*Letters*, I, 291, and J. E. Cabot, *Memoir*, I, 161). Emerson referred to Carlyle's essay on Jean Paul in October 1827, without knowing Carlyle's name (*Letters*, I, 218). In 1830 he read the translation of *Wilhelm Meister*, the essay on Novalis, and other of Carlyle's writings (*Journals*, II, 330 and 348-51).

[6] "Nature" (1836), in *Works* (Centenary Edition, Boston, 1903), I, 55.

Emerson and German Philosophy

of course, no such passage in Plato, and the whole passage is a literal reproduction of a sentence in the *Critique of Pure Reason*. It does not, however, come from the actual text of Kant, but is reproduced from Coleridge's *Friend*, where Coleridge coolly ascribed this passage he had read in Kant to Plato.[7] But not too much can be made out of this, since the passage is scarcely central for Emerson's argument. The question of the influence of Coleridge, Carlyle and the French eclectics has been studied extensively and cannot be discussed within our limits.[8] But Emerson knew the German thinkers also at firsthand, and there are plenty of comments which define his attitude toward them.

Among the German thinkers—to take them in their chronological order—Jacob Böhme was undoubtedly well known to Emerson. In 1835 he read the *Aurora* in English translation, and he quoted Böhme at length on inspiration and other subjects. He read him again in 1844.[9] Emerson valued him, as he did all mystics, very highly, and he even enumerated him, together with Swedenborg and Goethe, among men of "grander pro-

---

[7] *Die Kritik der reinen Vernunft*, A. 307. In Norman Kemp Smith's translation (London, 1929) this appears on page 306. Cf. Coleridge, *The Friend* (Essay V, Section 2), Bohn edition (London, 1890), 307.

[8] See F. T. Thompson, "Emerson and Carlyle," *Studies in Philology*, XXIV (1927), 438-53; "Emerson's Indebtedness to Coleridge," ibid., XXIII (1926), 55-76; and William Girard, "De l'influence exercée par Coleridge et Carlyle sur la formation du transcendentalisme," *University of California Publications in Modern Philology*, IV (1916), 404-11.

[9] *Journals*, III, 524 and 525; and VI, 517. The quotation on inspiration occurs in "Inspiration" (1872), *Works*, VIII, 277-78. Another quotation from Böhme is found in *Journals* (1841), VI, 142. This is derived from Barchou de Penhoen, *Histoire de la philosophie allemande depuis Leibnitz jusqu'à Hegel* (Paris, 1836), I, 123. The same passage is alluded to in "Swedenborg," *Works*, IV, 117.

Emerson and German Philosophy

portion" than Erasmus, Locke, Rousseau or Coleridge.[10] He preferred him even to Swedenborg, who seemed to him cold and rationalistic in his manner, while Böhme, "tremulous with emotion listens awe-struck, with the gentlest humanity, to the Teacher whose lessons he conveys." "His heart beats so high that the thumping against his leathern coat is audible across the centuries."

Böhme is "healthily and beautifully wise."[11] But even Böhme is not exempted from the general criticisms which Emerson directs against the mystics. "Mysticism," generalizes Emerson, "consists in the mistake of an accidental and individual symbol for an universal one. The morning-redness happens to be the favorite meteor to the eyes of Jacob Behmen, and comes to stand to him for truth and faith; and, he believes, should stand for the same realities to every reader."[12] But this is a mistake, just like his literal-minded adherence to Biblical symbol. He failed, with Swedenborg, "by attaching himself to the Christian symbol, instead of to the moral sentiment, which carries innumerable christianities, humanities, divinities in its bosom."[13] Böhme has no precision, no intellectual clarity. He shares the mystics' "narrowness and incommunicableness."[14] "His propositions are vague, inadequate, and straining. It is his aim that is great. The will to know, not one thing, but all things. He is like those great swaggering country geniuses that come now and then down from New Hampshire to college and soon demand to learn, not Horace and Homer, but also Euclid

---

[10] "Plato," *Works,* IV, 39-40.
[11] "Swedenborg," *Works,* IV, 142-43.
[12] "The Poet," *Works,* III, 34.
[13] "Swedenborg," *Works,* IV, 135.
[14] "Swedenborg," *Works,* IV, 143.

Emerson and German Philosophy

and Spinoza and Voltaire and Palladio and Columbus and Bonaparte and Linnaeus."[15] Emerson senses a tendency to egotism and insanity in him and concludes that "he cannot take rank with the masters of the world. His value, like that of Proclus, is chiefly for rhetoric."[16] He criticizes him substantially on the lines of the essay on Swedenborg and his frequent latent criticisms of Alcott. Emerson was no mystic, except in the very loosest sense of the term, though he agreed with the mystics in seeing God in nature and nature as an emblem of God. He claimed no illumination or any direct contact with the Unseen, and was skeptical about the supernatural implications of the occult, as we can see from his essay on demonology.

Leibniz, I think, remained almost unknown to Emerson, though there are several general references to him, one as early as 1823. In 1825 he borrowed the *Théodicée* from the Harvard Library.[17] In 1834 he quoted him, saying: "I have faith that man may be reformed when I see how much education may be reformed."[18] In 1841 Emerson copied a reference to a supposed zoological discovery of Leibniz from a French history of German philosophy by Barchou de Penhoen, a book which deserves investigation.[19]

Kant is frequently mentioned by Emerson, even as early as 1822, when he read Dugald Stewart, long before

---

[15] *Journals* (1844), VI, 517-18.
[16] *Journals* (1844), VI, 517-18. On Böhme's egotism see "Nature," *Works*, III, 187-88. On his insanity, see "The Over-Soul," *Works*, II, 231-32.
[17] Cameron, pp. 46 and 85; *Journals* (1823), I, 222.
[18] *Journals* (1834), III, 350.
[19] The passage from Penhoen is in *Journals* (1841), VI, 143; cf. II, 8 and 34.

Emerson and German Philosophy

he knew Coleridge. Emerson owned a copy of the 1838 translation of the *Critique of Pure Reason*, translated by Francis Haywood; and we are told that the copy still preserved in his library at Concord shows pencil markings.[20] I have not been able to ascertain their date or importance. In 1832 Emerson borrowed F. A. Nitsch's *View of Kant's Principles* from the Boston Athenaeum,[21] and late in his life he praised Edward Caird's book on Kant, which is in his library. Emerson must have also read Cabot's competent little introduction to Kant, since he himself recommended it for publication in the *Dial*.[22] This seems to be all the available evidence for Emerson's direct contact with Kant's thought. In numerous instances Kant is referred to by Emerson as he could have referred to any other great philosopher. He lists him among "teachers sacred or literary" with Spinoza and Coleridge, in contrast to men of the world such as Locke and Paley, and classes him implicitly with the mystic, "prophesying, half insane, under the infinitude of his thought," among those who speak "from within" or from experience, while the others speak only "from without, as spectators merely."[23] There are other passages of open or implied praise of Kant as a "great analyst," a term used in Cousin's characterization of Kant. Emerson, however, immediately qualifies this praise by saying that "Kant is rather a technical analyst than an universal one

---

[20] Harrison, *The Teachers of Emerson*, p. 288. Stanley Vogel, in *German Literary Influences on the American Transcendentalists* (New Haven, 1955), p. 106n, has examined the copy. "It shows some markings as well as an index with entries such as 'Locke and Hume,' 'Immortality,' and 'Oblate Sphericity.'"

[21] Cameron, pp. 19 and 94.

[22] Cabot's essay is in the *Dial*, IV (1844), 409-15; cf. *Letters*, III, 243.

[23] "The Over-Soul," *Works*, II, 287.

Emerson and German Philosophy

such as the times tend to form."[24] In discussing the term "transcendental" in the lecture "The Transcendentalist" (1842), he refers in more detail to Kant, explaining that the term is derived from him, though Emerson does not seem to recognize that it is used in America in a very un-Kantian sense, almost with the meaning of "transcendent." He then describes Kant as a foe of Locke and fairly well defines the *a priori* as "imperative forms which did not come by experience, but through which experience was acquired." But Emerson immediately called these *a priori* forms or functions "intuitions of the mind itself" and interprets the term "transcendental" as equivalent to "intuitive," though he realizes that this is a non-technical extension of Kant's usage. "The extraordinary profoundness and precision of that man's thinking have given vogue to his nomenclature, in Europe and America, to that extent that whatever belongs to the class of intuitive thought is popularly called at the present day *Transcendental*."[25]

Emerson thought of Kant as the originator of intuitionism, but was mainly interested in his moral philosophy. In a strangely phrased entry in the *Journals*, under the title "Belief and Unbelief," he comments that "Kant searched the metaphysics of the Self-reverence which is the favorite position of modern ethics, and demonstrated to the Consciousness that itself alone exists."[26] Though one might misunderstand this passage as an allusion to Kant's supposed solipsism or at least subjective idealism, Emer-

---

[24] *Journals* (1839), V, 306. Kant is called the "greatest analyzer of modern times" in V. Cousin's *Introduction to the History of Philosophy*, translated by H. G. Linberg (Boston, 1832), 169.

[25] "The Transcendentalist" (1842), in *Works*, I, 327ff., especially 340.

[26] *Journals* (1843), VI, 482.

Emerson and German Philosophy

son apparently uses "consciousness" here as moral consciousness and alludes to Kant's founding of morality in the autonomy of the moral will. Late in life, after 1862, Emerson several times refers to Kant's formula for the categorical imperative: "act always so that the immediate motive of thy will may become a universal rule for all intelligent beings."[27] In a late entry in the *Journals* we find, however, an almost grotesque caricature of Kant. Here Emerson pleads for allowance in favor of great men of one bent: those who "haunt the pond-sides, groping for plants" or those who "study the surfaces and mantles and runes on sea-shells." He singles out "Carnot buried in his mathematics," and Kant "climbing from round to round the steps of the mysterious ladder which is the scale of metaphysic powers."[28] Kant, needless to say, knows no "mysterious ladder" or "scale of metaphysic powers." Also another passage in which Emerson expressly exempts Kant from "microscopic subtleties and logomachy," as a "metaphysician who treats the intellect well"[29] seems to show that Emerson could not have penetrated into Kant's actual text very deeply.

Indirectly Emerson used several of Kant's concepts: the distinction of reason from understanding—which he learned from Coleridge—the idea that our moral sense supports our faith in immortality, and the subjectivity of space and time. But in every case one can speak of Kant as misunderstood by Emerson, or rather by Coleridge or Carlyle. The distinction between reason and understanding amounts frequently to little more than the difference

---

[27] "Civilization" (1862), *Works*, VII, 27; "Character" (1866), *Works*, x, 92. Here Emerson ascribes this saying, strangely enough, to Marcus Aurelius and Kant.
[28] *Journals* (1862-1872), x, 461.
[29] "Plutarch," *Works*, x, 306.

Emerson and German Philosophy

between faith and reason. Thus Emerson calls Jesus Christ a "minister of the Pure Reason," and speaks even of prayer as the "forcible subjugation of the Understanding to the Reason."[80] The Kantian proofs of immortality, the existence of God, and the freedom of will are mentioned as direct, intuitive insights; and the subjectivity of time and space is constantly misconstrued in terms of a psychological subjectivism. Time and space are even called "physiological colors which the eye makes."[81] This was, of course, a common misunderstanding of Kant, but the use Emerson makes of the figure of "colored and distorting lenses which" "we have no means of correcting" or of "computing the amount of their errors"[82] as an analogy to the space-time relation shows that Emerson had read the unfavorable accounts of Kant in Drummond, and possibly Thomas Brown, both of whom used this illustration derived from Villers, a Frenchman and one of the earliest expounders of Kant in Western Europe.[83] Thus all the evidence seems to point to only a perfunctory acquaintance with the actual specific characteristics of his thought. When Emerson expressly refers to him and uses his nomenclature, he seems to interpret him as an intuitionist who paved the way to faith in order to validate his own experience. On this point, Emerson's Kant seems quite close to Emerson's own philosophical position, as far at least, as it is expounded in the few epistemological reflections in the early *Nature* (1836) and the essay "Experience."

Jacobi and Schleiermacher scarcely enter upon Emer-

---

[80] *Journals* (1833), III, 236; also 1835, III, 435.
[81] "Self-Reliance," *Works*, II, 66.
[82] "Experience," *Works*, III, 75.
[83] See my *Immanuel Kant in England*, pp. 35 and 39.

Emerson and German Philosophy

son's horizon. In 1837 he borrowed two volumes of Jacobi's *Werke*,[34] and he refers to three sayings of Jacobi. One, in defense of Desdemona's beautiful death-bed lie, can be traced to Coleridge's *Friend*.[35] Another, on Understanding and Reason, he read in Carlyle's essay on Novalis.[36] The third, which says that "when a man has fully expressed his thought, he has somewhat less possession of it," I am unable to trace, but it may have come orally to Emerson since he refers to it on another occasion as "the famous saying of Jacobi (and of Mr. Dean)."[37]

In 1834 Hedge read to Emerson a "few good things" out of Schleiermacher. Emerson noted the distinction between physics and ethics, which he used later, a definition of sciences and art, and the term "ascetic" for the "discipline of life produced by the opinions."[38] In 1846 Emerson borrowed Schleiermacher's edition of Plato, and two years later, an English translation of Schleiermacher's *Introductions to the Dialogues of Plato*.[39] Late in his life, Emerson read a pamphlet on Schleiermacher which Herman Grimm had sent him, though in acknowledging it, he confessed that "his was never one of my high names."[40]

---

[34] Cameron, pp. 23 and 81.

[35] "The Transcendentalist," *Works*, I, 336-37, also *Journals*, II, 405; cf. *The Friend*, first section, essay 15, motto (Bohn edition, London, 1890), 204. Mme de Staël, *De l'Allemagne*, III, ch. 16, quotes the same passage.

[36] *Journals* (1834), III, 377. Cf. Carlyle's "Novalis," in *Critical and Miscellaneous Essays* (London, 1907), II, 205. Elsewhere (*Journals*, III, 237), Emerson ascribes the saying to Novalis.

[37] "Behavior," *Works*, VI, 191; also *Journals* (1853), VIII, 418.

[38] *Journals* (1834), III, 393. Cf. *Correspondence of Thomas Carlyle and Ralph Waldo Emerson*, ed. Charles Eliot Norton (Boston, 1888), I, 50.

[39] Cameron, pp. 48, 97, and 103.

[40] *Correspondence between Ralph Waldo Emerson and Herman Grimm*, ed. F. W. Holls (Boston, 1903), pp. 85 and 89.

Emerson and German Philosophy

But he noted in the *Journals* about this time that Schleiermacher said "the human soul is by nature a Christian."[41]

The contact with Fichte was also very slight, though Emerson borrowed the English translation of the *Popular Works* in 1863.[42] He refers to the "grand unalterableness of his morality" and to the "strength of his moral convictions which are the charm of his character."[43] He tells us that Fichte "would use any weapon to convert a hearer. He would trepan a person, if so he could pass his own edacious conceptions into the bared brain."[44] But he also repeats an anecdote which shows the usual misinterpretation of Fichte's thought in terms of solipsism. Fichte had declared his disbelief "in the existence of Heinrich Schlosser, who was worth two hundred thousand thalers. Nay, it was currently whispered that he did not credit the existence of Madame Fichte."[45] No doubt, the terms *Me* and *Not-Me* frequently used by Emerson, for instance in the preface to *Nature* (1836), are ultimately Fichtean in origin, but they came to Emerson through Cousin or Carlyle's essay on Novalis.[46] A passage which describes the progress of victorious thought, until

[41] *Journals* (1872), X, 380. Emerson quotes Schleiermacher also on university reform, from Varnhagen, *Journals* (1875), X, 445.
[42] Cameron, pp. 34 and 72.
[43] *Journals* (1834), III, 260; cf. *ibid.* (1870), X, 318.
[44] Charles J. Woodbury, *Talks with Ralph Waldo Emerson* (London, 1890), p. 54.
[45] *Journals* (1841), VI, 62, where "Schlossen" appears by mistake for "Schlosser." The anecdote seems to come from Heine's *Zur Geschichte der Religion und Philosophie in Deutschland* (1834). "Die Damen fragten: Glaubt er nicht wenigstens an die Existenz seiner Frau? Nein? Und das lässt Madame Fichte so hingehen?"
[46] "Nature" (1836), *Works*, I, 4; Carlyle, "Novalis," 204; and Cousin, *Introduction to the History of Philosophy*, pp. 159, 219, and *passim*.

Emerson and German Philosophy

"the world becomes at last only a realized will,"[47] is also Fichtean in its terminology. But it is again safe to assume only a slight acquaintance, because Fichte is rarely mentioned and is even left out of a fairly full catalogue of the German philosophers dating from 1867.[48]

It is different with Schelling. In 1831 Emerson quoted Schelling to the effect that "some minds think about things; others think the things themselves," and later he spoke of this as "by far the most important intellectual distinction." This quotation does not come from the text of Schelling but from *Guesses at Truth* (1827) by Augustus William and Julius Charles Hare, an early influential miscellany which shows considerable knowledge of German philology and philosophy.[49] A little later, Emerson became interested in De Quincey's attacks on Coleridge for his plagiarisms from Schelling, and thus found the source of many ideas in Coleridge which had attracted him profoundly.[50] In 1842 Schelling was called to Berlin as professor, and Emerson received from Stearns Wheeler, an American friend in Germany, an account of his reception by the students and the text of his inaugural lecture. Emerson "read it or rather in it," obviously in the German original, but it seemed to him "to have rather the interest of position than of thought."[51] He sent the lecture to his friend Hedge, who translated it for the *Dial*. Besides, Emerson wrote a note for the *Dial* on Schelling in Berlin based on the information he had received from

[47] "Nature" (1836), *Works*, I, 40.
[48] "Eloquence" (1867), *Works*, VIII, 131.
[49] *Journals* (1831), II, 422; repeated *ibid.* (1850), VIII, 126. Cf. *Guesses at Truth* (London, 1827), 1876 ed., p. 386.
[50] *Journals* (1835), III, 503.
[51] *Letters*, III, 98, November 21, 1842; cf. *ibid.*, III, 100.

Emerson and German Philosophy

Wheeler.[52] In a slightly earlier letter to another American student in Berlin, John F. Heath, Emerson says "to hear Schelling might well tempt the firmest rooted philosopher from his home and I confess to more curiosity in respect of Schelling's opinions than to those of any living psychologist." "There is grandeur," he comments, "in the attempt to unite natural and moral philosophy which makes him a sort of hero."[53] In 1845 James Eliot Cabot lent Emerson the manuscript of his translation of Schelling's early paper *Philosophical Enquiries into the Nature of Freedom* (1809), which shows Schelling's closest approximation to Böhme and the contemporary theosophist Baader. Emerson seems to have been very much impressed. He tells Cabot that "this admirable Schelling, which I have never fairly engaged with until last week, demands the 'lamp' and the 'lonely tower' and a lustrum of silence. I delight in his steady inevitable eye, and the breadth of his march including and disposing of so many objects of work." Emerson kept the manuscript for almost a year, apologizing for being so "ill a reader of these subtle dialectics." Deciding, at last, to "let it alone," he calls it "one of the books like my Alexandrian Platonists, which seems to require a race of more longevity and leisure than mankind, to sound all its depths, which yet do not pretend to be the sea, but only the swimming school."[54] Finally, Emerson made a fruitless attempt to find a publisher for Cabot's translation.[55] But he remembered the paper, since he referred

[52] *Letters*, III, 98-99; Schelling's lecture in *Dial*, III, 398ff.; and Emerson's note on Schelling in Berlin, *ibid.*, III, 136.
[53] *Letters*, III, 76-77, August 4, 1842.
[54] *Letters*, III, 293, 298-99, 303-304, and 343. On Schelling's "Enquiries," see my *Immanuel Kant in England*, p. 96.
[55] *Letters*, III, 345-46.

Emerson and German Philosophy

later to Schelling's "quoted Baader."[56] Emerson frequently referred to Schelling as one of the "fontal Germans" and quotes such a saying as that the "Absolute is the union of the Ideal and the Real" and the "daring statement" that "there is in every man a certain feeling, that he has been what he is from all eternity, and by no means became such in time."[57] Emerson approves expressly of the identity philosophy for its fundamental conception that object and subject are intimately one and that "all difference is quantitative,"[58] listing the identity philosophy as a "constant" together with Copernican and Newtonian theories in physics and Hegel's philosophy of history.

But there are also passages which reflect Emerson's distrust even of Schelling. He calls Swedenborg "a believer in the Identity philosophy, which he held not idly, as the dreamers of Berlin or Boston,"[59] a reference which must be directed against Schelling. In 1870, in praising American freedom, he speaks of Schelling as "called in, when Hegel dies, to come to Berlin, and bend truth to the crotchets of the king and rabble."[60] Besides the factual mistake (Schelling came to Berlin only eleven years after Hegel's death), the idea that Schelling wanted to please the rabble is scarcely a fair description of the motives behind his philosophy of revelation. Very late in his life Emerson wrote to Max Müller about a quotation on national mythology from Schelling which made

---

[56] *Journals* (1846), VII, 152, where "Maader" appears by mistake for "Baader."

[57] *Journals*, VII, 151-52, and VIII, 69; and "Fate," *Works*, VI, 13.

[58] "Literature," *Works*, V, 241-42. This proposition is prominently displayed in Stallo's *Principles* (Boston, 1848), p. 22.

[59] "Swedenborg," *Works*, IV, 106-107.

[60] *Journals* (1870), X, 337.

Emerson and German Philosophy

him "sit still to explore Schelling's rather nebulous light."[61] Emerson also found a story about Schelling in Henrik Steffens's *Memoirs* which he read in English translation. There Steffens relates that Schelling asked his students, in a lecture, to think of the wall. "All the class at once took attitudes of thought; some stiffened themselves up; some shut their eyes: all concentrated themselves. After a time, he said, 'Gentlemen, think of that which thought the wall.' Then there was trouble in all the camp." Emerson uses this story to express his distaste for too much introspection and self-analysis. He feels in it something "mean, as spying."[62] It throws some light on Emerson's method of work to see that this passage on spying was used by him, in identical words in the *Natural History of the Intellect*, where its original occasion, the story about Schelling, together with all references to German philosophy, has disappeared.[63] Thus Schelling's fundamental principles—his concept of the identity of subject and object, his use of the age-old idea of the world-soul, his conception of nature as the art of God—appealed to Emerson, while, as was often the case, he did not show any interest or knowledge regarding the technical detail, and disapproved of the method of dialectical deduction.

Most interesting and baffling, as well as completely unexplored, is Emerson's relation to Lorenz Oken. As early as 1842, five years before Oken's main book, *The Elements of Physiophilosophy*, was translated into English, Emerson refers to him definitely. "Oken," he says, "of

[61] *Letters*, VI, 245, August 4, 1873.
[62] *Journals* (1870), X, 317-18. H. Steffens, *The Story of My Career*, tr. W. L. Gage (Boston, 1863), p. 39, tells the story of Fichte.
[63] *Natural History of the Intellect*, in *Works*, XII, 14.

whose speculations I have read something, I take to be a scholar first, and then a continuator of Schelling's thought."[64] By "scholar" Emerson, in contradiction to his usual wider use, seems to mean here a "scientist." We must assume that Emerson had read the German journal *Isis*, which Oken had edited for years, or knew, at least, some article in an English periodical. He might have heard about Oken from Bronson Alcott who picked up a number of German books in London, in the very same year, 1842. Emerson refers to Oken several times later, always in complimentary terms. He chides England that it "cannot receive Oken, but nibbles, gnaws, accommodates, by Owen and Chambers"; he mentions Oken as a scientist of imagination, as a "poet in science" with Goethe, Saint-Hilaire, Agassiz and Audubon.[65] He lists him among the proponents of evolution which gave the "poetic key to Natural Science";[66] he describes the Romantic revolt against materialistic science beginning with Goethe and lists Schelling's and Oken's ideal natural philosophy as resulting in "a return to law in literature and the general mind."[67] Law seems here to mean a nonmechanistic order of the universe. Emerson refers also to specific theories as Oken's. He calls the "theory of the skull as a metamorphosed vertebra" Oken's,[68] though it was first propounded by Goethe, and tells us about Oken's vesicles in some detail. "A vesicle in new circumstances, a vesicle lodged in darkness, Oken thought, became animal; in light, plant. Lodged in the parent animal, it suffers changes which end in unsheathing mi-

---

[64] *Letters*, III, 76-77, August 4, 1842.
[65] *Journals* (1852), VIII, 337; (1851), VIII, 177; also (1871), X, 364.
[66] "Poetry and Imagination" (1872), *Works*, VIII, 7.
[67] "Life and Letters in New England" (1867), *Works*, X, 338.
[68] *Journals* (1871), X, 364.

Emerson and German Philosophy

raculous capability in the unaltered vesicle, and it unlocks itself to fish, bird, or quadruped, head and foot, eye and claw."[69] Indirectly, through Alcott, Emerson referred, as we have already mentioned, to Oken's curious theory that the extremities appear metamorphosed in the skull: "the hands being now the upper jaw, the feet the lower jaw, the fingers and toes being represented this time by upper and lower teeth."[70] There is elsewhere much of that fanciful natural science in Emerson which can also be found in Oken, though I am not competent to decide whether it could not have been derived from elsewhere: e.g. the plants are the young of the world, trees are imperfect men, or rooted men, etc.

But more important than such details is the similar outlook, at least on nature, which Emerson and Oken had. Let me quote a few passages from Oken to show that they sound Emersonian: "Animals are irregular men." "The universe is the language of God." "Nature is spirit analyzed." "Spirit is nothing different from Nature, but simply her purest outbirth or offspring, and therefore her symbol, her language." "The universal spirit is Man. Man is the entire image or likeness of the world. . . . All the functions of animals have attained unto unity, unto self-consciousness in Man." "That is beautiful which represents the will of nature."[71] There is no question of a source for Emerson, nor am I inclined to ignore the dissimilarities between the two men: the range of interests in Emerson unknown to Oken and the quite un-Emersonian technicality of Oken's physiology, zoology and botany. But in defining Emerson's position

---
[69] "Fate," *Works*, VI, 14.
[70] "Swedenborg," *Works*, IV, 108.
[71] *Elements of Physiophilosophy*, pp. 16, 373, 655-56, and 662-63.

Emerson and German Philosophy

in relation to the history of German thought, everything points to his affinity with Schelling and Oken, even though it is impossible to ignore such personal and national differences as Emerson's deeper religious roots, his stronger individualism, his finer artistry, his preoccupation with practical morality.

Hegel is the only German philosopher still left for our consideration. He came late to England and America—there was no translation of any major work before 1855[72]—and he is highly technical and personal in his vocabulary. There is thus little likelihood that he could have meant much to Emerson. But there is a surprising number of references to and discussions of Hegel in Emerson's writings, though little evidence of actual reading in Hegel's works. He seems to have been impressed by what a German, Emmanuel Scherb, told him of Hegel in 1849. "I caught somewhat that seemed cheerful and large, and that might, and probably did, come by Hindoo suggestion."[73] Very soon afterwards, Emerson read Stallo's *Principles of the Philosophy of Nature*, which contains a full exposition of Hegel. In 1855 Cabot sent to Emerson something of Hegel, either *The Philosophy of Right* or more probably the *Subjective Logic*, which had been translated in England in that year. Emerson found the text obviously unintelligible. He wrote to Cabot that he "did not find his way into Hegel as readily as I hoped, nor was I as richly rewarded as probably better scholars have been."[74] In 1865 Emerson bor-

---

[72] See list in B. Q. Morgan's *A Critical Bibliography of German Literature in English Translation*, second edition (Palo Alto, California, 1938).

[73] *Journals* (1849), VIII, 69.

[74] *Letters*, IV, 530-31. *The Philosophy of Right* was translated by

Emerson and German Philosophy

rowed Sibree's translation of the *Lectures on the Philosophy of History*, which he kept for four months; and in 1866 he read at least part of James Hutchinson Stirling's bulky *Secret of Hegel*.[75] He certainly later paraphrased closely a passage on page 10, on the "Zymosis" or fermentation of philosophy in Germany,[76] and became interested personally in the author, partly because he recognized Carlyle's influence on Stirling's writings. When Stirling applied for a professorship at Edinburgh, Emerson wrote glowing letters of recommendation for him, and he was pleased when Stirling nominated him as a candidate for the Lord Rectorship of the Scottish University.[77] To William Torrey Harris, Emerson even wrote that "in England they have never yet acknowledged his genius though he is a more subtle metaphysician than any other in their island. I long to see him famous."[78] Through Harris, the leader of the St. Louis Hegelians, who visited Emerson and later came to live in Concord, Emerson was brought into further contact with Hegelianism. He read the first numbers of the *Journal of Speculative Philosophy* (1867), but wrote to Harris that he found Hegel "at first sight not engaging nor at second sight satisfying. But his immense fame," he added with his customary trust in the collective judg-

---

T. C. Sandars in *Oxford Essays* (1855); *Subjective Logic* by J. Sloman and J. Wallon (London, 1855).

[75] Cameron, pp. 37 and 73; *Correspondence of Thomas Carlyle and Ralph Waldo Emerson*, II, 329-31.

[76] "Eloquence" (1867), *Works*, VIII, 131.

[77] *Letters*, VI, 18 and 259. Further letters to Stirling are in Amelia H. Stirling, *James Hutchinson Stirling* (London, 1912). Emerson's statement is printed also in J. H. Stirling's *Secret of Hegel*, second edition (Edinburgh, 1898), VIII, 169, 176, 209, 263-66.

[78] *Letters*, VI, 291, March 1876.

Emerson and German Philosophy

ment of mankind, "cannot be mistaken, and I shall read and wait."[79]

Emerson's knowledge of the doctrines of Hegel is, as far as one can ascertain from his writings, fairly varied. He quotes a passage on the life of sensation, which he had read in Varnhagen's *Memoirs*, one of the few German books he seems to have known in the original.[80] Elsewhere he alludes to Hegel's term "die List der Natur," illustrating it by the lover who "seeks in marriage his private felicity and perfection" and fulfills also nature's end, "progeny, or the perpetuity of the race."[81] But Emerson obviously was most impressed by Hegel's philosophy of history and evolution. He speaks of Hegel's teaching that "an idea always conquers, and, in all history, victory has ever fallen on the right side," commenting that it was expounded by Cousin and that Carlyle found for it "a fine idiom, that Right and Might go together." But he calls it a "specimen of Teutonism," among a strange list of other writers which includes Schelling, Baader, Goethe, Swedenborg and Novalis.[82] "Teutonism" seems to imply some doubt of its truth and validity, but later he lists "Hegel's study of civil history, as the conflict of ideas and the victory of the deeper thought" among the "constants," along with Schelling's philosophy of identity and Newtonian physics.[83] In describing the slow progress of the idea of evolution or, as he phrases it, "the idea that the form or type became transparent in the actual forms of successive ages as presented in geology," he ascribes it to an

[79] *Letters*, v, 521, June 1867.
[80] *Journals* (1873), x, 423; Cameron, p. 111.
[81] "Nature" (1844), *Works*, III, 187.
[82] *Journals* (1846), VII, 151-52.
[83] "Literature," *Works*, v, 241-42.

Emerson and German Philosophy

aperçu of Schelling, telling that Oken was ridiculed for expounding it, and that Hegel, "a still more robust dreamer, clung to this identical piece of nonsense."[84] But "nonsense" is used here ironically, as Emerson goes on to describe how the idea was popularized by Goethe and Saint-Hilaire, and finally reached America through Agassiz. Emerson also knows of Hegel's view that nature is objective spirit, the "Idea in its otherness," but formulates this in a way which shows that he is not aware of any distinction from the teaching of Schelling or, for that matter, of Swedenborg. He says that the "Natural Sciences have made great strides by means of Hegel's dogma which put Nature, and thought, matter and spirit, in right relation, one the expression or externalization of the other."[85]

Emerson seems even to have admired Hegel's dialectics and logic. He knew something of its ancestry, saying "Hegel pre-exists in Proclus, and, long before, in Heraclitus and Parmenides,"[86] and he picturesquely describes Hegel's claims to finality. "Hegel seems to say, 'Look, I have sat long gazing at the all but imperceptible transitions of thought to thought, until I have seen with eyes the true boundary. I know what is this, and that. I know it, and have recorded it. It can never be seen but by a patience like mine added to a perception like mine. I know the subtle boundary, as surely as the mineralogist Haüy knows the normal lines of his crystal, and where the cleavage must begin. I know that all observation will justify me, and to the future metaphysician I say,

---

[84] *Journals* (1849), VIII, 76-77. An exposition of Schelling's and Oken's views of evolution is given in Stallo's *Principles*, 224, 226-28, and 230ff., a book Emerson read at the very time of this entry.
[85] *Journals* (1862-1872), X, 462-63.
[86] "Originality" (1859), *Works*, VIII, 180.

Emerson and German Philosophy

that he may measure the power of his perception by the degree of his accord with mine.' "[87] But Emerson adds somewhat ambiguously: "This is the twilight of the gods, predicted in the Scandinavian mythology," meaning apparently that philosophy, in that direction at least, has reached its limits with Hegel. He also somewhat hesitatingly accepts the first triad in Hegel's *Logic*—the synthesis of Something and Nothing in Being. "Well," he comments resignedly, "we have familiarized that dogma, and at least found a kind of necessity in it, even if poor human nature still feels the paradox."[88]

There are few pronouncements which show that Emerson had heard of the political implications of Hegel's thought and of the development of Hegelianism. As late as 1870, praising American freedom, Emerson alludes to Hegel's concessions to contemporary politics. "A superior mind, a Hegel, sincerely and scientifically exploring the laws of thought, is suddenly called by a necessity of pleasing some king, or conciliating some Catholics, to give a twist to his universal propositions to fit these absurd people, and not satisfying them even by these sacrifices of truth and manhood."[89] The point about concessions to Catholics seems doubtful, and a curious ignorance is also shown of the "dreary names and numbers of volumes of Hegel and the Hegelians,"[90] when Emerson comments that "they shunned to apply the new arm to what most of all belonged to it, to anthropology, morals, politics, etc. For this at once touched conservatism, church, jurisprudence etc."[91] In puzzling contradiction to this passage, another entry in the very same

[87] *Journals* (1866), x, 143.   [88] *Journals* (1868), x, 248.
[89] *Journals* (1870), x, 337.   [90] *Journals* (1868), x, 248.
[91] *Journals* (1862-1872), x, 462-63.

Emerson and German Philosophy

notebook preceding the passage quoted, at least in the collected edition, says: "'Tis fine, that Hegel 'dared not to unfold or pursue the surprisingly revolutionary conclusions of his own method,' but not the less did the young Hegelians consummate the work, so that quickly, in all departments of life, in natural sciences, politics, ethics, laws, and in art, the rigorous Dogma of Immanent Necessity exterminated all the old tottering, shadowy forms." Emerson adds that this is like "Goethe and Wordsworth disowning their poetry."[92] Obviously Emerson remained dissatisfied with Hegel. He expected the revelation of some further mystery from German philosophy. Speaking of Hegel's dialectics, he says, "it needs no encyclopedia of volumes to tell. I want not the metaphysics, but only the literature of them."[93] This saying seems to sum up Emerson's attitude, not only to Hegel but to all German philosophy.

Emerson's attitude toward German philosophy was, thus, somewhat paradoxical. On the one hand, he saw its high value and greeted it as the right philosophy. He speaks of Germany "as the paramount intellectual influence of the world."[94] He chides the English for their empirical science, though he praises Robert Owen for having imported the German "homologies," a reference to the analogizing speculative natural science of Goethe, Schelling and Oken. English science in general to him stands "in strong contrast with the genius of the Germans, those semi-Greeks, who love analogy and, by means of their height of view, preserve their enthusi-

[92] *Journals* (1862-1872), x, 460.
[93] *Journals* (1868), x, 248; cf. *Natural History of the Intellect*, in *Works*, XII, 13.
[94] "Thoughts on Modern Literature," *Works*, XII, 312; originally in *Dial*, I (1840), 137.

209

Emerson and German Philosophy

asm and think for Europe."[95] But Emerson expected something even greater from Germany. "In Germany," he writes, "there still seems some hidden dreamer from whom this strange, genial, poetic, comprehensive philosophy comes, and from which the English and French get mere rumors and fragments, which are yet the best philosophy we know." Neither Schelling, nor Oken nor Hegel (the list is significant) ultimately satisfies. "On producing authenticated books from each of these masters, we find them clever men, but nothing so great and deep a poet sage as we looked for. And now we are still to seek for the lurking Behmen of Modern Germany."[96] The lurking Böhme—greater than any actual German philosopher Emerson knew—refused to reveal himself, and thus Emerson turned from the Germans as he turned from all abstract philosophy. Before quoting from Schelling, he says that "All abstract philosophy is easily anticipated—it is so structural, or necessitated by the mould of the human mind."[97] When he was only twenty-one, he had entered in his *Journal* that "Metaphysics teach me admirably well what I knew before."[98] In one of his last works, the *Natural History of the Intellect*, Emerson repeats that philosophy is still "rude and elementary." The metaphysician "loses that which is the miracle."[99] Emerson, one feels, was looking among the Germans for support for his faith. He found it there, and that is why he praised them, though mostly from a distance. He was not interested in the processes of their

---

[95] "Literature," *Works*, V, 254-55.
[96] *Journals* (1846), VII, 151-52.
[97] *Journals* (1849), VIII, 69.
[98] *Journals* (1824), I, 378-79.
[99] *Natural History of the Intellect*, in *Works*, XII, 14; also *Journals*, X, 336-37.

Emerson and German Philosophy

thinking. He was merely interested in their results, which seemed to him a confirmation of a world-view which contradicted and refuted the materialism of the eighteenth century. All the Transcendentalists have this in common with Emerson in their approach to German philosophy.

If in a final survey we compare the American thinkers with the German philosophers, we must, I think, come to the conclusion that the Transcendentalists do not share the specific characteristics of the Germans: their dialectical method, their preoccupation with and special approach to the problem of knowledge, their philosophy of history and of the institutional life of man. What attracted the American thinkers was the fact that the German philosophy shared with them a common enmity to the methods and results of eighteenth-century British empiricism and to the tradition of skepticism and materialism in general. Among the Transcendentalists, one can distinguish two groups: the metaphysical, comprising Emerson and Alcott; and the theological, which includes Ripley, Parker and Brownson, and which advocates, in effect, an intuitive philosophy of religion. The latter are akin to the French eclectics, to the commonsense philosophers (though they were less empirical in their methods), and to German thinkers who, like Herder, Jacobi, and Schleiermacher, were in constant warfare with the main representatives of German speculative philosophy. Brownson, who stands somewhat apart, most clearly realizes the dangers of German subjectivism, expounding an extreme objectivist intuitionism. Emerson and Alcott, though they share their friends' trust in intuition, are far more interested in a philosophy of nature in which nature appears as a symbol or emblem of the

Emerson and German Philosophy

internal world of our mind and of the mind of God. In spite of the obvious distinctions between the two friends, they thus both continue the Neo-Platonic tradition. But this appears in them somewhat modified and strengthened by mysticism such as that of Böhme or Swedenborg and by contemporary German scientific or pseudo-scientific speculations as they found them in Oken or Schelling. Essentially, in a history of ideas, American Transcendentalism, it seems to me, should not be coupled with German philosophy; nor, of course, should it be described as a result of German idealism. This does not mean a summary dismissal of the existing contacts and sympathies: it is rather a conclusion based on the simple fact that none of the Transcendentalists ever adopted the specific tenets of German idealism as, for example, they were adopted and elaborated later in England by thinkers such as Edward Caird or in America by Josiah Royce. The Transcendentalists were merely looking for corroboration of their faith. They found it in Germany, but ultimately they did not need this confirmation. Their faith was deeply rooted in their minds and in their own spiritual ancestry.

✲ Index

Abrams, M. H., 25n, 26
Adams, John Quincy, 154
Adelung, Johann Christoph, 127
Agassiz, Louis, 202, 207
Alcott, Bronson, 153n, 160, 164, *166-169*, 170, 185, 191, 202, 203, 211
Alcott, Louisa, 169
Alexis, Willibald (W. G. Haering), 11
Allingham, William, 106n, 110n
Alves, George, 95
Andrés, Juan, 142
Ariosto, Lodovico, 69
Aristophanes, 130
Aristotle, 140, 147, 168
Arnim, Achim von, 5, 11, 12, 19, 20, 28, 42
Arnold, Matthew, 14
Arnold, Thomas Dr., 122
Arx, Bernhard von, 18
Ascham, Roger, 140, 141n
Audubon, John James, 202
Aulard, A., 107n

Baader, Franz von, 166, 168, 199, 200, 206
Bach, Johann Sebastian, 66
Bacon, Francis (Lord Verulam), 119, 168, 175
Bäumler, Alfred, 127n
Baker, Herschel, 25n
Ballantyne, Thomas, 74n
Balmes, Jaime, 182
Bancroft, George, 154, 158
Barchou de Penhoen, 189n, 191
Basile, Giambattista, 16
Baumgarten, Alexander Gottlieb, 126
Beach, Joseph Warren, 124n
Beck, Thor J., 144n
Beckers, Gustav, 20n
Beckford, William, 45
Beddoes, Thomas Love, 5, 21
Beethoven, Ludwig van, 6, 24

Behmen, see Böhme, Jacob
Bentham, Jeremy, 35, 66
Bently, William (Rev.), 154
Berend, Eduard, 66
Berington, Joseph, 95
Berkeley, George, 124, 125
Bernhardi, Sophie, 6
Bertram, Ernst, 61
Black, John, 143
Blake, William, 4, 8, 9, 10, 19, 22, 31
Boas, George, 84n
Boccaccio, Giovanni, 17
Boeckh, Phillip August, 134
Böhme, Jacob, 12, 124, 164, 166, 185, 188n, 189, 190, 199, 210, 212
Börne, Ludwig, 42, 60
Bonner, William H., 114
Bonnerot, Louis, 15n
Bonnet, Charles, 88
Boswell, James, 97, 100n, 101n
Boucke, Ewald A., 90n
Bouterwek, Friedrich, 93, 129, 130
Brentano, Bettina (von Arnim), 5, 7, 8, 11, 12, 13, 15, 16, 17, 19, 20, 21, 32, 42, 183
Brooks, Richard A. E., 108
Brown, Charles Brockden, 185
Brown, John, 144
Brown, Thomas, 184, 195
Browne, Thomas Sir, 69, 124, 147, 148
Browning, Elizabeth Barrett, 131, 135
Browning, Robert, 110n
Brownson, Orestes, 153n, *174-183*, 186, 211
Brüggemann, Fritz, 31n
Bruford, W. H., 27n
Buckminster, Joseph Stevens (Rev.), 155
Büchner, Georg, 6, 20

Index

Büchner, Ludwig, 171
Bürger, Gottfried August, 41
Buhle, Johann Gottfried, 184
Burke, Edmund, 123, 147
Burkhard, Artur, 49n
Burns, Robert, 13, 97
Burton, Robert, 63, 66
Bury, J. B., 84n
Bush, Douglas, 134n
Butler, Joseph (Bishop), 164
Byron, George Gordon, Lord, 4, 7, 9, 10, 11, 19, 22, 28, 29, 36, 44, 49n, 135

Cabot, J. E., 187n, 188n, 192, 199, 204
Caird, Edward, 192, 212
Calderón de la Barca, Pedro, 32
Callot, Jacques, 44, 45
Calvin, Jean, 164
Cameron, Kenneth Walter, 188n, 191n, 192n, 196n, 205n, 206n
Campbell, Thomas, 4, 95
Canat, René, 136n
Carlyle, Jane (née Welsh), 55, 63, 93n
Carlyle, John, 43n
Carlyle, Thomas, v, 10, 15, 16, 30, *34-113*, 124, 135, 141, 143, 148, 149, 154, 164, 178, 188, 189, 194, 196, 197, 205, 206; and German Romanticism, 34-81; and E.T.A. Hoffmann, 43-45; and Zacharias Werner, 45-48; and the Schlegels, 49-54; and Tieck, 54-55; and Novalis, 56-59; and Jean Paul, 60-80; and the philosophy of history, 82-113; and the Saint-Simonians, 84-86; and Herder, 88-90; and literary history, 92-98; his concept of historical development, 100-106; his practice of history writing, 106-111
Carnot, Nicolas-Léonard-Sadi, 194
Carré, Jean-Marie, 38, 41
Cassirer, Ernst, 90n, 119n, 121n

Cervantes y Saavedra, Miguel de, 17, 18, 32, 66, 69
Chambers, Robert, 96, 202
Chamisso, Adalbert von, 17, 23
Channing, William Ellery, 161, 184
Channing, William Henry, 183n
Charpentier, Julie von, 58
Chateaubriand, François-René de, 135
Chaucer, Geoffrey, 96
Chizhevsky, Dmitri, 24n
Clagget, Charles, 26n
Clare, John, 5
Clowes, John (Rev.), 125n
Cofer, D. B., 100n
Coleridge, George, 26n
Coleridge, Samuel Taylor, vi, 4, 6, 7, 8, 9, 10, 11, 12, 19, 22, 26, 28, 29, 31, 32, 36, 56, 62, 57, 69n, 88, 110, 120, 122, 123, 124, 128, 132, 134, 138, 143, 145, 148, 154, 156, 157, 158, 159, 164, 168, 169, 170, 184, 188, 189, 190, 192, 194, 196, 198
Coleridge, Sara, 184n
Collin, Mathias, 48
Collins, William, 33
Commager, H. S., 173n
Comte, Auguste, 84, 85, 86, 99, 103, 104, 106
Condillac, Étienne Bonnot de, 139
Condorcet, Marie-Jean-Antoine Caritat, Marquis de, 84
Constant, Benjamin, 164
Copernicus, Nicolaus, 200
Corneille, Pierre, 51
Courthope, William J., 98
Cousin, Victor, 164, 174, 188, 192, 193n, 197, 206
Cowper, William, 96
Creuzer, Friedrich, 134
Cromwell, Oliver, 105n, 108, 109

Dante Alighieri, 55

Index

Darley, George, 5
Dean, Mr., 196
De Quincey, Thomas, v, 4, 8, 9, 10, 11, 14, 25, 96, *114-152*, 198; and Kant, 116-119; and philosophy, 116-121; and Christianity, 121-122; his concept of nature, 124-125; his concept of genius, 125-127; on distinction of Classical and Romantic, 128-134; on Greeks, 133-138; on development in literature, 138-146; on literature of power, 145-147; on rhetoric, 147; and German literature, 149
Descartes, René, 119, 179, 180, 182
Dewey, John, 157n
Diderot, Denis, 138
Dieckmann, Liselotte, 125n
Dilthey, Wilhelm, 87
Diogenes, 72, 77
Döring, Heinrich, 68, 71
Donne, John, 147, 148
Dostoevsky, Fyodor, 24
Dowden, Edward, 9n, 143n
Drake, Nathan, 95
Drummond, William, 188, 195
Dubos, Jean-Baptiste, 142
Duffy, Sir Charles G., 110n
Dumas, Georges, 84n
Dunn, William A., 117, 118n

Eaton, Horace Ainsworth, 114, 117
Eichendorff, Joseph von, 5, 13, 28, 30
Eichhorn, Johann Gottfried, 93
Eichthal, Gustave d', 99n
Eliot, Thomas Stearns, 13
Ellis, George, 95
Emerson, Ralph Waldo, v, 16n, 42n, 105n, 110n, 124, 160, 162, 164, 167, 168, 180, 186, *187-212*; and Böhme, 189-191; and Kant, 191-197; and Fichte, 197-198; and Schelling, 198-201; and Oken, 201-204; and Hegel, 204-209
Emmerich, Katharina, 32
Erasmus of Rotterdam, Desiderius, 190
Ernesti, J. A., 156
Euclid, 190
Euripides, 93
Everett, Edward, 155, 157

Fehr, Bernhard, 61
Feuerbach, Ludwig, 171
Fichte, Frau (née Johanna Rahn), 197, 198
Fichte, Johann Gottlieb, 6, 31, 37, 49, 72, 77, 78, 80, 86, 88, 91, 92, 112, 119, 120, 153, 155, 158, 159, 160, 161, 162, 165, 166, 171, 175, 176, 179, 180, 183, 184, 185, 197
Firth, Charles H., 107n, 109n
Fischer, Otokar, 23n
Fittbogen, Gottfried, 30n
Flint, Robert, 84n
Florian, Jean-Pierre Claris de, 135
Florus, Lucius Anneus, 140
Foerster, Norman, 112n
Follen, Carl, 153n, 160, 161, 162, 170n
Fouqué, Friedrich Heinrich, Karl de la Motte, 17, 42, 43
Fourier, Jean-Baptiste-Joseph, 164, 171
Francis, Convers (Dr.), 156
Frederick the Great, 64, 107, 108, 109
Freiligrath, Ferdinand, 10
Fries, Johann Jacob, 157, 160, 162, 172
Frothingham, Octavius B., 153n, 170n, 172n, 187n
Froude, James Anthony, 55n, 61, 62n, 63n, 88n, 108, 110n
Fueter, Eduard, 87, 107n
Fuller, Margaret (Marchesa Ossoli), 153n, 183, 184, 185, 186

Index

Galinsky, Hans, 10n, 120n
Galluppi, Pasquale, 182
Gautier, Théophile, 131
George, Stefan, 60
Gessner, Salomon, 39, 41
Gillman, James and Anne, 7
Gioberti, Vincenzo, 182, 183
Girard, William, 153n, 187n, 189n
Gisborne, John, 25n
Glücksmann, Hedwig Luise, 134n
Goddard, Harold C., 153n, 187n
Godwin, William, 185
Goethe, Johann Wolfgang von, 5, 7, 10, 12, 14, 17, 32, 33, 37, 38, 41, 50, 54, 60, 61, 65, 70, 72, 73, 74, 75, 77, 83, 86, 88, 90, 97, 126, 131, 132, 133, 141, 148, 149, 164, 165, 166, 183, 184, 188n, 189, 202, 206, 207, 209
Gooch, G. P., 107n
Gozzi, Carlo, 16
Grabbe, Christian Dietrich, 6
Gray, Henry David, 187n
Gray, Thomas, 33, 98, 139
Green, Joseph Henry, 10n
Grillparzer, Franz, 6, 19, 48, 49
Grimm, Herman, 196
Grimm, Jakob, 127n
Gruppe, Otto, 137n
Guérin, Maurice de, 136
Gutzkow, Karl, 10

Händel, Georg Friedrich, 24
Haering, Theodor, 31n
Hamann, Johann Georg, 60, 124, 126
Hamburger, Käte, 13
Hamilton, Sir William, 120
Hardenberg, Friedrich von, see Novalis
Hardenberg, Karl von, 134n
Hare, Augustus William, 198
Hare, Julius, 10, 120n, 122, 149, 198

Harich, Walther, 60, 66, 76, 77n, 78n
Harris, William Torrey, 169, 205
Harrison, John Smith, 87n, 192n
Harrold, Charles Frederick, 40n, 88n, 93n, 108, 124n
Hartmann, Eduard von, 171, 172
Hatfield, James Taft, 158n
Hauff, Wilhelm, 11
Haüy, l'abbé René-Just, 207
Hayward, Abraham, 54
Haywood, Francis, 192
Hazlitt, William, 4, 8, 9, 25, 31, 95, 110, 135, 139, 145
Heath, John F., 199
Hedge, Frederic Henry, 153n, 158, 160, 171, 196, 198
Hegel, Georg Wilhelm Friedrich, 6, 22, 78, 86, 103, 104, 106, 112, 120, 134, 158, 160, 162, 165, 169, 173, 174, 175, 180, 181, 182, 185, 189n, 200, *204-210*; influence on Emerson, 204-209
Heine, Heinrich, 6, 11, 14, 42, 43, 60, 178, 197n
Heinse, Johann Jacob Wilhelm, 10n, 41
Hemsterhuis, Frans, 124, 128
Hensel, Paul, 88n
Heraclitus, 207
Herder, Caroline (née Flachsland), 65, 146n, 149
Herder, Johann Gottfried, 38, 41, 47, 50, 60, 65, 66, 67, 72, 78, 79, 80, 86, 88, 89, 90, 91n, 94, 98, 103, 104, 112, 124, 131, 145, 146, 149, 155, 157, 165, 170, 171, 172, 174, 184, 211
Hewett-Thayer, Harvey W., 5n, 30n
Heyne, Christian Gottlob, 52
Heyse, Paul, 17
Hippel, Theodor von, 63
Hirsch, Donald Eric, 12
Hitzig, E., 39n, 44, 45
Hobbes, Thomas, 119

Index

Hölderlin, Friedrich, 5, 30n, 60, 133
Hoffmann, E.T.A., 5, 10, 11, 12, 14, 15, 16, 17, 18, 19, 20, 22, 23, 24, 26, 27, 28, 30, 39, 42, 43, 44, 45, 67
Hogg, James, 5
Holbach, Paul Heinrich Dietrich, Baron d', 175, 181n
Homer, 93n, 138, 143, 190
Hooker, Thomas, 69
Horace (Horatius), 190
Horn, Franz, 37, 39, 61, 67, 93
Hume, David, 51, 119, 140, 141n, 142, 177, 178, 180, 192n
Hunt, Leigh, 4, 25
Hurd, Richard (Bishop), 139

Ilgen, Karl, 138
Irving, Edward, 62

Jacobi, Friedrich Heinrich, 56, 67, 72, 79, 80, 112, 162, 165, 173, 183, 184, 185, 195, 196, 211
Jäggi, Frieda, 61n
Jahn, Ludwig, 161
James, Henry (the elder) 85n, 86, 110
Jantz, Harold S., 154n, 155n
Jean Paul (Johann Paul Friedrich Richter), 5, 14, 15, 16, 23, 37, 38, 39, 42n, 50, *60-80*, 88, 97, 112, 124, 126, 129, 130, 146n, 148, 149, 164, 165, 183, 188n; influence on Carlyle, 60-80
Jeffrey, Francis, Lord, 4, 14
Jocelin of Brakelond, 102, 108
Joël, Karl, 124n, 125n
Jördens, Karl Heinrich, 41n
John I (King of England, called Lackland), 105
Johnson, Samuel, Dr., 59
Jordan, John E., 114
Jouffroy, Théodore, 164

Kamerbeek, J., 142n

Kant, Immanuel, v, 6, 31, 50, 51, 56, 72, 76, 77, 78, 79, 80, 86, 92, 105, 106, 112, 116, 117, 118, 119, 120, 126, 127n, *151-162*, 164, 165, 168, 169, 170, 172-180, 182, 183, 186, 187n, 188, 189, *191-195*; impact on De Quincey, 116-119; criticized by Brownson, 175-179; influence on Emerson, 191-195
Kayser, Wolfgang, 20
Keats, George, 25n
Keats, Georgiana, 25n
Keats, John, 4, 8, 9, 10, 22, 25, 28, 29, 33, 34, 110, 135
Keller, Gottfried, 14, 61
Kerner, Justinus, 183
Kierkegaard, Søren, 22
Kleist, Heinrich von, 5, 17, 18, 19, 20, 31, 42, 119
Klopstock, Friedrich Gottlieb, 6, 154
Klotz, Reinhold, 131
Körner, Josef, 31n
Körner, Theodor, 161, 183
Kommerell, Max, 13
Korff, Hermann, 50
Kotzebue, August von, 38, 41n
Küchler, F., 41, 61
Kühn, Sophie von, 57, 58

Laing, David, 87
Lamb, Charles, 4, 8, 22, 25, 28, 110, 148
Lambert, Johann Heinrich, 120
Landor, Walter Savage, 135, 148
Lanson, Gustave, 139n
Larrabee, Stephen A., 134n
Law, William, 166, 188n
Leavis, F. R., 14n
Leibniz, Gottfried Wilhelm von, 119, 160, 162, 165, 166, 182, 189n, 191
Lempicki, Sigmund von, 89n, 98n
Lenau, Nikolaus, 6, 11
Leopold, Werner, 39n, 52n, 93n
Leroux, Pierre, 164

Index

Lessing, Gotthold Ephraim, 39, 41, 131, 132, 145, 149
Lewis, George Cornwall, 134n
Lewis, Matthew Gregory, 18
Linberg, H. G., 193n
Lobeck, Christian August, 137
Locke, John, 35, 119, 120, 168, 175, 190, 192, 193
Lockemann, Fritz, 17n
Loève-Veimars, Adolphe-François, 45n
Lomas, S. C., 88, 105n, 107n, 110n
Long, O. W., 156n, 158n, 160n
Longfellow, Henry Wadsworth, 32, 158
Longinus, 140, 146
Lovejoy, Arthur Oncken, 3
Lowell, James Russell, 62
Lukács, Georg, 29
Luther, Martin, 31, 45, 47

Macaulay, Thomas Babington, 135
Mackintosh, Sir James, 184
Majut, Rudolf, 20
Maler Müller, see Müller, Friedrich
Mallet, Paul-Henri, 144
Marburg, Clara, 140n
Marsh, James, 156, 157, 170n
Mason, Eudo C., 8
Meinecke, Friedrich, 87, 89n, 90n, 142n
Mendelssohn-Bartholdy, Felix, 6
Menzel, Wolfgang, 42, 172, 184
Mérimée, Prosper, 18
Metcalf, John Calvin, 114n
Metternich, Prince, 28
Meyer, Herman, 23n
Michelsen, Peter, 149n
Mill, John Stuart, 35, 42n, 85, 86, 93n, 110n
Miller, J. Hillis, 125n
Miller, Samuel, 155
Milton, John, 32, 33, 69, 140
Mörike, Eduard, 6

Molière (Jean-Baptiste Poquelin), 23, 69
Moore, Thomas, 13
More, Hannah (Mrs.), 121
Morgan, Bayard Quincy, 204n
Morley, Henry, 98
Motley, John Lothrop, 158
Mozart, Wolfgang Amadeus, 24, 25
Müller, Adam, 30, 133
Müller, Friedrich (called Maler Müller), 39, 41
Müller, Johannes, 47, 92, 93n
Müller, Max, 200
Müller, Otfried, 137
Müllner, Adolf, 19
Mueschke, Paul, 114
Muirhead, J. H., 153n, 187n
Murphy, Ella M., 100n
Murray, Thomas, 63
Musäus, Karl August, 38, 39, 41, 67
Musset, Alfred de, 20

Napoleon (Bonaparte) Emperor, 29, 30, 191
Newman, John Henry, Cardinal, 122
Newton, Isaac, 200, 206
Nicolson, Marjorie H., 157n
Nietzsche, Friedrich, 19, 61n, 100, 134
Nitzsch, F. A., 138, 168, 192
Norton, Charles Eliot, 89n
Novalis (Friedrich von Hardenberg), 5, 11, 15, 16, 28, 29, 31, 37, 38, 39, 49, 55-59, 73, 90, 91, 124, 125, 131, 132, 149, 164, 165, 188n, 196, 197, 206

O'Connell, Daniel, 110n
Oegger, Guillaume, 164, 167
Okely, Francis, 166
Oken, Lorenz, 160, 162, 165, 166, 167, 168, 186, 201, 202, 203, 204, 207, 209, 210, 212
Orsini, Gian N. G., 9n

Index

Ovid, 125
Owen, Robert, 202, 209

Paine, Thomas, 121n
Paley, William, 192
Palgrave, Reginald F. D., 109n
Palladio, Andrea, 191
Pape, Henry, 62
Parker, Theodore, 153n, 170, 172, 173, 174, 186, 211
Parmenides, 207
Pater, Walter, 134n
Paterculus, Velleius, 96, 140, 141n
Paul, Herbert, 110n
Peabody, Elizabeth, 167n
Peacock, Thomas Love, 24
Percy, Thomas, Bishop, 144n
Peyre, Henri, 136n
Pfeiler, W. K., 134n
Plato, 12, 31, 119, 124, 128, 145, 164, 165, 168, 171, 188, 189, 196, 199, 212
Plautus, 23
Pochmann, Henry A., 153n, 187n
Poe, Edgar Allan, 18
Pollitt, Charles, 123n
Poole, Thomas, 6n
Pope, Alexander, 51, 98, 127, 148
Price, Lawrence Marsden, 11n, 164
Proclus, 191, 207
Proctor, Sigmund, 114, 115, 116, 117, 119, 121, 124, 125, 127, 130, 143, 147, 150, 151
Pückler (Count), Hermann zu Pückler-Muskau, 42
Pushkin, Alexander, 18

Rabelais, François, 45, 70n
Ranke, Leopold von, 104
Raphael (Raffaello Sanzio), 20, 133
Rauch, Frederick, 162
Reed, Sampson, 164
Rehm, Walther, 131n, 134n
Reid, T. Wemyss, 110n, 181, 182

Renker, Arnim, 20n
Ricardo, David, 123
Richter, Johann Paul Friedrich, see Jean Paul
Riley, I. W., 153n, 155n, 187n
Ripley, George, 153n, 170, 171, 172, 173, 174, 185, 186, 211
Robertson, William, 101, 107
Robinson, Henry Crabb, 6n, 7, 8, 10n, 24n
Rogers, Samuel, 4
Roscoe, William, 141
Rosenmüller, Johann Georg, 156
Rosmini Serbati, Antonio, 182
Rothacker, Erich, 87, 142n
Rousseau, Jean-Jacques, 12, 19, 190
Royce, Josiah, 212
Rubens, Peter Paul, 69
Runge, Phillip Otto, 133
Runze, G., 187n
Ruskin, John, 30, 34, 135

Sackville-West, Edward, 114
Sainte-Beuve, Charles-Augustin, 15n
Saint-Hilaire, Étienne-Geoffrey, 202, 207
Saint-Martin, Louis Claude, 124
Saint-Simon, Claude-Henri de Rouvroy, Count, 82, 83, 84, 85, 86, 88, 89, 91, 92, 93, 96, 99, 100, 141, 175
Samuel, Emanuel, 65
Sandars, T. C., 205n
Sandys, J. E., 138n
Schelling, Friedrich Wilhelm von, 6, 12, 31, 47, 78, 86, 92, 112, 120, 124, 134, 153, 158n, 159, 160, 162, 165, 166, 168, 173, 175, 180, 184, 198, 199, 200, 201, 202, 204, 206, 207, 209, 210, 212; influence on Emerson 198-201
Scherb, Emmanuel Vitalis, 162, 204
Scherer, Edmond, 62

Index

Schiller, Johann Christoph Friedrich, 5, 7, 19, 37, 41, 48, 50, 51, 63, 69, 72, 85, 97, 124, 126, 131, 132, 133, 135, 148, 149, 154, 164, 165
Schlegel, August Wilhelm, 5, 6, 7, 8, 9, 11, 28, 32, 39, 49, 50, 51, 52, 53, 54, 65, 93n, 110, 128, 129, 130, 137, 143, 164
Schlegel, Friedrich, 5, 8, 9, 11, 14, 21, 28, 30, 31, 32, 46, 49, 50, 51, 52, 53, 54, 92, 93, 94, 98, 128, 129, 130, 133, 149, 160, 164, 165
Schleiermacher, Friedrich Daniel Ernst, 6, 158, 165, 170, 171, 172, 173, 174, 175, 186, 195, 196, 197, 211
Schlesinger, Arthur M., Jr., 183n
Schlosser, Heinrich, 197
Schneider, Elisabeth, 145n
Schopenhauer, Arthur, 27, 160
Schubart, Christian Friedrich Daniel, 41
Schubert, Franz Peter, 6, 26n, 168
Schultz, Arthur R., 153n
Schumann, Robert, 6
Scott, Walter, Sir, 4, 8, 10, 11, 12, 14, 22, 28, 36, 45, 101, 135
Sehrt, E. T., 114, 120n, 123n
Seneca, 147
Shaftesbury, Anthony Ashley Cooper, Third Earl of, 140
Shakespeare, William, 7, 19, 20, 23, 32, 37, 51, 52, 69, 94, 95n, 148
Shelley, Mary, 9n, 143n
Shelley, Percy Bysshe, 4, 8, 9, 10, 12, 13, 19, 22, 24, 28, 29, 31, 110, 135, 143, 144, 145n
Shepard, Odell, 166, 167n, 168, 169n
Shine, Hill, 40n, 41n, 82, 83, 84, 85, 86, 88, 90n, 92, 93, 94n, 99
Sibree, J., 205
Sidney, Sir Philip, 145

Sloman, J., 205n
Smith, Adam, 35
Smith, Norman Kemp, 189n
Smith, William, 185
Socrates, 72, 124, 164
Solger, Karl Wilhelm Ferdinand, 21
Sophocles, 133, 137n
Southey, Robert, 4, 95, 96, 98, 122, 124, 139, 140
Spence, Joseph, 131
Spengler, Oswald, 113
Spenser, Edmund, 32
Spinoza, Benedictus, 79, 119, 161, 180, 183, 184, 191, 192
Spranger, Eduard, 140n
Squire, Samuel, 109
Staël, Anne-Louise-Germaine, Madame de, 8, 28, 49, 73, 164, 188, 196n
Staiger, Emil, 13
Stallo, Johann Bernhard, 162, 171, 200n, 204, 207n
Stamm, I. S., 119n
Steffens, Henrik, 165, 201
Sterling, John, 64
Sterne, Laurence, 14, 21, 22, 62, 63, 66, 69, 70n, 80
Stevenson, Robert Louis, 23
Stewart, Dugald, 184, 188, 191
Stifter, Adalbert, 14, 60
Stirling, Amelia H., 205n
Stirling, James Hutchison, 117, 118, 169, 205
Strauss, David Friedrich, 171
Streuli, Wilhelm, 62
Ströle, A., 88n
Stuart, Moses, 155, 156, 157
Swedenborg, Emanuel, 124, 125n, 164, 167, 189, 190, 191, 200, 206, 207, 212
Swift, Jonathan, 69, 70n
Swinburne, Algernon Charles, 134n

Taine, Hippolyte-Adolphe, 107n
Taylor, Jeremy, 147, 148

Index

Taylor, Thomas, 164
Taylor of Norwich, William, 40, 69, 97, 155
Teggart, F. J., 140n
Temple, William, Sir, 140n
Teniers, David, 45
Tennemann, W. G., 184
Tertullian, 147
Thompson, F. T., 189n
Thompson, J. W., 107n
Thoreau, Henry David, 62
Thorpe, Clarence D., 114, 117, 148
Ticknor, George, 154, 158
Tieck, Ludwig, 5-*12*, 16, 17, 19, 21, 28, 31, 39, 49, 50, 51, 54, 55, 56, 58, 67, 94, 120n, 149
Tiraboschi, Girolamo, 142
Townsend, Harvey Gates, 153n, 187n
Trevelyan, G. M., 107n
Troeltsch, Ernst, 84n, 87, 142n
Tulk, Alfred, 167n
Turgot, Robert-Jacques, 84
Tymms, Ralph, 23n

Uhland, Ludwig, 6
Unger, Rudolf, 38, 89n, 91n

Varnhagen, von Ense, Karl August, 42n, 197n, 206
Vaughan, C. E., 41
Verkoren, Lucas, 145n
Verlaine, Paul, 14
Vico, Giambattista, 182
Villers, Charles de, 195
Vogel, Stanley M., 153n, 192n
Voltaire, François-Marie Arouet de, 53, 58, 91, 191
Voss, Johann Heinrich, 138

Wachler, L., 37, 93
Wackenroder, Wilhelm Heinrich, 5, 27, 50
Wade, Mason, 185n

Wahr, Fred B., 187n
Walker, James, 156
Wallon, J., 205n
Walpole, Horace, 139n
Walzel, Oskar, 128n
Warren, Austin, 169n
Warton, Thomas, 94, 95, 139
Weber, Carl Maria von, 6
Webster, John, 19
Wedgewood, Thomas, 28
Weill, Georges, 85n
Weiss, J., 173n
Welsh, Jane, *see* Carlyle, Jane
Werder, Karl, 173
Werner, Zacharias, 19, 30, 39, 42, 45, 46, 47, 48, 57, 149
Wette, W. M. L. de, 156, 172, 173, 184
Wheeler, Stearns, 198, 199
Wieland, Christoph Martin, 41, 154
Williams, Daniel Day, 156n
Williams, Jane, 24, 25
Willich, Anthony Florian Madinger, 155, 168
Wilson, D. A., 54n, 74n, 106n, 110n
Winckelmann, Johann Joachim, 126, 133
Windelband, Wilhelm, 82
Wolf, Friedrich August, 137, 143
Wolff, Christian, 120
Woodbury, Charles I., 197n
Wordsworth, William, 4, 6-10, 12, 19, 22, 24, 28, 29, 31, 36, 124, 145, 148, 209
Wright, H. C., 8n
Wright, W. Aldis, 109n

Young, Charles, 7n
Young, Louise Merwin (Mrs.), 82-86, 100, 103, 107, 109
Young, Norwood, 109n

Zeydel, E. H., 54n, 55n

GPSR Authorized Representative: Easy Access System Europe - Mustamäe tee 50, 10621 Tallinn, Estonia, gpsr.requests@easproject.com

www.ingramcontent.com/pod-product-compliance
Lightning Source LLC
Chambersburg PA
CBHW051521230426
43668CB00012B/1697